Global Trading System at the Crossroads

Is the contemporary global trading system, after the debacle at Seattle, really on the brink of collapse?

Beginning with a detailed discussion of the World Trade Organization and the Uruguay Round and its achievements, this book delves into the reasons behind the failure to launch a new round of multilateral trade negotiations in Seattle in December 1999. Dilip Das tries to determine the precise location of the global trading system and to map a way forward, pondering items likely to be included in the agenda of the latest round of multilateral trade negotiations, and providing contours for a post-Seattle global trading system.

Global Trading System at the Crossroads comes up with new perspectives on the benefits of trade liberalization, lessons to be learned from its success stories, and why it often receives weak political underpinning. The author believes the launch of the Seattle negotiations was foredoomed, but that an action agenda, if crafted in a prioritized manner, could strike a balance between conflicting interests despite its complexity. The old negotiating process has outlived its utility and the contemporary trading system needs to devise a new one. Das explores the transparency or opacity of the negotiation process, as well as the improvements needed to make it functional. Various computable general equilibrium exercises also reveal that the new round of multilateral trade negotiations would bring substantial welfare gains.

This book provides an excellent overview of the contemporary global trading system and will be very useful to advanced students and professional economists. It will also greatly benefit policy makers and active participants in trade and global diplomacy.

Dilip K. Das is a former professor, and has authored and edited numerous books, including *International Finance* (Routledge 1993). His latest, *Asian Exports*, was published in 2000. He also contributes regularly to international professional journals. Das is Senior Economist at the Economic and Research Division of the Asian Development Bank.

Routledge Studies in the Modern World Economy

Global Trading System at the Crossroads

A post-Seattle perspective

Dilip K. Das

London and New York

First published 2001
by Routledge
11 New Fetter Lane, London EC4P 4EE

Simultaneously published in the USA and Canada
by Routledge
29 West 35th Street, New York, NY 10001

Routledge is an imprint of the Taylor & Francis Group

© 2001 Dilip K. Das

Typeset in Times by
Florence Production Ltd, Stoodleigh, Devon
Printed and bound in Great Britain by
MPG Books Ltd, Bodmin

British Library Cataloguing in Publication Data
A catalogue record for this book is available from the British Library

Library of Congress Cataloging in Publication Data
A catalogue record for this book has been requested

ISBN 0–415–26015–9

To Vasanti,
for the songs we didn't sing,
for the dances we didn't dance

Contents

Illustrations

Figures

Tables

Preface

> No sane person can say with complacency, "Your end of the boat is sinking."
> In terms of economic, financial and social development, we are all in the same
> boat. We must set sail together.
>
> Mike Moore (2000)

The global trading system, a valuable and significant public good, has been in a state of flux. The third Ministerial conference of the World Trade Organization (WTO) in Seattle may well have been its crescendo. Eight rounds of multilateral trade negotiations (MTNs) under the aegis of the General Agreement on Tariffs and Trade (GATT) succeeded in lowering trade barriers, particularly tariffs. Until not long ago, GATT negotiations were largely confined to industrialized nations and a handful of developing economies. The latter country group showed interest only in demanding "special and differential treatment". Consequently, MTNs essentially focused on issues and products of interest to industrial economies. The trade policy stance taken by developing economies began to change in the mid-1980s. This reflected their reaction to the debt crisis of 1982, the demonstration effect of the benefits of the neutral external policy stance taken by the dynamic East and Southeast Asian economies, and policy advice from the Bretton Woods institutions. These institutions have been influential in policy decisions leading to gradual but extensive trade reforms in developing countries. Their influence may have come through a number of channels in addition to the direct effects or requirements of policy conditionality attached to adjustment lending.

As domestic trade policies were liberalized in the developing economies and the interest in obtaining better access to industrialized country markets expanded, the willingness to engage in the MTNs increased. This period coincided with many large industrial economies becoming less interested in abiding by the multilateral rules of the game. A perception of "free riding" by more advanced developing countries was one element behind the turn to protectionistic policies. Added to it was the decline in the relative importance of the United States (US) as a power in world trade.

Recurring macroeconomic imbalances and external shocks were yet another factor responsible for turning the industrial economies towards such policies. Adherence to the most-favored-nation principle declined, as industrial economies applied non-tariff barriers (NTBs) to protect domestic industries. Examples included voluntary export restraint agreements, orderly marketing arrangements, steady expansion of the reach and time period of the Multifiber Arrangement, intensified use of antidumping action, and ever greater subsidization of agricultural production and exports. Thus both internal and external factors – pull and push, if you like – worked to usher developing economies into the fold of the GATT. During the Uruguay Round, particularly during the latter half of the prolonged negotiations, MTNs were no longer limited to the industrial economies. By the end of the round, many developing economies had become active, on occasion vociferous, participants in the MTNs.

Thus the kaleidoscope of the global trading system has turned. Global trading environment and system, both have been transformed significantly in the short span of a decade, and dramatically since the debacle of the third Ministerial meeting of the WTO in November–December 1999 in Seattle. Failure to launch a new round of MTNs in Seattle was essentially caused by deep chasms of disagreement among the WTO members. In the past, the stands taken by the European Union (EU) and the US were reasonably close, except on agriculture. In Seattle, the transatlantic divide was as great as the North–South divide. They *inter alia* disagreed on agriculture, labor, the environment, investment, competition, antidumping and on how to deal with developing economies' problems with implementing some of their Uruguay Round commitments.

As to why the disagreements persisted, there are a host of reasons. Before the third Ministerial, the atmosphere at the WTO was made noxious by the deadlock over the appointment of a Director General. After the disputed appointment was made, there were only three months to prepare for the Ministerial. The deputies at the WTO were appointed weeks before the Ministerial. As if this poor preparation and the inexperience of the new Director General were not enough, in Seattle, Ministers tried to reach agreement in three days on issues where agreement had eluded ambassadors in Geneva for years. They were unreasonably ambitious and tried to negotiate an agreement at Seattle, rather than laying down groundwork for the round. None of the major stakeholders was flexible enough. In addition, the street theater did not help. The timing for launching a new round of MTNs was wrong and the political will was missing.

During the period between the culmination of the Uruguay Round and the third Ministerial several features of the global trading system had changed. First, a wider range of controversial issues was on the trade agenda. Second, the WTO had far more members than the GATT, and many developing economies that had never played a role in MTNs now demanded their say. This indicated that they recognized the significance of multilateral trade liberalization and its benefits. Third, lack of leadership and flexibility among major players in the WTO gave the WTO the image of a rudderless organization. In the arena of global trade, the US was not a hegemonic power any more because the EU had emerged as an equal. Their interests in and perspective on the global trading system often diverge. Fourth, although the developing economies were never in unison, they became progressively more assertive in the global trade fora. Brazil, Egypt, India, Mexico, and the ASEAN governments began to wield discernible influence in the WTO. China's accession, likely in 2001, will make this scenario more complicated. Fifth, adapting to a multipolar world was proving to be difficult for the global trading system.

While Seattle was a daunting experience, if not a shock, and numerous challenges still exist, international trade and investment have continued to flourish. Although there were several downside risks, world trade growth for 2000 was estimated at 10 percent by the WTO Secretariat, matching the best annual trade growth in the 1990s. The value of world merchandise trade grew by 14 percent in value terms, four times faster than in 1999. In addition, WTO members recognize that the global trading system is a valuable and significant public good. It is evident from the fact that during 2000 they have continued to engage in regular meetings of various councils and committees, established under multilateral agreements. WTO members also participate in the various committees established to consider specific issues like trade and development, and trade and the environment. Working groups have been established to examine the relationship between trade and investment, the interaction between trade and competition policy, as well as transparency in government procurement. Other activities by WTO members include the monitoring of trade policy regimes in the Trade Policy Review Body, and dispute settlement in the Dispute Settlement Body. Thus what happened at Seattle has not squelched the life out of the global trading system. However, crises are great opportunities for upgrading policies. The WTO as an institution is making a concerted attempt to do that. It is gradually making progress towards the new round of MTNs. Knowing how the "bicycle theory" has applied to global trading system, it is necessary for the stakeholders to succeed.

At the end of 2000, widespread expectations among academics and trade mandarins were that the new round of MTNs would be launched at the time of the fourth Ministerial in November 2001. The new round will need to recognize the progressively globalizing nature of the world economy and the interconnections of national and international policy initiatives, including trade initiatives. All the participants in the new round will need to recognize trade as an integral part of a broader strategic effort to build a more prosperous global economy. They will need to work flexibly and creatively towards the creation of a global trading system that makes a difference. Special efforts need to be made to ensure that they build a genuinely inclusive system. For instance, a number of developing economies have been highly successful in competing in world markets. But they are a small minority. We can little afford to compound the old division of rich and poor countries with a new division between the successful few and the marginalized many. On their part, the not-so-successful developing economies will need to learn in a pragmatic manner from the repertoire of the successful ones.

Writing a preface is like writing an apology for writing the book. It is necessary to explain why the author embarked on a seemingly lengthy and monotonous endeavor. One of my motives was that while there is a flurry of journal articles and papers, this is the first book on an important topic. Another objective of the book is to map out a way forward for the global trading system in the aftermath of Seattle. It *inter alia* explores what progress has been made since the failure at Seattle and then explores the likely themes that could be included in the agenda of the new round of MTNs. The book takes an unbiased stand, that is, its stance is neither developing-country nor industrial-country. It takes a pro-trade perspective, with potential expansion and liberalization of free trade in goods and services as its principal concern. This approach has decisive welfare implications for the global economy, which includes both the country groups, the developing and the developed.

The subject matter of the book falls in disciplines like international economics, international trade, and international trading relations. It starts with a relatively general approach to the WTO and the problems plaguing it. It moves into a more detailed discussion of the WTO, the Uruguay Round, and the crucial issues that they addressed. The analysis takes for granted an understanding of the GATT and the WTO and requires some existing background of international economics. It deals in great detail with the issues that were to be taken up for negotiation during the round of MTNs following the Seattle Ministerial. The final chapter focuses on the empirical analysis of the impact of the negotiations and requires some knowledge of computable general equilibrium models. As regards the structure of the book, the first chapter introduces the reader to the global trading system, how it reached its present contours and shape. The second analyzes the failure at the third Ministerial at Seattle, an important event for academics and policy makers, and all those who have an interest in global trade in goods and services. The third chapter focuses on the Uruguay Round, the most comprehensive – if the most difficult – round of MTNs thus far. The chapter also provides its implementation-related details, which include both successes and failures. The fourth chapter is a lengthy one because it enumerates and dwells on the probable foci of the agenda of the new round. Completed in December 2000 and updated in March 2001, it includes developments on the global trading system until that time point. The fifth chapter provides the empirical results of various exercises in trade liberalization. The results contain important lessons for policy makers. It is intended to provide guidelines for students, negotiators, and policy makers in adopting various trade liberalization stands.

There is a strong interest among academics, researchers, and policy makers in literature of this genre. The book should be of interest to master's level and doctoral students in international economics, international trade, and international relations. It will also benefit MBA students and senior level undergraduate students. It is likely to be added to reading lists as specialist reading for students doing coursework assignments or research on this or related topics. Lastly, it is intended to be of particular help to policy mandarins in the area of international trade. Basic knowledge of international economics and familiarity with the basic features of the GATT, the WTO, and the Uruguay Round would help the reader in appreciating the book.

An endeavor of this kind cannot be completed without incurring heavy debts to several knowledgeable scholars. I owe a debt of gratitude to three of my intimate friends. In alphabetical order, they are Professor Christopher Findlay, of the Australian National University, Canberra; Professor Linda Low, Graduate School of Business, National University of Singapore; and Dr Peter Tulloch, Director, the World Trade Organization, Geneva. All three of them provided me with extensive comments on the first draft of my manuscript, notwithstanding the fact that they are exceedingly busy individuals in their own right. I was touched by their generosity. The usual disclaimer applies. The views expressed in this book are those of the author. They do not represent those of the organization he is associated with. In addition, this book has absolutely nothing to do with the organization the author works for.

Dilip K. Das
March 2001

Abbreviations and acronyms

ADB	Asian Development Bank
ADFAT	Australian Department of Foreign Affairs and Trade
AFTA	Asian Free Trade Area
AGOA	Africa Growth and Opportunity Act
APC	Australian Productivity Commission
APEC	Asia Pacific Economic Co-operation
APG-cubed	Asia–Pacific G-cubed
ASEAN	Association of Southeast Asian Nations
ATC	Agreement on Textiles and Clothing
BITs	Bilateral Investment Treaties
CAP	Common Agricultural Policy
CGE	Computable General Equilibrium
CPs	Contracting Parties
DSB	Dispute Settlement Body
DSM	Dispute Settlement Mechanism
DSU	Dispute Settlement Understanding
ECM	European Common Market
EEC	European Economic Community
EU	European Union
FDI	Foreign Direct Investment
FTAA	Free Trade Agreement of the Americas
FTAP	GTAP model with foreign direct investment
GATS	General Agreement on Trade in Services
GATT	General Agreement on Tariffs and Trade
GDP	Gross Domestic Product
GM	Genetically Modified
GNP	Gross National Product
GTAP	Global Trade Analysis Project
HS	Harmonized Commodity Description and Coding System
ICTSD	International Centre for Trade and Sustainable Development
IDB	Integrated Database
ILO	International Labor Organization

IMF	International Monetary Fund
IPRs	Intellectual Property Rights
IT	Information Technology
ITC	International Trade Center
MAI	Multilateral Agreement on Investment
MERCOSUR	Mercado Comm del Sur or Southern Common Market
MFA	Multifiber Arrangement
MFN	Most-Favored-Nation
MNC	Multinational Corporation
MTN	Multilateral Trade Negotiation
NAFTA	North American Free Trade Agreement
NGO	Non-governmental Organization
NIEs	Newly Industrialized Economies
NTBs	Non-tariff Barriers
OECD	Organization for Economic Co-operation and Development
OMAs	Orderly Marketing Arrangements
PCMs	Price Control Measures
PECC	Pacific Economic Co-operation Council
PRC	People's Republic of China
PSI	Pre-shipment Inspection
QR	Quantitative Restriction
ROW	Rest-of-World
RTA	Regional Trading Agreement
SEM	Single European Market
SITC	Standard International Trade Classification
SPS	Sanitary and Phytosanitary
TCF	Textiles, Clothing, and Footwear
TCMD	Trade Control Measure Database
TFP	Total Factor Productivity
TNCs	Transnational Corporations
TPR	Trade Policy Review
TPRB	Trade Policy Review Body
TPRM	Trade Policy Review Mechanism
TQR	Tariff Quota Rate
TRIMs	Trade Related Investment Measures
TRIPs	Trade Related Aspects of Intellectual Property Rights
UN	United Nations
UNCTAD	United Nations Conference on Trade and Development
UNDP	United Nations Development Program
URAA	Uruguay Round Antidumping Agreement
US	United States
VERs	Voluntary Export Restraints
WIPO	World Intellectual Property Organization
WTO	World Trade Organization

1 Global trading system

Contemporary scenario

Hope is a thing with feathers,
That perches in the soul.
Emily Dickinson

1.1 The new global trading system

Although imprecisely defined, economic globalization has almost become
a catch phrase at the end of the twentieth century, and for good reason.
Globalization is a multifaceted phenomenon. It covers a range of trends in
economic, finance, technology, business, and international relations, which
may be mutually reinforcing but which have diverse origins. As conven-
tionally understood, international trade and capital flows are central to the
globalization process. Although capital flows are important in their own
right, trade in goods and services has captured a great deal of attention.
Along with rapid technological developments – especially in information
and communication technologies, telecommunications, and transport –
international trade has been a significant driving force behind globalization.
Trade has contributed to the enormous benefits that have flowed from
mutual interdependence among nations and from integration of the global
economy.

The objective of this opening chapter is to introduce the reader to the
World Trade Organization (WTO)[1] and recent transformations in the global
trading system. Over the last half-century a great deal of liberalization has
taken place in both developing and industrial economies, albeit the process
moved at an uneven pace. This chapter analyzes its welfare effects –
including effects on poverty – over different countries and country groups.
Despite its salutary economic effects, trade liberalization and the opening
up of economies have always been an onerous process. We analyze here
the how and why of this seeming irrationality. Employment-related decisions make this process of opening up even more difficult to handle for the
policy makers. In addition, not all developing economies benefit from liberalization. These sections coalesce to present a cohesive scenario of the
current challenges in front of the global trading system.

The WTO is a vitally important, if not indispensable, multilateral body in a globalized economy. It was established as the successor to the General Agreement on Tariffs and Trade (GATT). It is correct to say that the WTO is nothing but the mutated GATT, although its political and legal base is broader than that of the GATT. It is one of the younger and smaller international organizations.[2] The WTO, according to Sampson (2000), is a set of agreements that create legally binding rights and obligations for all members (Section 1.2). The schedules of tariffs and other limitations and restrictions on imports of goods and services attached to the respective agreements create similar legally binding rights and obligations for the members. These schedules bind the degree of openness of domestic markets. The agreements and schedules are negotiated mutually and agreed to by all WTO members. The WTO is an intergovernmental forum where delegations from member countries meet to discuss and negotiate a number of trade-related matters. It is essentially a member-driven organization. For instance, in the Trade Policy Review Body (TPRB) established under the aegis of the WTO governments periodically review the trade policies of other members. They analyze and discuss recent developments in the multilateral trading system. WTO members also negotiate to liberalize trade and to change the rules when they consider it necessary. This, however, is done within the context of formal multilateral "rounds" of negotiations (Sampson, 2000).

The Marrakesh Agreement, formally adopted in April 1994, contained the obligations of WTO members. It comprises twenty-nine individual legal texts and twenty-eight additional ministerial declarations, decisions, and understandings that spell out further obligations and commitments, together with approximately 26,000 pages of computer printouts detailing each member's schedule of tariff concessions and schedule of services commitments. The Ministerial Conference is the all-important body, which meets every two years to decide on strategic issues. Thus the authority to create, interpret, and enforce rules lies in the hands of the member governments. The Marrakesh Agreement, in its Article IV, gave the Ministerial Conference complete "authority to take decisions on all matters under any of the multilateral trade agreements" (GATT, 1994). Unlike the Bretton Woods twins, the Director General of the WTO has little power. He can neither formulate policies nor comment on the policies of the member governments. As the Ministerial Council meets only infrequently, the General Council exercises its functions. The latter also comprises the full membership of the WTO.

The basic philosophy of the WTO, enshrined in Article I of the Articles of Agreement, is non-discrimination. Member governments agree not to discriminate against the trade in goods and services of other members, either between supplying countries or between domestic and foreign suppliers of the same goods and services. Although WTO obligations are legally binding, they do not rule out the possibility of members agreeing to forgo their rights by undertaking obligations in other agreements that provide for measures that would otherwise violate WTO rules (Sampson, 2000).

The new, post-Uruguay Round[3] global trading system has been built upon the old. Consequently, it is similar to the old one as well as different from it. Over the past half-century there have been eight rounds of multi-lateral trade negotiations (MTNs) under the aegis of the GATT. The WTO has inherited, and it embodies, half a century of MTN-related knowledge and expertise of the GATT, which established a substantial body of trading regulations. However, WTO obligations apply to larger share of global commerce than did those of the GATT. The most significant difference between the GATT and the WTO is the so-called "single undertaking", which implies that members must accept all the obligations of the GATT and its corollary agreements negotiated in the Tokyo and Uruguay Rounds (Schott, 1996).

In the past when developing countries received benefits from the GATT system and codes without reciprocity or having to undertake new obliga-tions in return for the benefits, they have been asked under the new system to terminate their "free ride" and abide by all the codes of conduct of the WTO. Consequently, the level of obligations for many developing economies has been raised substantially. The level of obligations *per se* for the members of the WTO is higher than what it was for the contracting parties of the GATT. That being said, for the large trading economies – both industrial and developing – the level of obligations under the single undertaking has not led to additional commitments. The new WTO system has only drawn down the special provisions for the developing economies. During the Uruguay Round negotiations, fuller integration of developing economies into the global trading system was being repeatedly emphasized. The single undertaking helps meet this objective.

Various provisions of the dispute settlement mechanism (DSM) under the GATT have been consolidated by the WTO into a unified dispute mech-anism. The new mechanism avoids several weaknesses of the GATT regime in this respect. The new DSM is more effective than its predecessor. It can function more efficiently and has eliminated long delays in the panel proceedings. Under the new DSM disputants cannot block the consensus needed to approve panel findings. Binding procedures for timely compli-ance with the panel ruling have been established, which could not be done under the GATT regime. It should, however, be noted that, if all else fails, retaliation is still possible.

Membership of the WTO is much larger than that of the GATT. The GATT had twenty-three signatories when it came into effect in January 1948, and eighty-four signatories at the beginning of the Tokyo Round in 1973. More than 110 countries signed the Uruguay Round accords in Marrakesh in April 1994, including several countries that had observer status in the GATT. Thus the developing economies are much more heavily represented in the WTO than they ever were in the GATT. As of March 2001, the WTO had 140 members, with an additional twenty-eight in the process of accession.[4] The two institutions have different structures. For instance, the GATT was an accord or had provisional application; the legal status of the WTO is that of an international treaty. Therefore, countries could be "contracting parties" to the agreement, not "members". Unlike the GATT, the WTO is a membership organization. The new institutional structure of the WTO provides greater legal coherence among its wide-ranging rights and obligations, which partly explains heightened non-governmental organization (NGO) interest in the WTO. It has also established a permanent forum for consultations and negotiations. As noted earlier in this section, the Trade Policy Review Mechanism (TPRM), which provides regular monitoring of trade policies of the member economies, has a high degree of utility for the developing economies. During the GATT regime, meetings of the Trade Ministers were called on an *ad hoc* basis and were few and far between. The WTO has a mandate of biennial Ministerials, which provides political leaders with an opportunity to periodically review the work of the WTO and provide direction to it.

1.2 Institutional structure

Thus viewed, the WTO regime is a decisive and discernible improvement over the GATT regime in terms of the area of global commerce covered, the rights and obligations conferred on the member countries, the sheer number of participating countries, the process for resolving trade disputes, and the ability to promote trade negotiations and trade (Schott, 1996). Consequently the contemporary global trading system will be able to provide greater discipline over the US$7 trillion[5] in annual trade in merchandise and commercial services. A down side of this is that the global trading system will also attract greater interest from those who want to use its powers for other objectives than trade.

As an institution, the WTO lays the legal foundation of the global trading system. It is not a "best endeavor" organization (Blackhurst, 1998). There are some examples of international economic institutions placing legally binding obligations on their members.[6] However, the WTO is unique both in the extent of its contractual obligations and in the enforcement mechanism built into its system for resolving disputes. At the end of an integrated dispute settlement process, there lie multilaterally agreed and authorized trade sanctions. This is a critically important feature of the WTO, and colors everything that occurs in the WTO context.

Between meetings of the Ministerial Conference, the main governing body is the General Council. The Council meets in two other forms, namely as the Dispute Settlement Body (DSB) to oversee the dispute settlement procedures, and as the TPRB to conduct regular reviews of WTO members' trade policies. The main bodies that report to the General Council are the

Council for Trade in Goods, the Council for Trade in Services, and the Council for Trade Related Aspects of Intellectual Property Rights. All the WTO councils and committees are open to all members. This is in contrast to an institutional arrangement in which the body that meets regularly is composed of a subgroup of members, with the entire membership meeting only to decide matters that require action by all members. There is nothing in the WTO that corresponds to the International Monetary Fund's (IMF's) or World Bank's executive boards, interim committee, and development committee. A mere mention of it here should suffice because these and related issues are discussed in Chapter 4.

Unlike the IMF and the World Bank, which have weighted voting, the WTO is a "one country, one vote" organization. Except for waivers and accessions, where mail ballots were used, voting was rare during the GATT regime. Contracting Parties preferred to operate on the basis of consensus. The WTO regime expects the same. Article IX on decision making states, "The WTO shall continue the practice of decision-making by consensus followed under GATT 1947. Except as otherwise provided, where a decision cannot be arrived at by consensus, the matter at issue shall be decided by voting."[7]

Seattle was a shock to the global trading system, but this cloud had a silver lining. It highlighted the importance of the WTO to the member countries, both industrial and developing. Seattle also brought the need to build further on the institutional framework provided by the WTO to ensure further liberalization of trade in goods and services and further opening up of global markets.

1.3 Spasmodic trends in trade liberalization

The proportion of goods and services produced in the global economy and traded internationally progressively went on expanding. International trade now encompasses a much larger share of commodities than it did at the beginning of the twentieth century. Their share has risen from 20 percent in the late nineteenth century to more than 40 percent at the end of the twentieth. Likewise, trade in services has swelled from insignificance to nearly one-third of total global trade (Bordo *et al.*, 1999). Against the background of a general decline in direct trade restrictions, market openness has increased significantly over the preceding half-century. The present volume of global merchandise trade is sixteen times what it was in 1950; it has almost tripled as a share of global GDP. Trade in service transactions has also grown at a rapid pace, becoming one of the fastest growing components of world trade since the early 1980s.

Four trends can be clearly identified in the global trading system during the last half-century: uneven liberalization of markets for trade in goods in both developing and industrial economies (excluding agriculture), increasing differentiation of treatment for different levels of developing countries, a growing number of regional trading agreements (RTAs) among both developing and industrial economies, and the expanding scope and strength of trade regulations (*WDR*, 2000). Trade liberalization has been an ongoing feature of global economic activity over the past half-century. A notable amount of unilateral trade liberalization has also taken place, especially in the East Asian economies. It also occurred in the US, where the majority of quantitative restrictions (QRs) were dismantled without any *quid pro quo* from trading partners. The benefits of trade liberalization have been intensively studied and are well documented.[8] What is important now is the distribution of the gains rather than their aggregate scale.

At the dawn of the twenty-first century, however, the global trading system finds itself at a crossroads. The reason is that free trade has rarely been a popular cause. The brief history of the international trading system presents numerous glaring examples of this. Several compromises had to be made in the creation of the GATT. During the 1960s and the early 1970s, industrial economies increasingly adopted trade liberalization. The GATT provided them with a framework for a co-ordinated multilateral liberalization of trade. Successive GATT rounds of MTNs helped in reducing tariffs. In contrast, developing economies over this period shunned liberalization and pursued inward-looking strategies. In their endeavors to modernize their economies, they adopted "infant industry" support of nascent industries, as well as "import substitution" for the development of domestic industry. As a part of this inward-looking strategy, tariffs, quotas, and exchange payment restrictions in many developing countries were increased. Generally, domestic political opposition blocks liberalization moves. Entrenched interests fight hard, and frequently with prolonged success, to maintain their protected positions.

Although GATT's success during the early 1960s was well admired, by the early 1970s it was moribund. The Tokyo Round of multilateral trade negotiations, launched by the large trading economies in 1973 with the intention of achieving substantial tariff cuts, was erratic and protracted. In the mid-1980s, leading trade experts thought that the GATT was "in a state of breakdown" (Das, 1990). The Uruguay Round of MTNs, which was launched in September 1986, seemed doomed to failure as the European Union (EU) and the United States found themselves locked in a politically complex struggle over agricultural pricing and subsidies. It did collapse and had to be pulled back to its feet by the extraordinary perseverance and diplomatic skills of Arthur Dunkel, the erstwhile Director General of the GATT. International trade continues to be an important area of policy debate for both developing and industrial economies.

Developing economies were not able to ignore liberalization for very long. Theoretical and empirical evidence gradually mounted on the costs of protection to develop intellectual support for trade liberalization. The high cost of import substitution as well as the benefits of outward-oriented development strategies, emphasizing the development of competitive export sectors, was demonstrated by the success of the rapidly growing economies of East Asia. This became increasingly visible and debatable in the 1980s. Soon, rapid growth in output and trade and efficient industrialization came to be associated with a liberal regime. The benefits from liberal and outward-oriented strategies were clearly determined to outweigh the costs of protection. During the 1980s, the accumulated evidence became so large that its weight began to be felt on policy making in many developing countries.

Trade in service transactions became the new area of trade liberalization. Industrial economies, the US in particular, took increasing interest in opening up global trade in services. However, there was widespread skepticism concerning the political feasibility of a reduction in the protectionist bias that characterized most countries' policies towards services. Besides, protectionist practices in the area of services were often entangled with pervasive webs of domestic regulations that affected service industries around the globe. Owing to these difficulties, trade in services was not included in various GATT rounds. Until the Uruguay Round services were not seriously considered for inclusion in a round of MTNs. Discussions and information exchanges between the contracting parties of the GATT in this regard were highly informal. However, exports of commercial services[9] have expanded rapidly. Their value was US$62.9 billion in 1970, US$362.8 billion in 1980, and US$751.6 billion in 1990. The value of commercial services traded soared to US$1,340 billion (UN, 1993; WTO, 2000e). Between 1970 and 1980, exports of commercial services grew by 18.5 percent; between 1980 and 1990, their growth rate decelerated to 7.7 percent. The value of commercial services almost doubled between 1990 and 1999. The growth rate accelerated to 78.4 percent for this period.

By creating the General Agreement on Trade in Services (GATS) the Uruguay Round brought services into the fold of multilateral trading system. Since the launching of the Uruguay Round, numerous developing economies initiated liberalization movements that covered their commercial services industries as well. This trend was a natural extension of a broader reform movement focusing on trade in goods. By the early 1990s, developing economies were liberalizing their service transactions faster than the industrial ones (UN, 1993). As the statistics in the preceding paragraph testify, the global expansion of exports of services during the 1990s was much faster than ever in the past. This was in spite of a contraction (of 1.5 percent) in trade in merchandise in 1998.

As a group, industrial countries are the larger traders in commercial services. This does not imply that developing economies do not have a significant stake in the performance of international trade in services. Over the last three decades, developing countries as a group have recorded faster growth of trade in commercial services than the industrial economies.

Among the developing economies, the dynamic East Asian economies have been posting the most rapid expansion in trade in services. However, the degree of liberalization in services in absolute terms has been relatively meager, with many GATS schedules involving simple standstill commitments. However, in practice liberalization has gone a good deal further than the commitments. It is widely agreed that there is still considerable scope for liberalization in service sectors.

Debate on trade-related aspects of intellectual property rights (TRIPs) started in the Tokyo Round (1973–79), but this discussion had a narrow focus on the issue of counterfeit trading. It broadened during the Uruguay Round and became a major, if contentious, topic of negotiation. The consequential Agreement on Trade Related Aspects of Intellectual Property Rights, including trade in counterfeit goods, turned out to be the most comprehensive international agreement on intellectual property rights ever negotiated. TRIPs, GATS, and trade-related investment measures (TRIMs) were named the "new" issues.

Against all odds, eventually, the Uruguay Round did succeed. Shakespeare would have called it a "barful strife". In all, twenty-eight substantive agreements were completed during the Uruguay Round. Some of its achievements were, beyond any shadow of doubt, remarkable. For instance, trade discipline was extended to intellectual property rights and trade-related investment measures, a more complete procedure for dispute resolution was created, and a schedule for dismantling the Multifiber Arrangement (MFA) was agreed. Another important new issue covered in the Uruguay Round was agricultural trade, which was not covered by the trade liberalization measures of the Tokyo Round. The Uruguay Round agreement revealed the high levels of protection and began a process of negotiation to reduce them.

The WTO, as noted above, was established as the successor to the GATT, and GATS was established to extend multilateral regulatory discipline to trade in service transactions. Establishment of these two was an institutional achievement of major dimension. WTO and GATS suit the contemporary international trading environment much more than their predecessor GATT. All the Uruguay Round accords are now up and running, although TRIPs and TRIMs are two exceptions. A lot of debate on their implementation is still raging. In most cases, liberalization commitments are being fulfilled while in some progress is lethargic. The requisite domestic programs and practices have been notified to the WTO, and the new trading rules have been or are being implemented through changes in national commercial laws.

In 1995, the members of the Quadrilateral Group, or the so-called Quad, namely Canada, the EU (of fifteen), Japan, and the US, launched a post-Uruguay Round initiative to eliminate tariff barriers in the information technology sector, which included computers, semiconductors, telecommunications equipment, and software. The Quad members also tried to align technology-related policies as part of a broader global information infrastructure strategy. During the First WTO Ministerial Conference in Singapore in November 1996, agreement was reached to eliminate these tariff barriers by the year 2000. Three sectoral agreements were completed during the post-Uruguay Round period. They were on information technology (1997), telecommunications (1998), and financial services (1999). (Refer to Chapter 2, Section 1 for more details.)

Will the momentum of global trade liberalization be maintained in the new century? The answer to this query is crucial for the global economic growth, *a fortiori* for the economic prospects of developing economies. There is a backlash against trade liberalization and globalization. Seattle was one example of this backlash. There is little likelihood that the global economy will succumb to the recent backlash against trade reforms. However, if the apprehension is realized, both developing and industrial economies will squander substantial opportunities for growth. Consequently, global integration will suffer.

1.4 Benefiting from trade liberalization

The discipline of economics has had an enduring debate on trade liberalization and openness. Adam Smith extolled the virtues of trade liberalization, openness, and competition in *The Wealth of Nations*. It is easy to see the three essential sources of economic growth, namely, growth in inputs, improvements in efficiency of allocation, and innovation. Being open to trade and investment contributes to each of the sources of growth. While the potential benefits of openness from the perspective of growth and global welfare have been obvious for a long time, appreciation of their potential in full measure has been slow in coming.

A large number of scholarly studies have contrasted the growth performance of East Asia at one extreme and South Asia and sub-Saharan Africa at the other. To be sure, the contrast is striking and much has been written about it. The process of trade liberalization addresses the removal of incentives to import substitution. Growth spurred under an import substitution strategy slows over time, trade liberalization is associated with more rapid growth than the final phases of the import substitution strategy which precede it. It is in response to this phenomenon that trade liberalization offers the only known way to escape from the ever-slowing growth rates of developing countries. Any significant degree of relaxation of restrictiveness can result in gains, unless there are other policies in force in the economy that thwart their impact. Trade liberalization undertaken from a period of declining growth rates or even falling real GDP can lead to a period of growth above the rates previously realized (Dollar, 1992; Krueger, 1998, 2000).

Greenaway *et al.* (1998) modeled the impact of liberalization on growth. They tried to "encompass" the previous literature by estimating a new growth model on a large panel of developing countries, using a range of alternative methodologies for capturing trade liberalization. Their results are illuminating. They suggest that liberalization does indeed impact favorably on growth of GDP *per capita*. The impact does not necessarily have to be linear. The response in all probability should be lagged. They found that there may be a J-curve type effect of liberalization on GDP growth. This must not appear surprising because liberalization strategies vary in depth from economy to economy. They vary in intensity as well and almost never amount to an immediate shift to free trade. The liberalization episodes that are picked up for study are often in their first stages. Through time these very economies become more open, partly as a consequence of incremental trade reforms. But these economies also become more open as a consequence of other factors or the so-called second channel, discussed below. Greenaway *et al.* concluded that previous researches that failed to capture the growth effect of liberalization did so because they failed to model the dynamics adequately. They concluded that openness is a function of many factors, including liberalization.

Continual progress in trade liberalization is essential because economies, both developing and industrial, benefit immensely from it. As noted above, the first set of benefits accrues when tariffs are lowered, as relative price changes force resource reallocation in the economy. Resources are reallocated to production activities that have higher comparative advantage and, therefore, they raise national incomes to higher levels than before. This effect is known as the static benefits of liberalization. Several empirical studies show that the Uruguay Round raised national incomes in the developing economies by an estimated 0.3 percent to 0.4 percent, *only* when its static impact was taken into account[10] (Srinivasan, 1998; Francois *et al.*, 1996; Harrison *et al.*, 1996). Econometric studies suggest that trade liberalization has a much larger impact on economic growth. Frankel and Romer (1999) found that a one percentage point increase in the trade of GDP ratio raises *per capita* income by 2.0 percent to 3.0 percent, depending upon the countries sampled.[11]

The second channel of benefits accrues through reduction in transport and communication costs, technological change, and so on. The benefits are reinforced when developing economies make economic adjustments to technological innovation, new production structures, and changing patterns of competition. The second set, or dynamic, benefits are far larger than the first and have long-run implications. Economies that have participated in the various rounds of MTNs and have liberalized have benefited in a significant manner in the past. Their future participation is expected to lead to similar benefits in the future.

A broad range of empirical studies have established that trade liberalization and open trade policies are conducive to growth. Although the benefits of trade liberalization do not accrue immediately, they do over time through stimulating investment and growth. Most empirical studies find positive feedback from the openness of trade regime to economic growth. A revealing and much cited study by the World Bank (1987), and its later expansion by the International Monetary Fund (1993), classified forty-one developing economies into four categories on the basis of trade orientation: (1) strongly inward oriented, (2) moderately inward oriented, (3) moderately outward oriented, and (4) strongly outward oriented. The trade orientation was then compared with average *per capita* growth over three periods, 1963–73, 1974–85, and 1986–92 (WB, 1987; IMF, 1993). Results led to the clear conclusion that outward oriented economies grow faster on average than inward oriented economies. As this study did not control for other factors, the openness indicator may capture the joint influence of the trade regime and omitted variables that are correlated with the trade regime. For instance the soundness of the trade regime is likely to be correlated with the overall soundness of the macroeconomic policy regime, which decisively influences growth. To be sure, studies that controlled for other variables found a less pronounced impact of trade regime *per se*, but still a significant one.

The traditional neoclassical or "Solow model" (1956) views capital accumulation as an engine of growth. However, the model posits that factor productivity may differ from economy to economy, but openness of the trade regime influences growth in a favorable manner. Indeed, there are several other variables that influence growth. Barro (1998) provides an exhaustive review of empirical growth studies. It should be noted that nothing in these models suggests that trade liberalization will stimulate growth permanently. The growth impulse will eventually fade out once the economy is restructured and integrated in the global economy. Yet Barro (1998) concluded that empirical evidence does exist that open economies grow faster than closed ones for a prolonged period of time.

Broadly conceived trade liberalization plays a critical role in supporting growth and poverty reduction, which is a shared responsibility of the global community, if not a moral imperative. Although rapid growth in many parts of the world has led to a fall in the global population living on US$1 or less a day, population growth has kept the absolute number of poor steadily at some 1.2 billion (WDR, 2000). Although the linkage between trade and poverty is not direct and immediate,[12] trade expansion can affect the income opportunities of the poor in numerous ways. It can be instrumental in bringing about convergence in incomes between countries. Trade-related income convergence is accompanied by faster growth in the liberalizing countries. Many of the primary measures and institutions that facilitate the capturing knowledge spillovers emanating from trade – such as widespread and improved education, a sound infrastructure, protection of property rights, and the like – are inherently the same measures that facilitate a move to faster growth and alleviation of widespread poverty.

Trade can affect the income opportunities of poor people through several channels. It allows people to exploit their productive potential, curtails arbitrary policy interventions, and helps to insulate against shocks. Opening up an economy and expanding trade often reduces risk and variability because *in general* global markets are more stable than the domestic ones.[13] Most trade-related policy reforms do create some losers. The appropriate policy response is to alleviate the hardships of the losing groups and move ahead with the adjustment process rather than abandon the reform process (Ben-David *et al.,* 1999). Whether trade expansion or a trade reform measure is pro- or anti-poor depends on induced price effects, which in turn depend upon which tariffs are being reduced and how much of the price changes is being passed on to the poor. It also depends on how the poor earn and spend their income in an economy (Ben-David *et al.,* 1999).

Over the 1980s and the 1990s around eighty developing economies liberalized their economies. Some did it unilaterally, others under various structural adjustment programs of the International Monetary Fund and the World Bank. To be sure, these liberalization endeavors had varying depths. Available evidence suggests that while close to twenty high and middle-income developing countries have done a laudable job of integrating into the global economy over the last two decades, many low-income developing economies have not yet been able to integrate successfully into global markets. They have failed to participate in the growth-inducing and potentially poverty-reducing benefit of trade. Research into the pace of integration, which divided a sample of ninety-three developing countries into rapid, moderate, and slow or weak integrators, has shown that only one of the twenty-eight so-called least developed countries in the sample fell into the rapid integrator category, and only seven more were moderate integrators. Thus the majority of the poorest countries – those most in need of the spur to growth that trade integration can provide – are being left behind in the race towards effective participation in global markets. Their share in global trade has declined steadily, from 0.8 percent in 1980 to 0.4 percent by 1997 (WB, 2000b). This subgroup of economies is not only not globalizing but is making a retrograde motion.

Gains from liberalization are not limited only to the macro part of economy: liberalization has a decisive firm-related impact. Economies like India that did not liberalize trade for decades ended up with high-cost firms and high-cost industrial output. Under long-term tariff and non-tariff shelter, firms were allowed to grow into high-cost producers, to the detriment of the domestic economy. As opposed to this international competition forces firms to be more innovative. Their credo is "compete or die".[14] Consequently, they eagerly absorb the latest technologies in their respective areas and remain efficient producers. A good deal of empirical evidence is available to indicate that the benefits of trade liberalization extend to the micro part of the economy and that it has a discernible and significant impact on firms' performance. Culling data from numerous firm-related empirical studies, Evenett (1999) has provided evidence for the following:

1   Increased imports were found to discipline domestic firms in Côte
    d'Ivoire, India, and Turkey, forcing them to bring prices close to
    marginal cost, thereby reducing distortions created by monopoly
    power.
2   Trade liberalization can permanently raise a firm's productivity. The
    firm is able to access more modern capital equipment and high-quality
    intermediate inputs at lower prices. It was found that firms in Korea
    and Taiwan were able to increase their productivity markedly by diver-
    sifying their use of intermediate inputs.
3   Productivity rises when businesses are exposed to demanding interna-
    tional clients and the "best practice" of international competitors. Dom-
    estic firms may also benefit from the opportunity to re-engineer foreign
    firms' products, sometimes at lower prices. Studies in Colombia,
    Mexico, Morocco, and Taiwan have indicated that exporting firms have
    higher factor productivity than non-exporting firms.

Fujita *et al.* (1999) have posited a spatial theory of trade liberalization.[15]
According to them, trade liberalization triggers a chain reaction that
catalyzes the growth of secondary and tertiary economic activities in a
city or a region. Consequently costs fall and output rises, attracting more
firms in the same or related areas. A chain reaction is set in motion, with
one stage of development reinforcing the next stage. As more firms start
and move in, an agglomeration of economic activity is formed. As exports
rise, these agglomerations become more successful, average costs and
profits rise, providing further impetus for expansion. Output expands
further and the agglomeration expands. Responding to the needs of end
product producers, intermediate input producers and non-tradable service
producers set up businesses and the process of agglomeration expansion
gets further impetus. New intermediate inputs make production more
efficient in the agglomeration, lower the costs of production, and enhance
the profitability of the end product producers. They also raise quality standards. More businesses are attracted and the cycle continues until it is
curtailed by congestion. It stops when the infrastructure becomes a
constraint. Such agglomerations lead to higher productivity and output
(*WDR*, 2000).
   Trade reform is a well researched area. Static trade models suggest that
movements towards openness can increase growth rates owing to gains
from the reallocation of resources, which establishes a nexus between
change in the degree of openness and GDP growth. The new growth
literature also identifies numerous avenues through which openness
may affect long-term growth – the dynamic impact of trade liberalization.
For instance, technological change is a positive function of both a country's
openness and the gap between a country's technology level and the rest
of the world. Intuitively, by reforming their trade regime, developing
countries create more opportunities to absorb new ideas and tend to

converge to international norms (Edwards, 1998). Exporting firms in these countries provide externalities by serving as conduits for the dissemination of world class technology to less dynamic domestic market oriented firms. Recent models of economic growth also imply a positive relationship between degree of openness to trade and total factor productivity (TFP). According to these models, TFP can be explained by either an expanding number of inputs or higher input quality. To the extent that countries which are more open to trade can either learn more quickly how to produce these inputs, or can import them, openness can be positively related to TFP (Coe and Helpman, 1995; Krishna *et al.*, 1998; Krueger, 1998).

Various estimates of benefits from trade liberalization were given in the preceding section. The preceding exposition of trade liberalization was related to multilateral liberalization, but it has been well established that there are welfare gains to be had from unilateral liberalization. Economies benefit from unilaterally bringing down tariff barriers and eliminating non-tariff barriers (NTBs). This process suffers from a classic dilemma, that is, the costs of unilateral trade liberalization are suffered by a small number of import-competing firms, while the benefits are distributed among a large population of consumers. Therefore, the prospective beneficiaries of liberalization have little incentive to work for unilateral trade liberalization, more so when the import-competing firms are strongly lobbying against it. The WTO indirectly works to resolve this tangle. Although it exists for facilitating multilateral trade liberalization, in so doing it creates a clutch of successful exporting firms which stand to benefit from lower tariffs in their potential export markets. In order to achieve lowered tariffs in their export markets, they need to persuade their policy makers to lower the domestic tariff. To this end, they need to create a constituency for trade liberalization and oppose the stand taken by the import-competing domestic firms. A progressive government looks to maximize the number of exporting firms and globalize its economy, therefore it has a definite incentive to liberalize and lower domestic tariffs.

A tangible and visible benefit of trade liberalization is the integration of the global economy through the expansion of trade in goods and services, albeit not all the global economies have been able to integrate as yet. Trade expansion can also be a source of growth and employment. Trade has expanded faster than output by a significant margin in the last fifty years. While real output in the global economy has grown at an average annual rate of 3.7 percent over the 1948–97 period, the comparable figure for trade is 6 percent. In other words, trade flows have multiplied by a factor of 17 in real terms, while output has grown sixfold (WTO, 1998d). Increased trade volume was facilitated by the market-opening and trade liberalization measures of governments. Both developed and developing countries have progressively opened their markets to trade and investment during the last two decades. The ratio of imports and exports to GDP rose from 16.6 percent to 24.1 percent between 1985 and 1997 in developing economies, and from 22.8 percent to 38 percent in the industrial economies during the same period (WTO, 1998). As for the two largest trading entities, the EU and the US, the share of imports and exports in the GDP of the US approximately doubled over 1980–2000. If intraregional trade is excluded, the same is true of the EU (of fifteen).

There is very little evidence that countries, in general, are converging towards one another in terms of their *per capita* income gaps. If anything, income gaps between the majority of countries appear to be growing over time. That said, among those countries whose income gaps are converging, an important thread that appears to tie together many of them is trade in goods and services. Countries that formally enacted trade liberalization policies exhibited a convergence in income once they implemented trade reforms. An empirical study that examined this issue with data for middle and high-income countries inferred that while no intragroup income convergence was evident prior to the inception of the individual trade reform programs, significant income convergence began to occur simultaneously with the removal of trade barriers and increase in the volume of trade (Ben-David and Loewy, 2000). If we generalize this finding, we can say that countries that liberalize their trade regimes and trade extensively with one another tend to exhibit a relatively high incidence of income convergence. An increase in the extent of trade by these countries is associated with an even faster rate of convergence.

The trade-related convergence did not appear to have come at the expense of the high-income countries. Not only have the relatively lower-income countries been able to move to higher and steeper growth paths, so have their higher-income trade partners. Not opening the economy by dismantling tariff and non-tariff barriers becomes the principal constraining factor for the country group whose income is not converging. However, the contribution of several critical institutions in providing the overall environment so that openness to trade can contribute to growth is extremely important.

Trade as a proportion of GDP is not very high for either the EU or the US: large economies trade less with others because they trade more internally. However, merchandise trade as a share of merchandise value added is very high in these economies. According to calculations by Feenstra (1998), between 1913 and 1990 the ratio of merchandise trade to merchandise value added increased from 13.2 percent to 35.8 percent for the US, from 39.4 percent to 69.8 percent for Canada, from 66.2 percent to 85.9 percent for Denmark, from 23.3 percent to 53.5 percent for France, from 29.2 percent to 57.8 percent for Germany, and from 21.9 percent to 43.9 percent for Italy. Other than trade liberalization and fast declining transport costs, there is the disintegration of the production process itself. Since the mid-1980s it has led to intermediate inputs crossing national borders, sometimes several times over. To be sure, this was a significant factor in the export surge from the newly industrialized economies of Asia. The ultimate outcome is closer integration of global markets. Companies now find it profitable to outsource increasing amounts of the production process, a process that can happen domestically or abroad. This has come to be known as the "slicing of the value chain" (Krugman, 1996).

1.4.1 Alternative channels of trade liberalization

The WTO (or MTNs) is the most important mechanism of trade liberalization. The other important channel is the growing number of regional trading agreements (RTAs) which industrial and developing countries are signing with neighboring countries. Regionalism is almost half a century old. Many regional initiatives began in the 1950s and 1960s; this was the so-called "old regionalism". They accomplished little, except in Western Europe. The relationship of this European integration to multilateral liberalization was usually regarded as benign, largely because of the success of the Kennedy Round (1964–67). Two quiet decades followed the old regionalism. The Single European Market was launched in 1985 and completed in January 1993. (See Chapter 4, Section 4.5.9.) This triggered the second wave of RTAs. In the late 1980s a new bout of regional integration began, which is still continuing. This is the so-called "new regionalism".

As the international economic environment of the 1990s differed dramatically from that of the 1950s and 1960s, the characteristics of the new regionalism differ from those of the old. Ethier (1998) has identified the new regionalism with five principles. First, one or more small countries link up with a large country or entity. For instance, with the US in the North American Free Trade Agreement (NAFTA), or Brazil in MERCOSUR, or with the European Union (EU). Second, small countries undertake significant economic reforms prior to, or simultaneously with, the regional integration. Third, the degree of trade liberalization is moderate. This is necessarily so in comparison with the old regionalism, because trade barriers are significantly lower now than they were in the 1950s and 1960s. In addition, the new arrangements do not eliminate all internal barriers. Fourth, the agreements are asymmetric. The small countries make significantly more concessions than the large ones. Fifth, the partners in an RTA do not confine themselves to reducing tariff barriers. They also harmonize or adjust diverse assortments of other economic policies. This is known as deepening regional integration.

The number of RTAs has soared since 1990. Over the 1990–98 period, eighty-two RTAs came into force. In contrast, during 1950–59 only three RTAs were formed, during 1960–69 an additional nineteen were created, and during the next decade of 1970–79 thirty-nine more came into being. However, during 1980–89 the number of RTAs formulated declined to only fourteen. The RTAs that came into being during the 1990s covered not only trade in goods but also trade in services, investment regimes, and regulatory practices. They have substantially increased not only intra-regional trade but also intraregional investment flows (Frankel, 1997; *WDR*, 2000). Supporters of RTAs contend that these agreements have enabled member countries to liberalize trade and investment barriers far more than multilateral trade negotiations. Also, RTAs have generated welfare gains for participants, with little possibility of negative spillovers into the rest of the world (Baldwin and Venables, 1995; Fernandez and Ports, 1998).

Sectoral agreements are another alternative mechanism of liberalization. After the Uruguay Round was completed, liberalization agreements were negotiated in information technology (March 1997), in telecommunications services and products (February 1998), and in financial services (March 1999), under the aegis of the WTO. Although sectoral agreements offer a means of achieving additional trade liberalization, they carry the risk of limiting the sort of productive trade-offs that are possible in larger trade negotiations. The broader the array of sectors subject to negotiation, the greater the potential for securing agreements with larger economic gains that are in every participating economy's interest.

Since the beginning of the 1980s developing economies have liberalized their trade regimes fast, much faster than the industrial economies whose trade regimes were already quite liberal.[16] Consequently, the degree of export orientation, as measured by the share of exports in GDP, in the developing economies has progressively increased. Since the late 1980s, developing countries have steadily increased their share in global merchandise exports, while the share of industrial economies has declined. What is more noteworthy is that the share of manufactures in merchandise exports increased at a faster rate for the developing economies than for the industrial economies, throughout the 1980s and the 1990s. Thus the share of the developing economies in world exports of manufactures increased from 12 percent in 1980 to 25 percent in 1996, and further to 31 percent in 1998. Conversely, the share of the industrial economies declined from 83 percent in 1980 to 72 percent in 1996 and further to 61 percent in 1998 (WTO, 1999d).[17]

1.4.2 Some lessons from successful episodes

Several significant lessons have emerged from the liberalization experiences of the last two decades. We saw in Section 3 that the majority of the poorest countries – those most in need of the spur to growth that trade integration can provide – are being left behind in the race towards effective participation in global markets. In general, low-income developing countries have paid little attention to liberalization and have remained more restrictive than the high-income developing economies. This restrictive stance is perceived by most stakeholders as a major impediment to accelerating growth. Distorted trade regimes are a serious impediment to both macroeconomic reform and structural adjustment. Here lies an important lesson for the policy mandarins. Liberalization and trade reform can contribute importantly to improving the efficiency of resource allocation, reducing the anti-export bias of the economy, exposing it to competition, promoting realistic exchange rates and balance of payments adjustments, spurring domestic and foreign investment, and diversification of the economy (Mussa, 1998).

Lessons, however, are often misperceived. It is imperative not to draw simplistic conclusions and head for easy targets. Trade liberalization *alone* cannot be an engine of growth in the absence of complementary action in other macroeconomic and structural areas. Often trade reforms are narrowly defined to include tariffs and non-tariff barriers. But foreign exchange restrictions and exchange rate adjustments, price controls, state trading monopolies, are all an intimate part of trade liberalization. The effectiveness of trade liberalization is enhanced considerably when it is "accompanied or preceded by" reforms in all these policy areas (Mussa, 1998). Experience shows that most successful liberalization and trade reforms were those that were a part of comprehensive economic adjustment packages. The ones that were narrow in design either had limited impact or could not be sustained.

Liberalization programs that were bold and implemented vigorously proved more durable than the ones that took a more hesitant approach. Past experience shows that if liberalization of restrictive tariff and non-tariff regimes was undertaken along with broader structural reforms on a sustained basis – for six to seven years – the consequences were far reaching. For high credibility among economic agents, the liberalization programs must be announced in advance. The element of surprise in the policy structure must be completely eliminated.

Mussa (1998) found that poor macroeconomic management has generally led to poor results and even the reversal of liberalization programs. Particularly, fiscal prudence is an important precondition to a successful liberalization program. Conscious policy measures must be taken to minimize the adverse short-term impact of liberalization on external and fiscal positions. The adverse impact on the balance of payments can be kept to manageable proportions by managing domestic demand policies and by phasing trade liberalization appropriately. As a matter of strategy, QRs must be dismantled first because they are less transparent and more restrictive. They distort an economy more than tariff barriers. Attempts must be made to eliminate QRs during the first two years of the liberalization program. One way of dismantling them on a priority basis is replacing them with tariffs, which could be temporarily higher than normal maximum tariff rates in the economy. However, they must not exceed their tariff equivalents.

Successful trade liberalization episodes suggest that liberalization and reforms become easier to initiate and sustain when they move *pari passu* with real exchange rate depreciation. This is particularly true when the initial level of protection is high and it is rampant in the economy. The high level of protection itself artificially raises the value of the currency compared with the equilibrium level in the absence of the restrictions.

1.5 Discomfiture from trade liberalization

Although causation remains an issue, as we saw in the foregoing exposition, static and dynamic gains from improved resource allocation and efficiency that follow from trade liberalization have been well researched and well documented in the literature. Yet mercantilist hesitation and discomfiture among policy mandarins persist. They also tend to reinforce their protectionist policies because "others are doing so". As Frederic Bastiat put it, it makes no more sense to be protectionist because other countries have tariffs than it would to block up our harbors because other countries have rocky coasts.[18]

Policy makers are often reluctant to implement liberalization measures owing to fear of excessive adjustment costs. There are some misperceptions regarding the adjustment costs. A survey of fifty studies establishes that adjustment costs are much smaller than the benefits of trade liberalization (Matusz and Tarr, 2000). Studies that focused on manufacturing employment in developing economies found that it had not declined one year after the advent of trade liberalization. Collectively, the weight of so many studies of various types all pointing more or less in the same direction makes it difficult to avoid the conclusion that adjustment costs are relatively much smaller than the benefits of trade liberalization. They are smaller than generally visualized because (1) they are typically short term and terminate when displaced workers find employment, while the benefits continue to accrue and grow larger with the economy, (2) estimates of the duration of unemployment in most industries are not very high, (3) in many industries normal labor turnover exceeds the dislocation from trade liberalization, so downsizing can be achieved without much forced unemployment, and (4) it has been observed that a great many interindustry shifts occurred after trade liberalization, which minimized the dislocation of factors of production. However, the political dynamics of liberalization is not conducive to promoting it. Politicians find that in the short term they incur the wrath of the owners of displaced resources, while the benefits accrue in the medium or long term. The logical result is the scuppering of political enthusiasm for liberalizing the trade policy structure.

Developing economies, in particular the more capable, better developed newly industrialized economies (NIEs), benefited from the GATT discipline, and as supply-side improvements became standard features of their economies they gradually increased their exports to the industrial economies. Consequently, many industrial economies in the EU and the US found that their merchandise imports exceeded their merchandise output. This led to increased competition in merchandise products in the industrial economies (Feenstra, 1998). Over the last few decades, the composition of exports from the developing economies, particularly from the NIEs, has also undergone a substantial transformation. Many of them are now exporting engineering and medium-technology products. NIEs from Latin America and India fall into this category. After 1980, China also became a successful and large exporter of medium-technology products to the industrial economies. The proportion of high-technology products like electronics, electrical goods, and machinery from the NIEs based in East and Southeast Asia increased substantially during the decades of the 1980s and the 1990s. These economies have come to acquire an impressive competitive advantage in high-technology products and, therefore, have become competitive in several product ranges in the industrial economy markets.

When several developing economies move up the industrialization curve, acquire competitive advantage in medium and high-technology goods, and under the liberalized trade regime export to the industrial economies, they enhance global welfare. However, the flip side of the coin is that they may destabilize firms in the importing countries. Thus progressively increasing trade liberalization is making workers and industries feel victimized in some economies (Mandel and Magnusson, 1999). The import-competing firms in the industrial economies that cannot compete against the imports have to shut down. The immediate result is lobbying against import liberalization. Therefore, the next phase of trade liberalization or globalization could be seen as more unsettling because it will be in direct collision with economic interests and cultural and political beliefs in the industrial economies. It is interesting to note that the same is true of the impact of domestic competition, which is not resented by the firms that fail to compete.

In the past, lobbying against more competitive imported products, and, therefore, trade liberalization, was limited in the developing economies. Developing economies, particularly the high and medium-income ones, have always been under pressure from the industrial economies to liberalize rapidly. They also raise concerns about job losses. When they do, they receive the doctrinaire response that markets create jobs and that resources released from the protected sectors can be redeployed productively elsewhere. However, jobs do not appear quickly enough for those who have been displaced. Besides, the displaced workers do not have any resources to buffer themselves. Few developing countries have public safety nets like those common in the industrial economies. These were genuine concerns of policy makers in the developing economies; therefore, further opening of markets was not a popular cause.

Thus trade liberalization causes loss of jobs in both developing and industrial countries in industries that are losing comparative advantage. While it is true that protectionism can provide job security in the short term, it can do so in the long term only at enormous cost, including at the cost of employment in non-protected industries. Comparative advantage is a dynamic phenomenon. The dynamics of economic growth is such that while one sector loses comparative advantage, another gains. Job losses in one sector are often offset by job creation in another. In addition, the new jobs are likely to be higher-productivity jobs than the old ones. It is this movement from low-productivity jobs to high-productivity jobs that represents gains from the national perspective.[19] It also explains how, in principle, everyone can be better off as a result of trade liberalization. If the policy makers decide to save the sector that is losing comparative advantage by way of protection, they are not able to benefit from the development of those sectors that are newly gaining comparative advantage. It is possible that by abandoning the so-called sunset sectors and moving into the sunrise sectors, they provide the economy a new direction towards high-productivity sectors and better job opportunities. Thus while negative effects are incurred in specific industries or sectors, the net impact of trade liberalization is overwhelmingly positive in the long run (WTO, 1998d).

Since the early 1990s successful exporters among the developing economies began to be seen as a threat to prosperity in the industrial economies. These apprehensions were, albeit unintentionally, exacerbated by World Economic Forum in the early 1990s.[20] Influential European politicians and opinion leaders like Jacques Delors[21] agreed with this kind of thinking. A White Paper on the economic problems of Europe, particularly the long uptrend in European unemployment rates, blamed competition from the emerging market economies for it (EEC, 1993). Although such views are less widespread in the US, which was busy "Japan bashing", some otherwise respected think-tanks like the Economic Policy Institute maintained a drumbeat of warnings about the threat that low-wage competition from developing economies posed for US living standards. These fears are misleading and unjustified, not to say alarmist (Krugman, 1996).

When world productivity rises, as it does when productivity levels in some developing economies converge towards those in the industrial economies, average living standards must rise globally. The simple logic is that the extra output must go somewhere. Higher developing country productivity must, after a time lag, be reflected in higher wages in those economies, not in lower incomes in the industrial economies. One cannot ignore the basic fact that in any economy, producers and consumers are the same people. Krugman (1996) concludes that economic growth in low-wage economies is in principle as likely to raise as to lower *per capita* income in high-wage countries, although so far the real impact has been "negligible".

As most policy makers are erroneously convinced of the threat-to-prosperity theory, various safety instruments are devised. To save themselves from the cold wind of competition, the import-competing firms in the industrial economies do not stop at lobbying. They accuse the exporting firms of unfair trade practices, which allows them to resort to antidumping laws allowed by the GATT in the past and the WTO at present.[22] These laws allow importing countries to impose offsetting duties on the products of foreign firms found to be dumping on the domestic market and in the process causing "material injury" to a domestic industry. Antidumping actions are not only arbitrary but also seriously discriminatory and can be a major problem. After 1993, cases of imposing antidumping duties have increased sharply. In 1993 a total of 299 antidumping actions were reported, as against 165 in 1990. Although they declined during 1996 and 1997 to 221 and 233, respectively, this was a very high level of antidumping action. Thus if an import-competing firm cannot compete with more efficient exporting firms in other parts of the globe, it can consider calling on antidumping laws to ward off competition. After the Uruguay Round, antidumping action has increasingly become a tool for diluting market access, annulling gains from trade liberalization brought about by the Uruguay Round. A new characteristic to be observed is that in the past antidumping action was taken almost exclusively by industrial economies only. Since 1993, several developing economies have also joined in. The non-traditional users of antidumping action are Argentina, Brazil, India, Korea, Mexico, and South Africa.

Such rampant use of antidumping duties not only undermines free trade but has several pernicious effects. One of the most significant is to eliminate stability and predictability in global product markets. More efficient domestic firms have the same impact on the less efficient firm as imports from the more efficient firms in the global market place. However, they are meted out a different treatment and not asked to shut down because other domestic firms are not able to compete with them. A pragmatic and economically reasonable resolution of the problem of excessive use of the antidumping defense by less cost-efficient firms is to establish parity between foreign and domestic firms by international agreement. Antidumping action should be taken only when an issue exists in reality, not to ward off competition from more cost-efficient exporting firms in the global market place. Another pernicious effect is that if policy makers use antidumping action against more cost-efficient firms abroad, they promote less cost-efficient firms domestically. The ultimate result is the creation and promotion of a high-cost industrial structure.

Organized labor and labor lobbyists in the industrial economies challenge global trade liberalization. They charge that international competition, especially from more capable developing economies, depresses wages in the industrial economies and worsens income distribution. Conversely, advocates of global trade liberalization argued that export jobs pay far more than the national average and that further trade liberalization, which is equated with increased trade, would lead to improved income levels. This controversy has spawned an enormous amount of economic analysis as well as political debate. The classic and oft-cited reason why trade liberalization may have increased wage inequality is the Stolper–Samuelson theorem, whereby trade increases the price of abundant factors of production and reduces that of the scarce factors. For the industrial economies, skilled labor is a relatively abundant factor of production and unskilled labor relatively scarce. Therefore, it is argued, trade expansion has had two effects in the industrial economies. It has (1) provided more opportunities for skill-intensive exports and (2) increased competition from low skill-intensive imports for the domestic producers. Using US wage data for the 1970–95 period, Leamer (1996) came to a somewhat different conclusion. He concluded that imported goods created a twist in the labor demand curve. It led to lower real wages for unskilled workers who resided in communities with abundant unskilled labor but raised the wages of unskilled workers who were fortunate enough to live in communities inhabited mostly by skilled workers. Thus trade liberalization does not necessarily work against the interests of unskilled workers.

After a comprehensive research survey, Cline (1997) concluded that trade expansion provides the most certain basis for economic growth and efficiency. There is no assurance that trade will lead to greater – rather than less – income and wage equality over time. The principal implication of this line of thinking is that a society adhering to free trade and other market-oriented policies will be able to make efforts in a whole array of other policies to assure that the resulting gains in efficiency and growth are shared in a fair way by the work force. One way of remedying the skilled–unskilled wage disparity is increasing the supply of skilled labor relative to unskilled labor, through education and training, rather than creating barriers to trade liberalization. When trade liberalization leads to job losses, income insurance policies can help in the short term. Such programs provide time for exploring other employment avenues. Besides, as noted above, there is little justification in treating workers affected by more efficient imports differently from those affected by domestic competition.

In the recent past, a high and rising current account deficit in the US (3.7 percent of GDP in 1999) and high and persistent unemployment in the large EU economies contributed to the same anti-free-trade bias and exacerbation of protectionist pressures. Over the years a crude argument has gained ground in the US that trading with low-wage countries is depressing US wages and incomes, therefore the US must not trade with them. Anti-globalization sentiment was strong in the EU because foreign competition makes a convenient scapegoat for dysfunctional domestic policies that produce chronically high unemployment (Lindsey *et al.*, 1999).

1.6 Intransigent labor issues

The so-called "core labor standards" have become a seriously contentious issue. Core labor standards represent (1) the physical conditions of work, (2) the rights workers have under national law, and (3) the extent to which people feel protected by legislation or can get redress. Core labor standards also relate to labor's right to organize.[23] If the labor force is not organized, the producer is at an advantage because it reduces his costs. Some think that this should be considered a subsidy to producers, and therefore as an unfair trade practice.

At the first Ministerial Conference in Singapore in 1996, the Scandinavian countries and the US were in favor of including the core labor standards in the WTO's mandate. The labor movement is the central constituency of the Democratic Party in the US, therefore taking a reformist stand on labor-related issues was politically correct for the Democratic administration. However, developing economies called this a "non-trade issue", and the labor issue was cautiously avoided. It was mentioned that as the International Labor Organization already exists, the WTO is not the correct forum for this issue. Many trade economists consider core labor standards as excess baggage for the WTO which may divert it from its basic mission. However, the issue cropped up again in the second Ministerial in Geneva in 1998.

Labor lobbies in the industrial economies, particularly the US, are after inclusion of core labor standards in the WTO because globalization has led to erosion of their bargaining power and in effect weakened them. If core labor standards are established in the developing economies, organized labor in the industrial economies expects to benefit from it by strengthening its bargaining power. The argument is often presented with an altruistic twist, that is, labor lobbies are essentially interested in advancing the cause of workers' rights worldwide and their mission is to achieve global equity and well-being.

The fears of US labor lobbies are exaggerated and do not stand up to careful scrutiny. While anti-trade polemicists in the US are constantly worried about the jobs shipped overseas, they ignore the jobs shipped inwards. In 1999, 12.3 percent, or one in eight, of manufacturing workers in the US were employed by a US affiliate of a foreign-owned company, like Honda, Toyota, DaimlerChrysler, Fuji, and the like (Griswold, 2000a). The argument that trade liberalization through the WTO has made Americans poorer contradicts the most obvious facts about the US economy in the year 2000. During the last five years, living standards have been rising for low and high-income workers alike. Over 80 percent of the jobs created in the US economy since 1993 were in occupations that paid above median wages (Griswold, 2000b). As in the case of trade, most of the US foreign direct investment (FDI) dealings are with other advanced economies, and 80 percent of foreign direct investment by US manufacturing companies in 1998 was in other high-wage countries. The largest destinations for US manufacturing FDI were the United Kingdom, Canada, the Netherlands, Germany, and Singapore, in that order. All of these are high-wage economies with labor, health, and environmental standards and regulations comparable with, or more restrictive than, the US. Labor lobbies in the US need not fear openness to trade and investment with developing economies.

Global trade liberalization encouraged by the WTO promotes growth and investment at home as well as globally (Griswold, 2000b).

The reason it is difficult for policy makers in the developing economies to accept this altruistic line of logic is that they consider it a concealed attempt at protection. To them it amounts to a threat to market access in the industrial economies under the guise of labor standards and humanitarian concern. They view standards of any kind as neo-protectionism, be they health and safety, or environment, or labor. Developing countries strongly resent the link made between labor standards and dispute settlement mechanisms (DSMs) because the latter are binding. In addition, enhancing the power of labor would disturb the established economic and political equilibrium in the developing economies. Policy makers also see core labor standards as a threat to the economic strategies that they have adopted to benefit from globalization. Aversion to core labor standards is not limited to the developing economies. As the transnational corporations (TNCs) also have cost benefits from the inability of labor to organize effectively in the developing countries, their enthusiasm for promoting core labor standards is low. The two country groups, the developing and industrial, have expressed polar opposite views in this regard, which could be harmful to the fragile structure of the WTO.

A related knotty issue is that of child labor. The use of child labor is prevalent in most developing economies. According to an estimate as many as 250 million children are employed in the developing countries, at least half of them full time (Fallen and Tzannatos, 1998). Sometimes, albeit not always, children have to work in harmful conditions. Some civil organizations have proposed that the use of child labor must be prevented by taking measures like trade sanctions and consumer boycotts. These proposals are not problem-free. Trade sanctions generally hit hard and the tendency is to move the production of the product in question into the informal sector, which is known to have worse working conditions than the formal sector. Besides, trade sanctions may be implemented in such a manner that they work as protectionist measures. It should, however, be pointed out that labor standards and child labor are development problems, calling for a domestic policy response. They exist in all low-income developing economies. Close on 5 percent of child laborers worldwide work in the export sector (Short, 1999). If trade sanctions are imposed on exports that are produced with the help of child labor, it will harm the low-income countries and drive children into worse forms of employment. Beside, trade sanctions do nothing to improve the fate of the 95 percent of child laborers in the non-traded sectors. Therefore, each WTO member government should fine-tune its domestic strategies and resolve the issues of core labor standards and child labor in a manner most suitable to its own circumstances. The mandate of the WTO is to expand international trade in goods and services in a non-discriminatory manner, which does not have a bearing on these problem policy areas.

1.7 Managing trade liberalization

The seemingly beneficial process of trade liberalization is fraught with inherent problems. Although the benefits of trade liberalization in terms of higher incomes and enhanced opportunities have been discussed, debated, and delved into for decades, controversies have continued to rage around it almost interminably. There are several reasons. The first is the psychology of change: no one likes to disturb the *status quo*. Paradoxically this includes change for the better, or change that can potentially lead to greater opportunities for the economy as a whole. Resistance to change becomes more intense if it promises betterment in the medium or long term. Second, this process of change through trade liberalization creates winners and losers, which complicates the situation further. It matters little to the losers that their losses may be ephemeral and that the winners from liberalization gain more than the losers lose (WTO, 1998d).

Third, not all the developing economies gain from the liberalization of trade. Those that are relatively more open and at a higher stage of development and industrialization benefit more than those that are at a lower stage and have less open economies. If anything, the latter category apprehends that it is being marginalized by trade liberalization. Fourth, trade liberalization is viewed by some, particularly the non-governmental organizations in the industrial economies, as undesirably intrusive upon societies. They believe that it mauls the diversity of social values among and within nations. Free trade and the unbridled play of market forces, some apprehend, would lead to the adoption of lower standards so that countries were able to compete. Sound public policy may be a casualty of this process. The oft-repeated expression is "race to the bottom", particularly the debate about trade and the environment as well as that about labor standards. These views are based on preconceived notions. There is little empirical evidence of a race to the bottom. If anything, trade liberalization and increased competition tend to put upward pressure on labor and environmental standards (Oman, 2000).

Trade liberalization carries negative distributional consequences for some economic agents or groups. They resist it and lobby for protectionist policies. The most pragmatic policy stand is to secure the larger overall gains from trade liberalization. To be sure, there will be complaining groups who stand to lose from import competition. Their concern should be domestically addressed. If not, the trade liberalization process will soon become politically impossible. Slowing down trade liberalization measures or the adoption of a protectionist strategy is not the appropriate response to the distributional challenges. If this policy response is adopted, the overall gains from trade liberalization will be eroded. A more appropriate policy response is to provide safety nets and facilitate adjustment to a transforming economic reality through human capital formation and flexible labor and capital markets (WTO, 1998d).

As the gains from trade liberalization are achieved largely through transformations in modes of production and consumption, it is common to have labor and capital idle for short intervals while they are still moving between different phases. Matusz (1997) contends that this is sure to cause a temporary reduction in incomes and output. If the factors employed are more employment-"specific" to the previous phase, the reduction in incomes and output will be larger. Also, it will be more expensive and time-consuming to put these factors of production to alternative use. A highly specialized textile professional is unlikely to be put quickly to work in the software industry when textiles lose their comparative advantage. Likewise, it can take a long while and a great deal of expenditure to shift capital from, say, steel to semiconductors. These costs are called the "social costs of adjustment" and should be included in the cost–benefit calculations of trade and liberalization. There are other non-economic costs involved as well which are excluded by economic analysis.

Many countries, particularly the industrial ones, have sufficiently well developed social safety nets to keep populations out of poverty. These nets comprise unemployment insurance, social assistance, and adjustment assistance programs. Some of these programs explicitly target those displaced by import competition. For instance, the trade adjustment assistance scheme of the US provides some cash benefit and retraining to workers who lose their jobs owing to trade expansion. This scheme also provides extended unemployment insurance payments, called Trade Readjustment Allowances, relocation expenses, job search assistance, and worker retraining. Reskilling or skill upgrading is another important method of shortening the adjustment period and reducing the adverse impact of future earnings. Several European countries also have comparable schemes in operation and a small number of high-income developing countries are trying to develop them. An oft-heard complaint about these schemes is that they do not often benefit the target groups. It has been observed that many of the programs are targeted at the middle classes in the industrial economies and effectively fail to benefit those who are displaced by trade. Therefore, meticulous design of such programs is essential for their success (WTO, 1998d; Burtless *et al.*, 1998).

1.8 Challenges for the new trading system

To be sure, increasing globalization of economic activity has created, and will continue to create, new challenges for the global trading system. In addition, the role of the developing economies, particularly that of the NIEs, is sure to assume a higher profile on the global economic stage in the short and medium term. As a result of domestic economic reforms, including trade liberalization undertaken unilaterally and pursuant to GATT negotiations, a meaningful number of developing economies have not only integrated well into the global trading system but also have a

greater stake in it (Section 1.3). They also have a greater claim to participation in the WTO's decision-making process. Rights and obligations
under the WTO regime must continue to adapt to the changing character
and dimensions of global trade, otherwise the system will lose its credibility and relevance. WTO members must faithfully implement the
agreements negotiated during the Uruguay Round, make the required
domestic policy changes, and begin to see and address the issues that are
likely to take on significance during the twenty-first century. Schott (1996)
has a small wish list of issues to be addressed. The most pragmatic issues
on this wish list are:

1   Promoting new trade liberalization initiatives, beyond the "built-in"
    negotiating agenda[24] mandated by the Uruguay Round accords.
2   Expanding the WTO agenda to new issues, although care should be
    taken that the new issues are those on which members have arrived
    at consensus.
3   Ensuring the complementarity of regional and multilateral trade re-
    forms.
4   Progressing with institutional reforms in the WTO.

Once the Uruguay Round recommendations are implemented, non-agricultural tariffs in industrial countries will be reduced to low levels (Chapter
3). However, in some selected industries and in agricultural products tariff
barriers will still remain exceedingly high. For instance, in the US tariff
spikes will continue in textiles and clothing and in the EU in electronics.
As a result of the tariffication of farm trade barriers in the Uruguay Round
the level of tariffs binding on agriculture (sugar, wheat) and dairy products
will be of a high order in the EU, Japan, and the US. Developing economies
also need to reduce their peak tariffs, in particular they need to reduce the
gap between the rates they are bound to and their currently applied rates.

In the aftermath of the Seattle fiasco, the WTO has come in for a great
deal of criticism for not having developed a functional, transparent, democratic, and inclusive negotiating process. Perhaps an appropriate response
to this criticism is that multilateral negotiations worked reasonably well
during the GATT period. It is the failure at Seattle that has revealed that
the WTO – with its much larger structure and mandate – has outgrown the
old process. The failure should lead the global community to evolve a new
or different negotiating process. WTO members need to ensure that the
process they evolve has the characteristics that were found most wanting
at Seattle. That said, it will not be easy to evolve such a process. (Refer to
Chapter 4, Section 4.7.)

Tariff spikes are one, but a host of other areas need to be addressed in
the next round of MTNs. They will soon be addressed in the following
chapters, in particular in Chapter 4.

1.9 Summing up

The brisk growth of international trade in goods and services and in capital flows is a part of the rapidly globalizing economy which has made the WTO an extremely important multilateral organization. If anything, the WTO has become a key institution of global governance. It was established as a successor to the GATT. It has inherited GATT's half a century of MTNs-related knowledge and expertise. The WTO regime is a decisive and discernible improvement over the GATT regime. The most significant difference between the GATT and the WTO is the "single undertaking", which requires that members accept all the obligations of GATT. Developing economies that formerly received the benefit of some GATT codes without having to accept obligations in return are now required to call an end to their "free ride" and abide by all the WTO requirements.

Over the preceding half-century a great deal of trade liberalization has taken place in both developing and industrial economies. They have benefited from it through a variety of channels. A vast empirical literature exists on the static and dynamic gains from trade liberalization. Yet trade liberalization has never been a popular cause. Negotiations went far from smoothly during the Uruguay Round. The failure at Seattle is one of the examples of the difficulties faced by the global trading system. At the turn of the century it finds itself at a crossroads.

Policy makers are frequently reluctant to implement trade liberalization policies, owing to their perceived misgivings regarding the adjustment costs. Growing merchandise exports from the NIEs and other developing economies have led to increased competition in merchandise products in the industrial economies. Successful exporters from the developing economies began to be seen as a threat to prosperity in the industrial economies. They were accused of destabilizing firms in the importing countries, which in turn lobbied for protection. A large number of policy makers are erroneously convinced of the threat-to-prosperity theory, and resorted to the antidumping laws allowed by the GATT–WTO system. Trade liberalization causes loss of jobs in both developing and industrial countries in industries which are losing comparative advantage. Protection is simplistically seen by some as an instrument of job security. Trade liberalization also carries negative distributional consequences for some economic agents or groups. Besides, not all the developing economies gain from trade liberalization. The generalization holds that those economies that are relatively more open and at a higher stage of development and industrialization benefit more than those that are at a lower stage and have less open economies. Thus the seemingly beneficial process of trade liberalization is fraught with inherent problems, which in turn have created snags for the global trading system.

The increasing pace of globalization of economic activity is sure to create more challenges in the future for the global trading system. In this milieu, as many as twenty developing economies have done a meritorious job of integrating into the global economy. By contrast the developing countries that are at the other extreme of the spectrum, that is, the least developed countries, have failed to integrate with the global economy. The role of the NIEs and other high-income developing economies is sure to assume a higher profile on the global economic stage in the short and medium term. They will be more active participants in the global trading system and WTO's decision-making process. Members need to faithfully implement the recommendations of the Uruguay Round. In addition, rights and obligations under the WTO regime must continue to adapt to the changing character and dimensions of global trade. Members must make the required domestic policy changes and begin to address the issues that are likely to be of significance in the immediate future.

2 Seattle and its aftermath

Imagination is more important than knowledge.
Albert Einstein

2.1 The need for another round of MTNs

The Uruguay Round of multilateral trade negotiations (MTNs) was complete in 1994. The formal agreement was signed on 15 April 1994 in Marrakesh, Morocco. Therefore, it is also referred to as the Marrakesh Agreement. The conclusion of the Uruguay Round generated substantial gains in market access for many countries, including developing countries. One tangible result of the Marrakesh Agreement was the birth of the World Trade Organization (WTO) on 1 January 1995. Increased transparency and predictability that emanated from the enhanced WTO rules improved the commercial environment for both exporters and importers (discussed in Chapter 1). Implementation of various agreements made under the Uruguay Round was to continue to run through to 2000 in some cases and beyond for others. Implementation of the accord on the Multifiber Arrangement (MFA) was scheduled to continue through to 2004. Three important achievements of the post-Uruguay Round period are signing off on the Information Technology Agreement at Singapore, crafting the Basic Telecommunications Agreement, and the adoption of the Financial Services Agreement (Table 2.1). All these three agreements were substantial achievements of the open trading system, even if they were not media spectacles.

The flip side of the coin is that during the Uruguay Round and post-Uruguay Round period several failures also occurred that adversely affected the movement of the global trading system towards free trade. Many felt that the Uruguay Round took too long and achieved too little, given the amount of time, energy, and resources deployed. Besides, the Uruguay Round missed deadlines. As if that was not enough, it collapsed and had to be pulled back to its feet. These developments were enough to promote the creation and strengthening of the alternative regional trading systems. The EU frequently seemed to focus heavily on its regional agenda to the exclusion of its global responsibilities. Likewise, the US seemed preoccupied with its own twin regional arrangements, the North American Free Trade Agreement (NAFTA) and Asia Pacific Economic Co-operation (APEC), whose structures are very different.

A high and rising current account deficit in the US (4.3 percent of GDP in 2000) and high and persistent unemployment in the large EU economies[1] were contributing to the same anti-free-trade bias and exacerbation of protectionist pressures. Over the years a crude argument has gained ground in the US that trading with low-wage countries is depressing US wages and incomes, therefore the US must not trade with them. Anti-globalization sentiment was strong in the EU because foreign competition makes a convenient scapegoat for dysfunctional domestic policies that produce chronically high unemployment (Lindsey *et al.*, 1999). The EU's interests and, therefore, proposals for the new round are much more focused on expanding international bureaucracy than on reducing national barriers to trade. The EU favored the negotiation of international rules on competition policy, and early EU proposals on foreign investment emphasize the need to "preserve the ability of host countries to regulate the activities of investors". At the same time the EU defends its own protectionism in a zealous manner.

Japan, the third largest trading economy after the EU (of fifteen) and the US, has never been a leader in MTNs. In spite of being highly successful at exporting during the post-war period, Japanese policy makers have been less than enthusiastic about market opening. Presently they are absorbed in reviving the domestic economy. Although it is running large surpluses (2.8 percent of GDP in 2000), Japan's domestic market liberalization was traditionally perceived by its major trade partners as grudging. Slow market opening has tended to have a steep cost for the Japanese consumers. Sazanami *et al.* (1995) measured the consumer cost of trade barriers as 3 percent to 4 percent of Japanese GDP. They concluded that Japanese trade barriers reduce imports by at least US$50 billion annually. The dynamics of market liberalization is such that market liberalization wins domestic support only when major trading partners are also liberalizing and contributing their share to the liberalization process. Thus just before the launching of the Seattle Ministerial the international trading system was devoid of any enthusiasm for market liberalization.

Trade liberalization had suffered from a serious backlash during the post-Uruguay period. Some of the notable failures of this period were: the Free Trade Agreement of the Americas (FTAA) was stalled, the enlargement of the European Union (EU) was slowed down, the Early Voluntary Sectoral Liberalization proposals in the APEC forum at Kuala Lumpur in November 1998 were defeated, the Multilateral Agreement on Investment (MAI) was killed in December 1998, the US Congress initially stalled a twin vote on NAFTA parity for the Caribbean Basin countries, and the Africa Growth and Opportunity Act (AGOA). The measures were not passed until 2000. In addition, in the US, which had championed the free trade system in the post-war era, renewal of the "fast track" negotiating authority was defeated twice in the Congress. Despite the strong performance of the US economy in recent years, political support for continued trade liberalization has deteriorated in the face of misbegotten fears of globalization. Consequently, despite its success in the past, the WTO is having difficulty in promoting further trade liberalization on a multilateral basis.

Notwithstanding the Asian crisis (1997–98), most assessments show that the Asian economies stayed open (Das, 2000). However, policy mandarins did question the need to launch a new round of MTNs. Their query becomes more pointed when juxtaposed against the fact that several developing economies are either concluding or struggling to implement the commitments they made during the Uruguay Round. Paradoxically, these very arguments provide a sound rationale for initiating a new WTO round. As trade is widely accepted to be a driving force behind growth, further trade liberalization would have a stabilizing effect on the crisis-led economic dislocations. The new WTO round will not only help keep global markets open but will also further liberalization, which in turn will help policy mandarins manage calls from domestic constituencies for more protectionist responses. A larger imponderable is the scope of the next round.

The zen of trade policy liberalization is that when we stop, we fall.[2] Unless we continue to move forward, there is a considerable risk of back-sliding into protectionism, as non-tariff barriers (NTBs) replace tariff barriers and as countries resort to competitive regionalism. Thus, even to stay still, the global trading system should continue to liberalize. When trade liberalization is not progressing, efforts to maintain existing trade barriers and undo liberalization commitments with other protectionist measures make headway. The changing composition of national output, and in particular the increasing role of services, implies that we must broaden the scope of international trade agreements. The half-century of trade policy liberalization under the aegis of the General Agreement on Tariffs and Trade (GATT) and the WTO testifies to the fact that failure to move steadily forward condemns the trading system to start making retrograde movements. For instance, protectionism scored major successes, especially in the US, during the prolonged periods when the GATT became moribund immediately after the successful conclusion of the Kennedy Round (1964–67) and the Tokyo Round (1973–79). When endeavors towards MTNs are weak, RTAs proliferate, which sap support for WTO initiatives and create new obstacles to multilateral liberalization.

It should not be surprising that protectionism is on the rise despite the strength of the global economy. After the three sectoral agreements scheduled by the Uruguay Round were complete (Table 2.1), no multilateral negotiations of a serious nature and no unilateral liberalization initiatives were taken anywhere in the world. The 1990s are known for the second wave of regional trading agreements (RTAs). The global trading system

Table 2.1 The GATT/WTO trade rounds

Year, place/name, and negotiation details

1947, Geneva. **The birth of GATT**. On 30 October, the General Agreement on Tariffs and Trade (GATT) was signed by twenty-three nations. The Agreement contained tariff concessions agreed to during the first multilateral trade negotiations and a set of rules designed to prevent these concessions from being frustrated by restrictive trade measures.

1949, Annecy. **Second Round**. From April to August at Annecy, France, thirteen contracting parties exchanged some 5,000 tariff concessions.

1951, Torquay. **Third Round**. From September 1950 to April 1951, thirty-eight contracting parties exchanged some 8,700 tariff concessions in the English town, yielding tariff reductions of about 25 percent in relation to the 1948 level.

1956, Geneva. **Fourth Round**. Completed in May, the round produced some US$2.5 billion worth of tariff reductions. These tariff reductions were exchanged between twenty-six contracting parties.

1960–61, Geneva. **Dillon Round**. Named in honor of the US Under-Secretary of State Douglas Dillon, who proposed the negotiations, the fifth round was divided into two phases: the first was concerned with EEC member states for the creation of a single schedule of concessions for the Community, and the second with further tariff negotiations, which resulted in about 4,400 tariff concessions exchanged between twenty-six countries covering US$4.9 billion of trade.

1964–67, Geneva. **Kennedy Round**. For the first time, negotiations departed from the product-by-product approach to an across-the-board or linear method of cutting tariffs for industrial goods. The working hypothesis of a 50% target cut in tariff levels was achieved in many areas. Concessions covered an estimated total value of trade of about US$40 billion. The number of participants increased to sixty-two.

1973–79, Geneva. **Tokyo Round**. Launched in the Japanese capital, the seventh round resulted in tariff reductions and bindings covering more than US$300 billion of trade. As a result, the weighted average tariff on manufactured goods in the world's nine major industrial markets declined from 7.0% to 4.7%. Agreements were reached on subsidies and countervailing measures, technical barriers to trade, import licensing procedures, government procurement, customs valuation, a revised antidumping code, trade in bovine meat, dairy products, and civil aircraft. In all, 102 contracting parties participated.

1986–94, Geneva. **Uruguay Round**. Results of the most comprehensive trade negotiations ever undertaken included average tariff cuts of 40% on industrial products; an average increase of tariff bindings from 21% to 73% for developing countries, from 78% to 99% for developed countries, and from 73% to 98% for transition economies; a comprehensive program of agricultural reform; phaseout of quantitative restrictions on textiles and clothing; new agreements on trade in services, intellectual property rights, sanitary and phytosanitary measures, and trade-related investment measures; and strengthened agreements on safeguards, technical barriers, customs valuation, import licensing, state trading, subsidies, and antidumping measures. In all, 123 contracting parties participated. The round also strengthened the dispute settlement systems and created the World Trade Organization.

1997–99, Information technology. In March, forty governments agreed to eliminate customs duties on IT products beginning on 1 July 1997 and eliminating tariffs altogether by 2000. International trade in these products amounts to some US$600 billion annually.
Basic telecommunications. Negotiations successfully concluded in February with sixty-nine governments agreeing to wide-ranging liberalization measures. The agreement entered into force in February 1998.
Financial services. Negotiations successfully concluded in December when seventy governments agreed to open their financial service sectors, covering more than 95% of trade in banking, insurance, securities, and financial information. The agreement entered into force on 1 March 1999.

1999, Seattle Ministerial. In all, 135 member countries of the WTO participated.

Sources: Das (1999); various GATT and WTO publications relating to the rounds.

seems stalemated. An oft-used metaphor for multilateral trade negotiations is that of riding a bicycle: either you move forward or you fall over. To all appearances, the bicycle has stopped. Therefore, it is essential to launch a new round of MTNs and keep the bicycle moving forward.

2.2 Seeds of discord

Notwithstanding the preparations by the WTO secretariat (Section 2.5) and the general perception of a strong global economy during 1999, seeds of discord existed before the Seattle Ministerial. There were deep divisions of opinion, beliefs, and expectations which could be divided into both North–South and East–West axes. A lot of division in opinion was more complex and could not be divided along these traditional axes. The differences of opinion and expectations between the US, the EU (of fifteen), and Japan on the one hand,[3] and among the industrialized and developing economies on the other, were too large to bridge in a short space of time (Section 2.5). Numerous contentious issues persisted between these countries and country groups. The resulting disharmony was enough to bedevil the preparations for the Seattle Ministerial. Besides, the WTO system had a strong tendency to work in a non-transparent manner. Lack of transparency can have enormous cost in international negotiations where 135 country delegations are involved (Section 2.6). Hindsight reveals that some of the largest trading economies and country groups tried to manipulate the WTO system, which led to aggravation of mutual distrust and erosion of the credibility of the system.

Weeks before the Seattle Ministerial, developing economies had expressed their deep-seated disappointment with the WTO system. They believed that five years after the creation of WTO they had not seen the promised benefits. They also put forward several proposals for the forthcoming Ministerial, including changing some of the WTO rules. According to one count the WTO received 220 negotiating proposals from 135 developing economies (*BW*, 1999). However, the large trading economies and country groups dismissed the proposals.

Significant disagreements existed in the various basic areas to be taken up for future negotiations. The industrial economies put forward their own proposals to further empower the WTO by introducing new areas such as investment, competition, government procurement, and labor and environmental standards. Their objective was to broaden and deepen the WTO (Summers, 1999). The proposals were opposed by the developing economies because they thought that the result of accepting them would amount to opening their markets more to the large and highly competitive corporations of the industrial economies. Many developing economies wanted some relief from the obligations of the Uruguay Round, which they found difficult to meet. They had come with a list of exemptions from obligations negotiated during the Uruguay Round, but neither the EU nor the US and the developed members of the Cairns Group were willing to address them.

Over five decades after the signing of the original GATT treaty in 1947, global trade has continued to be bedeviled by strong agricultural protectionism. Although GATT technically applied to trade in agricultural goods, its requirements were roundly ignored. Consequently, agricultural protection and subsidies remained outside any real multilateral discipline despite several rounds of MTNs until implementation of the Uruguay Round in 1995. Agriculture can be called the last great bastion of protectionism. Trade in agriculture remains subject to profound and costly distortions. While average tariff barriers have plummeted steadily during the post-war period, those on agriculture have remained stubbornly high, especially in the industrial economies. While average agricultural tariffs on manufactures have plummeted to almost 5 percent, those on agricultural goods average more than 40 percent (Josling, 1998). This average conceals tariff spikes as high as 300 percent and virtual bans and prohibitive tariff rate quotas on certain goods.

In 1986, when the Uruguay Round began, agricultural subsidies within the OECD economies totaled some US$326 billion. In 1998 it was higher, at US$362 billion (Hill, 2000). The EU (of fifteen) spent nearly US$143 billion on farm support in 1998, the US US$102 billion, and Japan US$57 billion (OECD, 2000b; Smith *et al.*, 1999). Some EU economies, particularly France, are arguing about the forms of agricultural export subsidies. These subsidies have created enormous distortions in global agricultural trade. Eliminating or reducing them would have benefited not just US farmers but also farmers from developing countries, whose agricultural exports have been badly affected by the subsidies. Subsidized exports outcompete domestic producers. Trade distortions created by export subsidies, together with market access barriers, penalize developing economies by hampering the development of local agriculture. According to a recent study, if agricultural tariffs were slashed by half, it would enhance global welfare by US$89 billion. Of this almost half, or US$43 billion, would accrue to Japan, US$12.7 billion to the EU, and US$6.0 billion to the US (ADFAT, 1999). The welfare gains that are likely to accrue to the EU, Japan, and the US are six times the cumulative welfare gains for Africa, Latin America, the People's Republic of China (PRC), India, Indonesia, Malaysia, the Philippines, and Thailand. Given this distribution of welfare gains, liberalizing agricultural trade can be considered as less a concession to the developing economies than a favor the industrial economies can do themselves.

The EU and the US account for approximately half of global farm trade, and are two of the most important trading entities. That they have widely divergent stands on various issues, including trade in agriculture, was well known since the early period of the Uruguay Round, when the two nearly led it to the point of collapse. While the EU dragged its feet on opening agricultural markets, the US still tried to protect textiles and apparel, steel, peanuts, and dairy products. Their disagreements were further aggravated during 1999 on issues like bananas, hormone-treated beef, and genetically modified (GM) foods. No issue created as much bad blood in the runup to the Seattle Ministerial as did agriculture. Leading agricultural exporters like Argentina, Australia, Brazil, and the US wanted an all-out assault on closed agricultural markets. But the EU, Japan, and Korea with their allies were fighting to keep objectives much more modest during the Seattle Ministerial. The result was an impasse between the two country groups.

As regards the myriad areas of disagreement, negotiating delegations should have known that MTNs are exceedingly complex exercises and that not all participating countries can expect to achieve what they consider to be positive results in each area of interest to them. However, all the participants benefit from broad-based tariffs and NTB reductions. All the participating countries benefit even if there are temporary negative side effects. The Uruguay Round testified to this fact. While some results benefited all the participants, various aspects were identified as having potential negative implications for some.

2.3 Launching the third Ministerial

The Ministerial Conference is the highest-level decision-making body of the WTO. As required by the Marrakesh Agreement, it meets at least once every two years. The first WTO Ministerial was held in Singapore in December 1996, followed by the Geneva Ministerial in May 1998. It coincided with the commemoration of the fiftieth anniversary of the WTO's predecessor, the GATT, held during the Geneva Ministerial when President Clinton invited WTO members to hold the third Ministerial Conference in the United States.

Trade Ministers of the 135 member countries of the WTO[4] accepted the invitation to meet in Seattle during 30 November–3 December 1999, to define the international trade agenda for the beginning of the next millennium. Officials of thirty governments that were negotiating membership of the WTO and scores of international organizations also attended the Seattle Ministerial as observers. The Seattle meeting was dedicated to "developing the framework for the global trading system in the twenty-first century" (Moore, 1999). The Ministers were expected to review the implementation of the WTO agreements during four days of plenary sessions and at the closing session launch the next round of MTNs. They were possibly going to name the new round of MTNs the Millennium Round, or the Seattle Round, or the Clinton Round. Mike Moore, the Secretary General of the WTO, had already started referring to it as the Development Round, although in academic circles it was being referred to as the Millennium Round.[5] This nomenclature was apparently based on the timing of the launch of the new round. Eight rounds of MTNs were successfully completed under the aegis of the GATT. As Table 2.1 shows, if launched, this round would have been the ninth round of MTNs, the first under the aegis of the WTO.

The 1998 Geneva Ministerial set in motion preparations for the Seattle Ministerial. Expectations from the forthcoming round in all the member and observer countries were immense; so was interest among the policy mandarins, and the academic community. The number of WTO Internet users broke the 200,000 barrier as early as October 1999, when 201,101 users accessed the site from 161 countries. The quantity of documents and data downloaded reached a new record of 88,000 Mb, or the equivalent of about 88 million pages of text.

The WTO secretariat had made preparations for the forthcoming Ministerial and on 4 November 1999 the General Council had dealt with several potentially problematic issues, namely decisions regarding observer status at the Seattle Ministerial, Dispute Settlement Understanding (DSU) amendment, and a review of 1994 exemption granted to the US for the Jones Act which excluded foreign participation in domestic shipping.

As regards the conduct of the Seattle Ministerial, the plan was as follows. Five working or negotiation groups were planned to be established in Seattle. Each group was to be chaired by a Minister and could be divided into subgroups. Singapore was to chair the negotiating group on agriculture, Lesotho that on market access, and Hong Kong that on "New Issues". Brazil's name was proposed for presiding over the negotiation group on implementation, and the one on systemic issues (transparency and relations with civil society) was likely to be chaired by Chile. Although the negotiating procedure was yet to be decided, each group would have represented fifteen to twenty member countries. The country participation was to be determined according to a participating country's economic weight as well as the special interest a country might have in a given theme. If the working group managed to reach a consensus, the text was to be introduced in the "Green Room". (Refer to Section 2.4.) The Green Room was to comprise fifteen to twenty country delegations representing different regions and different levels of development. Finally, the Green Room consensus was to be presented to the full WTO membership, which ultimately needed to approve it. *Prima facie* it was a logical, functional, and even imaginative procedure (ICTSD, 1999).

The Global economic and trading environment was widely considered an encouraging background. It was hoped it would contribute to the success of the Seattle Ministerial. Despite the Asian crisis of 1997–98 the good sense of governments and the WTO framework kept markets open, providing a crucial base for recovery. The five crisis-affected Asian economies[6] were busy making their famous V-shaped recovery. Their GDP had contracted by an average of 7.7 percent in 1998, but in 1999 their average GDP growth rate had bounced back to 6.8 percent (ADB, 2000). Global GDP grew by 3.3 percent in 1999, which was substantially higher than

2.5 percent in 1998 (*WEO*, 2000). A strengthening of world economic output in 1999 reversed the slowdown of world trade in the first half of 1999 and led to a dynamic expansion of trade in the second half. Global merchandise exports grew by 3.5 percent in 1999 and those of commercial services grew by 1.5 percent (WTO, 2000b). The US economy continued to provide a major stimulus to the world economy and trade in 1999, as its domestic demand grew by 5.5 percent.

2.4 Mechanics of failure

2.4.1 Green Room consultations

Four out of five mandated working groups, mentioned in the preceding section, came together on 1 December. The fifth was to meet on 2 December. Aside from the release of some heavily bracketed texts in the areas of agriculture, implementation, and market access there were few advances made in reaching substantive agreement on most issues. Bracketed text implies disagreement over the bracketed parts of the text. During the negotiations it is common to have large parts of the text in parentheses or many parts under parentheses in a large part of the text. (See Section 2.6 below.) No text was issued on the New Issues because the views of the delegations were so far apart. There was substantial opposition among delegations about going forward with negotiations.

A preliminary Committee of the Whole comprised of representatives from all 135 WTO members and chaired by US Trade Representative Charlene Barshefsky met on the morning of 1 December. Barshefsky urged delegates to send senior officials with decision-making authority to the mandated working groups. Although she notified delegations that she reserved the right to hold Green Room meetings, she preferred an inclusive approach such as that afforded by the working group structure. However, delegations continued to meet in a number of informal and bilateral sessions. An impromptu mini-Green Room process evolved and continued. The pre-Seattle discord continued unabated, if anything it worsened. All-night negotiating sessions between Ministers turned into feuding and finished in abject failure.

Although theoretically the WTO operates by consensus, the reality is generally different. The members of the Quadrilateral Group, the so-called Quad, namely Canada, the EU (of fifteen), Japan, and the US, have traditionally functioned as an informal steering committee for the WTO system. They continued to function in a non-transparent manner and held informal meetings on crucial issues in small groups to which some of the developing countries' ambassadors were not invited. It must, however, be stated that the principal trading developing economies were normally invited for discussions. As these meetings took place in a Green Room, next to the office of the Director General of the WTO at the Centre William

Rappard in Geneva, the discussions were referred to as the "Green Room" meetings.

The Green Room[7] process came in for a lot of criticism and has been painted in a villainous light. Some analysts went so far as to call the process "medieval" and irrelevant. The Green Room process was considered one of the elements of failure at Seattle. It was a legacy of the GATT and was once a functional mechanism for trade negotiations. Participation in the Green Room process was decided on the basis of issues, and only the most active delegations in negotiations participated. As for the question of which country delegations participated in the Green Room consultations, they typically included the Quad, Australia, New Zealand, Switzerland, Norway, sometimes one or two transition economies, and some developing economies. The developing economies that often participated in the Green Room process included Argentina, Brazil, Chile, Colombia, Egypt, Hong Kong, India, Mexico, Pakistan, South Africa, and at least one ASEAN economy. Most of the other developing economies kept out for lack of adequate resources or capabilities (Schott and Watal, 2000). These delegations got together to decide on diverse issues. The number of participants had gone on increasing over time. For instance, in the Tokyo Round period Green Room consultations involved eight delegations, while by the time the Seattle Ministerial started the number had risen to twenty-five to thirty delegations. With growing WTO membership, the Green Room process excluded too many new members of the WTO and subsequently it became impossible to build any consensus on any important issue.

The Green Room process became dysfunctional at Seattle. A brazen conference dynamics was adopted. The US trade representative, Charlene Barshefsky, presided over a seemingly undemocratic process. On the second day she announced her "right" as chairperson to use procedures of her own choosing to get a declaration out of the meeting. She and the WTO Director General, Mike Moore, set up several Green Room meetings on key issues of disagreement. Putatively, the plan was to get the major trade powers to agree among themselves, apply pressure in the Green Room on a few influential developing countries to go along, and then pull together a declaration to launch a new round that all the 135 members would be asked to accept in a general meeting on the last day.

For the first time ever the number of participating developing countries was so large that as a majority of them did not participate in the Green Room process described above they found themselves totally marginalized. They were not even onlookers because they had no knowledge of what was going on in the Green Room meetings. Their discomfiture knew no bounds on the third day of the Ministerial when Ministers of African countries, the Caribbean Community, and some Latin American economies complained about lack of transparency in the negotiations.[8] They felt that they were excluded from deliberations on issues vital to their future growth, therefore they did not feel obliged to support a Ministerial text produced without consensus. Thus the draft declaration that was to be presented on the final day stood a good chance of being rejected by the developing economies. In the end the Seattle Ministerial was suspended without attempting even a brief declaration (Jonquieres and Williams, 1999).

2.4.2 A structural limitation

One result of the collapse in Seattle is that a major structural weakness of the WTO has been identified. The WTO was bitterly criticized for its lack of transparency in Seattle. Transparency is often called the mainstay of the WTO agreements, and members assign highest priority to the need for transparency in the conduct of global trade. Both GATT and GATS call on members to publish all measures that affect the operation of the agreements. As opposed to these expectations, rules and requirements, the GATT–WTO system has frequently been perceived as non-transparent. The famous Leutwilder Group of eminent persons' report[9] of 1985 had noted that a

> major reason why things have gone wrong with the trading system is that trade policy actions have often escaped scrutiny and discussion at the national level. Clear analysis and greater openness in the making of trade policy are badly needed, along with greater public knowledge of how the multilateral system works.
>
> (GATT, 1985)

A decade and a half went past, and the WTO had to face the same music in Seattle. That the WTO should be more transparent was an express wish of the Group of Eight (G-8) leaders in the Kyushu–Okinawa summit (G-8, 2000). There have been problems in obtaining information on the activities of the WTO. The critics, therefore, felt that the organization was being secretive because it was trying to hide something that was not in the interests of everyone.

Other than the opacity of the WTO system, the decision-making process that was developed half a century ago was found to be unsuitable for the contemporary period. (Refer to Chapter 4, Section 4.8.) Over the last half-century, a good number of developing economies became successful exporters and, therefore, they expected to have deeper involvement in the WTO. Other than deeper involvement, sixty-five of them had participated in the negotiations that led to the formation of the WTO. Current membership includes more than 100 developing economies. Together they can reflect strength in numbers. Growth and expanding trade made them more important than they ever were in the WTO scheme, yet the decision-making processes of the WTO have not evolved to accommodate their agenda items.

Along with rapid growth in interest and numbers, developing economies steadily increased the size and activity of their diplomatic missions in

Geneva. The participation of developing economies has also been encouraged by changes in the operating style of the WTO. The two-tier system of membership that held industrial economies to a higher level of obligations has been eliminated. The current system is a unified one, in which all member countries follow the same rules and operate under the same basic trade laws, although developing economies can have a longer period to make adjustments than the industrial economies.

To this arcane, non-transparent, non-democratic negotiating process, add the US insistence on putting labor standards in all trade agreements and endorsement of the use of trade sanctions to enforce them. The Singapore Declaration had clearly stated what numerous economists believe to be the case, that is, "the International Labor Organization is the competent body to set and deal with these standards". Piling non-trade issues on to an institution specifically designed to address trade issues was a travesty of logic. The US insistence was a bad-faith violation of the understanding reached at the WTO's first Ministerial in December 1996. In making this demand, it appears that US President Bill Clinton had caved in to pressure from labor interests (Irwin, 2000). Developing countries correctly apprehended that labor standards could become just a new pretext for restricting their exports. Several Asian economies (in particular India, Pakistan, and Thailand) were vociferously opposed to it; developing countries presented a consensual front opposing the US demand on core labor standards. Some analysts regard this as one of the largest stumbling blocks at the Seattle Ministerial.

Several developing economies that exported textiles and apparel in a big way were upset by the US press briefing during the Seattle Ministerial declaring that acceleration of its textile liberalization commitments and discussion of its antidumping mechanism were off the table. Likewise, the developing country delegations were unpleasantly surprised when Pascal Lamy, the EU Trade Commissioner, opposed negotiations on implementation. While he acknowledged that implementation was a problem in "certain areas", that could be addressed in the context of a comprehensive new round (ICTSD, 1999).

2.5 The agenda in parentheses

In preparation for the Ministerial, the WTO secretariat had prepared a long agenda document in October 1999 (WTO, 1999d), which had seventy-nine paragraphs. They were all bracketed, implying that nothing was agreed. The draft agenda was a catalogue of contradictory positions rather than a basis for negotiations. The EU and Japan did not countenance demands from the US and the Cairns Group for far reaching negotiations on agriculture. Partly to deflect this pressure on its highly protectionist Common Agricultural Policy (CAP), the EU was pushing for a broader negotiating agenda that covered such issues as investment and competition policy, which were laudable objectives in their own right. To the US delegation, the EU position looked like "negotiate on anything but agriculture" (*Economist*, 1999). A group of fifteen substantial traders among developing economies called the G-15 held a meeting during 17–18 August at Bangalore, in India, and prepared a fairly pragmatic agenda. This agenda could have been a starting point. In addition, a large number of agenda issues were proposed by developing economies (Section 2.2) but the Geneva decision-making machinery could not accommodate such diversity of views.

The US delegation pushed for a much narrower agenda, partly to speed up negotiations. However, their narrow agenda included a WTO working party on the links between trade and labor rights. The EU echoed this demand. Developing countries were bitterly against any linking of trade and labor issues. They correctly saw in it a new pretext for rich-country protectionism. Many developing countries were still discussing the Uruguay Round, which they thought gave them a raw deal. Some developing countries (including India, Pakistan, and the Philippines) were not interested in discussing any further liberalization until they were granted leeway in implementing previous commitments in such areas as intellectual property and customs practices. This was stringently opposed by the US and was considered tantamount to "reopening done deals". With such wide disparities in the stand taken by various delegations, any kind of consensus could not possibly emerge. Delegations were looking for canaries in a coal mine.

An agenda document littered with parentheses was a not uncommon incident. At the Punta del Este meeting in 1986, where the Uruguay Round was launched, the scenario was the same. Still, the prospects of a launch looked better from the outset because the outline of a balanced deal that needed to be clinched existed for the participating delegations. The ambience at Seattle was more like that in 1982 when efforts to launch in Geneva failed because France adamantly blocked any serious negotiations on agriculture.

After weeks of, often acrimonious, negotiation WTO ambassadors abandoned efforts to agree on an agenda one week before the Seattle Ministerial. They were aware that starting the four-day Ministerial without a script could plainly be catastrophic. Therefore, informal consultations continued until hours before the commencement. A last-minute attempt by the White House to generate political momentum by getting more than thirty world leaders to join President Clinton fell flat.

2.6 Breakdown of the old GATT process

As set out in the preceding sections, the Green Room process had evolved during the early days of the GATT and it worked well in achieving its objective of arriving at consensus among the contracting parties to the GATT. Consensus building engaged a small group of delegations, while the rest were relatively passive. That this process worked well is testified by the fact that eight rounds of MTNs were successfully completed under the sponsorship of the GATT. Delegations worked together more or less harmoniously to produce concrete benefits for all the contracting parties and the multilateral trading system. These delegations came to the GATT to "do business" in a pragmatic manner. Impasses occurred in the GATT period as well but ways were found to circumscribe them. Delegations left political rhetoric to other international fora like the United Nations (Schott and Watal, 2000). It should, however, be pointed out that the GATT system was more limited and neither covered agriculture and textiles nor had a Single Undertaking.

The old GATT system operated by consensus, although voting or majority rule were not excluded.[10] If none of the members present disagreed with a decision, it was assumed that a consensus has been arrived at. Country groups had fairly operational understandings about each other's stands. Large traders like the EU and the US took the lead in devising the GATT agenda and they did not insist on full participation by developing economies. The consensus rule was not abused. Full participation should be taken to mean "full and/or immediate" compliance. In turn, developing economies did not block progress in trade talks because of two reasons. First, trade accords made few immediate demands on them. There was no compulsion to join the Agreements. Second, developing economies made huge gains from the commitments of the industrial economies that were extended to them on a most-favored-nation basis. They were aware of the fact that, as the weaker partners in the GATT system, they benefited significantly from the well functioning of the multilateral rule-based trading system.

The consensus-building process outlined above has broken down in the WTO era. Two factors contributed to the breakdown, which had occurred before the Seattle Ministerial. First, as stated earlier, the WTO membership has expanded to many developing countries that were previously either not members or inactive players in the trade negotiations. As the global trading system evolved, developing economies had become better integrated in the trading system. They had a greater stake and claim in the WTO system than in its predecessor. Therefore they now participate more actively than they ever did in the past during the GATT period. More opinions simply lead to greater diversity of opinion. Second, unlike the GATT period the WTO members could not be "free riders" on negotiated agreements. The "single undertaking" clause of the Uruguay Round demanded that developing countries participate in all the negotiated agreements. This needed substantial commitment to greater reforms of their trade barriers and domestic regulations than during the GATT regime, making it mandatory for them to be better informed about the issues under negotiation and the negotiation process. Some of them were dissatisfied with obligations they had accepted under the Uruguay Round without participating in the negotiations. These developing economies were facing difficulties in the implementation of regulations that were required to fulfill their obligations. This made it even more difficult to craft an agreement on agenda.

2.7 Backlash against globalization

Another big challenge came from a growing international backlash against globalization, which was more than economic. A strong perception that globalization has created winners and losers has taken hold. The same enriching competitive, liberalization process that neoclassical economists laud does indeed exact costs. The doctrine of competitive advantage, *à la* Michael Porter, has a salutary influence in a globalizing economy if you have wherewithal with which to be competitive. However, if an economy has had a history of poorly trained manpower and institutional structure and an inefficient government system, globalization can do little good. This does not imply that some have to lose for the others to win, although globalization has worsened some people's lives. Instead of denying the failings of globalization, one needs to set them in some sort of context. One needs to try to work out what governments and people on the comfortable side of the "red-lacquered gate" can do to solve them (Micklethwait and Wooldridge, 2000). The principal reason this issue has continued to be so frustrating is that supporters and opponents of globalization rarely listen to each other. There is so much evidence available that each side can go on *ad infinitum* without ever bothering to acknowledge the other.

Some observers of the globalization process opine that it is ruled by the laws of the market applied to suit the powerful. Concerns regarding the negative influences have been expressed by a diverse range of individuals, from Pope John Paul II to George Soros.[11] Various global issues have huge political and cultural dimensions, and economics and the laws of the market often seem out of synch with them, leading to negative consequences (Mickelthwait and Wooldridge, 2000). That a backlash against globalization could derail the efforts to commence new international liberalization initiatives and promote protectionist pressure around the world was well known before the Seattle Ministerial. Although some backlash could be found in the developing economies, there was little reaction against trade liberalization in the crisis-stricken Asian economies. Paradoxically, despite the continuing strong economic performance, some worrisome tendencies were emerging in the US. This trend was disconcerting because the US was not only the largest exporting country in the world[12] but also played a vitally important role in the development of the global trading system.

The WTO had become to leftist mythology what the United Nations had become to the militia movement, the center of a global conspiracy against all that was good and decent (Krugman, 1999). Several thousand disparate anti-WTO demonstrators from about 1,200 non-governmental organizations (NGOs) protested in the streets of Seattle against free trade.[13] They made WTO the scapegoat for all that was wrong in an unequal world.

These citizens' groups become increasingly powerful at the corporate, national, and international levels, ranging from environment groups and labor unions to human rights activists, and development lobbies had differing agendas. They were well organized and used the media in masterly fashion. In the past they had succeeded in arousing enough public interest and pressure. They had succeeded during the Earth Summit in Rio de Janeiro in 1992 in pushing through an agreement on controlling greenhouse gases, during the World Bank's anniversary meeting in 1994 in forcing a rethink of the Bank's goals and in sinking the Multilateral Agreement on Investment (MAI) in 1998, which was a draft treaty to harmonize the rules of foreign investment under the aegis of the OECD.

In Seattle, these citizens' groups expressed their displeasure over everything from genetically modified crops to fishing subsidies. They decried a panoply of global ills: deforestation, child labor, overfishing, and pollution. It made for colorful television. Red-jacketed steelworkers marched alongside environmentalists dressed as endangered green sea turtles and monarch butterflies. They were determined to stop or delay the launch of the next round of MTNs. However, they achieved little more than publicity. The demonstrators did not torpedo the Seattle Ministerial but it was sunk *inter alia* by numerous and serious deadlocks at the negotiating table.

Lindsey (2000) has asserted that the game plan of the anti-globalization movement was clear. Attack the global economy by attacking the multilateral economic and financial organizations. To the movement international bureaucracies formed an unlovable symbol of the global economy. The International Monetary Fund (IMF), the World Bank, and the WTO had much to answer for when it came to their influence on economic development in low-income countries. By placing these multilateral organizations at the center of the debate, critics of free international markets in goods and services put their opponents on the defensive. The economists' case in favor of national governments adopting policies of openness and competition to spur growth and opportunity is overwhelming. However, when the issue for the anti-globalization movement is whether unelected and unaccountable international bureaucracies should impose their policy prescriptions on sovereign national governments, those same policies look much more suspicious (Lindsey, 2000). The targets of the anti-globalization movement have been incorrectly, if naively, chosen. The institutions they have chosen to attack are not fundamentally responsible for the policy outcomes they deplore. The real object of their hostility is the trend towards freer trade and freer markets, unrestricted mergers, the perceived powers of global corporations, which have swept the global economy over the past two decades. To be sure, that trend did not result from the machinations of international bureaucrats. Besides, it would be sure to persist even if the IMF, the World Bank, and the WTO were to melt in thin air.

We need to answer the question whether unelected and unaccountable international bureaucracies, like the WTO, should impose their policy prescriptions on sovereign national governments or not. To make international agreements work, international bodies have to have some quasi-judicial process and/or authority that determines when ostensibly domestic measures become trade barriers. When they do, they violate the treaty – that is the WTO. Before the birth of the WTO, this process was slow and cumbersome. During the WTO era, the process has become swift and decisive. It needs to be emphasized that the much feared and maligned power of the WTO to overrule local laws is strictly limited to enforcement of the spirit of the existing trade agreements. It cannot force sovereign countries that are skeptical about the benefits of globalization to open their markets to trade and their economies to foreign investment. Nonetheless, if most sovereign countries are eager, or willing, to join the WTO and participate in globalization, it is because they are convinced that the WTO and the globalization are in their own interest (Krugman, 1999).

The real backlash against globalization was more substantive than the above narrative has indicated. The principal causes underpinning it were created over the decade of the 1990s. Although several issues within the international finance and trade regimes can be identified easily, the causes were not limited to mere economic issues. Bergsten (2000) has pointed to income and social disparities that globalization has tended to increase in several countries. Globalization is widely blamed for leaving some countries and some groups of people in many countries behind. European aversion to genetically modified US food has become well known, and globalization gets the blame. American anxiety regarding "races to the bottom" in several spheres like labor standards and environmental standards is also a chestnut. Some developing economies are now raising doubts about the global trading system itself and wondering about specifics like certain aspects of intellectual property rights. Although not all, many of these are merely perceived wrongs. But perception is an aspect of reality. Paradoxically the backlash against globalization is severe in the US, which at the time of writing is experiencing the longest economic upswing of the business cycle.

2.8 Dragons' teeth

A Chinese proverb says that if you sow dragons' teeth you will harvest storms. Certainly there were more than a few dragons' teeth in Seattle: wide discord in the stands taken by two of the largest trading entities and other country groups noted earlier, the unwillingness of powerful WTO members to be flexible, sensitive, and contemplate serious liberalization, strong, diverse, and intransigent views on the agenda, the breaking down of the old GATT consensus-building process, a large number of developing economies trying to participate actively, lack of adequate preparation in the run-up to the Ministerial, the non-transparency of the negotiation and decision-making processes, a strong backlash against globalization, structural and institutional weaknesses of the WTO, the inexperience of the WTO's new Director General, and sheer unwieldiness of a meeting of 135 member countries.

A large number of developing economies became new members of the WTO. Many of these new – as well as old – developing country members became more assertive during the post-Uruguay Round period. They wanted to participate in defining the Seattle agenda. A good deal of mistrust existed between the developing and the industrial economies in the post-Uruguay Round period. Developing countries pointed out that they were having problems implementing their Uruguay Round commitments and that taking on further obligations could be more problematic for them. They were disgruntled over the poor implementation of agreements by the industrial economies, particularly in the areas of trade in textiles and clothing. Developing economies also complained that promises of technical assistance as well as "special and differential treatment" by the industrial economies were not being kept. Lastly, long-drawn-out and deep-seated disagreement over the choice of the Director General of the WTO during 1999 had caused a good deal of ill feeling among the developing countries.

A preliminary Committee of the Whole comprising representatives from all 135 WTO members was chaired by US trade representative Charlene Barshefsky. The leader of one of the "most self-interested WTO delegations" acting as an independent, and conceivably neutral, chairperson was considered little short of a charade by many delegations, including some members of the Quad (Fried, 2000).[14] As elaborated above, there were major fissures among WTO delegations and substantive differences of opinion in Seattle that were often split among subgroups. Some delegations, while pleading allegiance to free trade, lobbied furiously for trade regulations most favorable to their parochial national interests. All this coalesced to create a good deal of pressure for a major retreat from the principle of free trade. Demonstrators in the streets were given undue credit for stopping the global trade negotiations cold. There were serious and substantive disagreements among the WTO members, and the consensus-building process had broken down. The next round of MTNs was a non-starter even without the demonstrators.

2.9 Prognostications

After December 1999 Seattle became synonymous with failure of the WTO Ministerial. Notwithstanding the street theater in Seattle, few analysts believe that a retreat from free trade is on the cards. The real GDP growth of the global economy has been estimated at 4.2 percent for 2000 and projected at 3.9 percent for 2001 (*WEO*, 2000). A retreat is possible only if trade creates unemployment. A deep and prolonged recession encourages governments to change their trade policies. Although only the unsound or ill informed will be strongly optimistic about an early launch of the next round of MTNs, giving up hope is not rational. Failure at Seattle must not lead policy makers to conclude that there will be no rounds of MTNs in the foreseeable future. Despair is hardly warranted.

The foregoing exposition proves that the Third Ministerial was doomed to failure. Little wonder that it had to be suspended. Although disappointing, and even dismaying, the suspension was not a surprising conclusion. A suspension of this nature was not unprecedented in the history of the multilateral trading system. However, recent history testifies that after a suspension of negotiations, a breakthrough is always achieved. Two of the most recent examples of the suspension of MTNs followed by breakthroughs are:

1   At the time of the mid-term review of the Uruguay Round, in Montreal, on 9 December 1998, it was decided that the Trade Negotiating Committee should meet again in the first week of April 1989. The results achieved in Montreal – the agenda for the second half of the Uruguay Round – were put "on hold" until then. After stalling, a breakthrough was achieved in Geneva in April 1989.
2   The Brussels Ministerial Meeting in December 1990 was organized to complete the Uruguay Round negotiations. However, on 7 December the chairman declared that the Uruguay Round would have to be prolonged. Although substantial progress was made in the Uruguay Round negotiations, participants needed more time to "reconsider and reconcile their positions" in some key areas of the negotiations. The Director General of the GATT was asked to conduct consultations on how to narrow the gaps in the negotiating program. Endeavors continued and eventually the Marrakesh Agreement was signed on 15 April 1994.

The members of WTO have learnt from the debacle at Seattle, and the lessons will contribute to their learning curve. One of the most important and obvious lessons of the debacle is that, while the principle of consensus is indispensable, it must be an asset rather than a liability in ensuring efficient and fair decision making. In Seattle it proved to be a liability. What happened in Seattle also reflected poorly on the decision-making capabilities of the WTO. Expansion of the scope and size of the WTO, and its success, have exposed its old decision-making process. The WTO needs to evolve a creative and efficient decision-making process that ensures a balance of all interests – which is a tall order. If one were to take a holistic look at the process that led to Seattle, it is not difficult to see that the global trading system needs to ensure the right balance between transparency, democracy, inclusiveness, and representativeness among the entire membership of the organization on the one hand and efficiency in reaching an agreement on the other. Evolving such a decision-making process would indeed be the challenge for the WTO leadership. They need to pick up the gauntlet without a moment's delay.

Policy makers in the developing countries increasingly understand the value of a well oiled, efficiently functioning multilateral trading system. They realize how much is at stake. Policy makers also understand there is a pressing need to evolve such a decision-making process and that it is in the interests of both developing and industrial countries to re-engage in a new round of trade negotiations. It is not only the benefits of new trade negotiations that lie in the balance, but also difficult and sensitive issues that will soon arise in the WTO if the new round is not started. Past experience and the debacle at Seattle show that the task of launching a new round will not be an easy one. But most people connected with the round – be they trade economists or policy makers – are aware that it certainly is achievable and deliverable.

That the WTO leadership is not oblivious to the challenges is obvious. Following Seattle, several constructive and realistic measures were taken by the leadership at global and regional fora to build confidence to finesse the launching of the new round of MTNs. The General Council of the WTO decided in February 2000 (1) to organize negotiations to further liberalize trade in services and agriculture, and (2) to continue consultation on the outstanding issues that surfaced in Seattle. These decisions shifted WTO work back on track and provided a platform, not only for the mandated negotiations and reviews, but also for other issues that members would like to see included in the future WTO agenda. As regards progress in the institutional initiatives, in the first quarter of 2000 the agriculture and services negotiations had begun and capacity-building programs for the least developed countries were in full swing.

It must, however, be noted that while agriculture negotiations reached agreement over the timetable for the first phase of negotiations, there were serious differences over picking the chairperson. An interim solution had to be agreed by the WTO General Council in this regard, which did not augur well for the future of the agriculture negotiations. Member countries made general statements about their positions on agriculture; many of them nuanced their statements in a different manner from what they had said in Seattle. When the negotiations began in March 2000, the Cairns Group emphasized that agriculture negotiations should be "stand-alone" because they had obtained the commitment to resume negotiations in return for the moderate reforms agreed during the Uruguay Round. Japan, Korea, and the EU stressed that agriculture negotiations require a comprehensive round covering a wide range of issues. (Refer to Chapter 4, Section 4.3.1.)

Support for the launch of the new round was expressed in no uncertain terms in several significant international fora. In February 2000, the UNCTAD X conference in Bangkok considered the trade agenda in a development context, and gave the international community an opportunity to take stock and consider options for moving forward on the MTN front. It reaffirmed commitment to a multilateral trading system that was fair, rule-based, and transparent (UNCTAD, 2000a). Industrial economies are aware of the mistrust of the developing economies.[15] In a General Council meeting in May, the members of the Quad extended a package of benefits to the forty-eight least developed countries in terms of market access. The Quad package was intended to build confidence between the developing and industrial economies. However, it received a cool reception from potential recipients because it was insufficient.

Subsequently, Trade Ministers from the Asia Pacific Economic Co-operation (APEC) forum met during 6 and 7 June 2000 in Darwin, Australia, to brood over this issue. APEC's twenty-one members include the US, Japan, Canada, and China, and together they accounted for 60 percent of world economic output. This was the largest meeting of the kind since the collapse at Seattle. Although the final communiqué called for "renewed efforts to build the global consensus necessary for the launch of a round at the earliest opportunity", deep lines of disagreement persisted on issues like agriculture and investment. However, it was unrealistic to expect anything more than "modest" momentum towards a new WTO round to result from the APEC conference (Wyatt, 2000).

Another influential and heavyweight body on the global economic scenario, the OECD Council, met at Ministerial level on 27 June 2000, in Paris. It expressed determination to work towards the launch of the new round as soon as possible. It hoped that the new round would reflect the needs and aspirations of the WTO members and be "ambitious, balanced, and broad-based". The OECD Ministers agreed that "strong political will and greater flexibility on all sides are needed if we are to build a consensus for a new round". The Ministers stressed the need to "strengthen further the WTO system and open up opportunities for a more inclusive range of interests for all WTO members to be addressed in a manner responsive to the challenges of the twenty-first century" (OECD, 2000c). Thus there was no letup in endeavors to move in the correct direction. However, until sufficient synergy is created, WTO members will have to stay the course and persist.

That the global political leadership is seized with the loss caused by the failure at Seattle is evident from the G-8 communiqué of 23 July 2000. The Group of Eight comprises the seven largest industrial economies, plus Russia. The former group includes all four members of the Quad (refer to Section 2.4), which are exceedingly important to any global trade-related decisions. The G-8 leaders recognized their responsibility to ensure that the multilateral trading system was strengthened and "firmly committed to a new round of WTO trade negotiations with an ambitious, balanced and inclusive agenda, reflecting the interests of all WTO members". They agreed "that the objectives of such negotiations should be to ensure market access, develop and strengthen WTO rules and disciplines, and support developing countries in achieving economic growth and integration into the global trading system". They decided to "intensify [their] fruitful co-operation in order to try together with other WTO members to launch a round during the course of this year" (G-8 communiqué, 2000). Although agreement among the members of the Quad was important and necessary, it was not sufficient for a successful launch of a new round of MTNs. While welcoming the strong support of such an important group of global leaders for the launch, the Director General of the WTO said that "there can be no launch . . . without support from the world's developing countries" (WTO, 2000c).

The twelfth APEC Ministerial meeting and the eighth Leaders' meeting were held in Bandar Seri Begawan, Brunei Darussalam, on 12–13 November 2000. APEC Ministers and leaders reaffirmed their strong commitment to the launch of a new round at the earliest opportunity. They also agreed that the successful and expeditious launch of a new round would require an agenda "balanced and sufficiently broad-based to respond to the interest concerns of all WTO members". This had been said before in the other regional and global fora. The new step in this direction was that the Ministers from twenty-one APEC member countries called on their WTO delegations in Geneva to agree on an agenda for a round in 2001. At the Ministerial level, they agreed to decide areas for negotiation in 2001, although the issue of the timing was left undecided (APEC, 2000). The fourth Ministerial Conference of the WTO is scheduled for November 2001.

In the first quarter of 2001 (when this book was finalized), the message emerged loud and clear that the members were really desirous of seeing the next round of comprehensive trade negotiations launched. After convalescing from the collapse of its third Ministerial, in Seattle, the WTO was back on its feet. A year's soul searching had convinced its 140 members that the organization's problems might overwhelm the global trading system unless they were tackled soon. They unanimously approved Doha, capital of Qatar, as host to the fourth Ministerial Conference. The European Union and Japan, two of the four Quad members, called on the WTO to push for agreement by July 2001 on an agenda for a comprehensive round to be launched when WTO Ministers met in Qatar in November. These two influential members of the Quad were joined by a number of emerging market economies, indicating that the gaps between developed and developing members were bridgeable. Using its presidency of the G-7, Italy called on the United States to lend the EU and Japan its full support in calling for the new round. Developing countries have emerged from their period of mourning over implementation-related difficulties. In early 2001 they were talking about solutions and accommodations. The debate had moved on from demands to constructive suggestions. A change of atmosphere was felt; and "critical space" to move forward was discernible. One indication of the altered mood was that the WTO negotiations on agriculture were being described as "in good shape". The auguries for a December launch of the new round seemed promising.

3   The Uruguay Round

Implementation and consequences

The most incomprehensible thing about the world is that it is comprehensible.
Albert Einstein

3.1 Developing economies in the global trading system

For a long time, under the General Agreement on Tariffs and Trade (GATT) regime, most developing economies kept themselves away from participation during negotiations in the multilateral trade negotiations (MTNs). During the early phase, developing economies were interested only in obtaining preferential access to industrial country markets. They were passive participants in the MTNs and their participation in the global economy was also limited. Virtually all liberalization commitments in the Kennedy and Tokyo Rounds were made by industrial economies. Developing countries enjoyed a "free ride" because under the most-favored-nation (MFN) clause of the GATT Article I, a tariff reduction granted to one trading partner had to be granted to all the contracting parties of the GATT. The dark side of the "free ride" was that it encouraged the industrial economies to leave the sectors of greatest significance out of the MTNs. This is how textiles and apparel and agriculture, the sectors in which developing economies had the greatest export potential, were protected in the industrial economies through the GATT-sanctioned Multifiber Arrangement (MFA),[1] which is known to be highly distortionary.

This situation gradually changed as developing economies began interacting with other developing economies as well as with the industrial economies. The process of interlinking progressed and their participation in various rounds of MTNs also strengthened from marginal to substantial. The Uruguay Round was a veritable milestone on this journey. It was justly celebrated for the innovations it represented. When it was launched in September 1986, at the initiative of the United States and with limited support from the other industrial economies, the developing economies were somewhat apprehensive. By the time the round ended, most developing economies began to expect substantial gains from it and were impatient with the failure of the industrial economies to settle their outstanding trade differences (ODI, 1995). Its completion marked the beginning of the critical process of integrating the developing economies into the global economy.

The mind set of policy makers in the developing economies had begun to change markedly between the conclusion of the Tokyo Round (1979) and the culmination of the Uruguay Round (1994). The realization dawned on them that freedom to impose import controls was less important, and that getting over the obstacles to exports was more important. Policy makers in the developing economies saw the latter not just as barriers to static efficiency gains, but as constraints on a strategy for dynamic change and industrialization. This realization is important and would influence the approach to MTNs. Accident prone as it was, the successful conclusion of the Uruguay Round led to further change in the attitude of developing countries towards the role of international trade in their domestic economies. In this, they were encouraged by the manifest success of the outward oriented economic regime of the East and Southeast Asian economies. The lackluster long-term economic performance of the economies that followed an inward-looking *dirigiste* path (like the South Asian and East European economies) also reinforced the changing mind set of the policy makers. Slowly at first, but rapidly by the late 1980s, many developing economies began to undertake a radical liberalization of their trade regimes.

During the earlier GATT rounds only a small proportion of developing country exports were covered by the GATT regime. Therefore, following a strategy of import substitution and ignoring exports did not have a high cost. As high tariffs and other barriers existed in the industrial economies, developing countries paid more attention to getting preferential access to industrial country markets. The "special and differential" treatment clause of the GATT allowed them preferences in the industrial country markets. With the success of various GATT rounds, tariff barriers began to plummet and the lower MFN tariffs were available to all. This reduced the value and attraction of preferential treatment to the developing economies. In addition, with the passage of time, as a small number of so-called emerging market economies began to compete successfully with the industrial economies, it became more costly for them to offer special privileges to developing economies. Therefore there was pressure in the Uruguay Round to remove special and differential treatment.

This shift in the mind set of policy makers in developing economies towards a relatively liberalized trading system was reflected in their attitude to and participation in the Uruguay Round. For the first time, many developing economies abandoned their traditional passive posture and participated actively throughout the round. Many of them became increasingly active as the round evolved. Developing economies were slowly learning the MTN ropes. At the time of the commencement of the round, the World Bank published *The Uruguay Round: a Handbook for the Multilateral Trade Negotiations* (Finger and Olechowski, 1987), which became something of a bestseller.

If a comparison is made, from the perspective of the developing economies, the Uruguay Round was far more important than the preceding seven rounds of MTNs. The traditional area of GATT-regulated world trade, that is, manufactures excluding textiles and apparel, became progressively more significant for the developing countries over the years. By the early 1990s, developing economies were significant markets and competitors of the industrial countries and of each other. In 1970 developing countries exported 7 percent of total world exports of manufactures. By the beginning of the Uruguay Round in 1986 this proportion had risen to 12.5 percent, and by 1990 to 21.1 percent. According to the latest statistics, developing economies accounted for 23.0 percent of exports of manufactures in 1998 (Page and Davenport, 1994; WTO, 1999e). By the beginning of the Uruguay Round, manufactures had increased to more than half of their total exports; in 1970 this proportion was only one-third. Substantial cuts were made in tariffs on manufactures which were of immense benefit to the developing economies. The principal beneficiaries were the developing economies with large exports in this sector. Asian exports are dominated by manufactures; in 1998 83 percent of total exports originated from the manufacturing sector (WTO, 1999e).

During the Uruguay Round, developing economies not only participated in formulating the new rules of the global trading system but also made offers in conventional areas and "new" areas. The first area was trade in manufactures, while the second set included trade in services, trade in agriculture, and Trade Related Aspects of Intellectual Property Rights (TRIPs) and the like. According to Martin and Winters (1995a), among the most significant outcomes of the Uruguay Round were the following. Agriculture and textiles and apparel were included in the multilateral trade regime. Agreement to abolish the MFA was seen as having far reaching implications for the developing economies. Besides, food crops in which some developing economies compete directly with industrial ones and of which other developing economies are large-scale importers came back under the normal rules. Textiles and apparel and agriculture were both governed by separate regulations and quotas. With such important areas of global trade included in the multilateral trading system, thirty-one developing economies joined the GATT during the conduct of the Uruguay Round. The list included major trading countries like Mexico and Venezuela. These new members further increased the impact of GATT on existing members. It must, however, be noted that the agreement on agriculture achieved a great deal by defining rules for agricultural trade, but rather little in terms of immediate market opening.

Cuts in the protection of merchandise trade were estimated to increase real incomes in developing countries by between US$55 billion and US$90 billion at 1992 prices, or between 1.2 percent and 2.0 percent of real income, despite the cautious offers made by many developing countries (Martin and Winters, 1995b). The establishment of the World Trade

Organization (WTO), overseeing three multilateral agreements, namely the Marrakesh Agreement, the General Agreement on Trade in Services (GATS), and Trade Related Aspects of Intellectual Property Rights (TRIPs), and having wider responsibilities like dispute settlement, strengthened the global trading system substantially. By tightening controls on tariffs and non-tariff barriers (NTBs) the Uruguay Round had increased the depth of trade regulations. It had extended regulation to subsidies and regional trading agreements (RTAs) and strengthened and refined the system of monitoring global trade.

3.2 The final Uruguay Round agreement

The active participation of a good number of delegations from developing and industrial economies and the GATT secretariat finally led to the signing of the Final Act embodying the Results of the Uruguay Round of Multilateral Trade Negotiations.[2] The Final Act also covers the results of the "market access negotiations" in which individual countries have given binding[3] commitments to reduce or eliminate specific tariffs and NTBs to merchandise trade. These concessions are recorded in national schedules that form an integral part of the Final Act.

It is easy to appreciate that the Uruguay Round agreement covered a large area of international trade policy. It will take us too far afield to discuss in detail the agreements reached in the Uruguay Round, which is hardly needed for this study. Complete details of the Final Act are available in the *Legal Texts* of the WTO, although in a skeletal form it comprises the following:

1 *Agreement establishing the World Trade Organization.* It called for a single institutional framework encompassing the GATT, as modified by the Uruguay Round, all agreements and arrangements concluded under its auspices, and the complete results of the Uruguay Round. Institutionally, it is headed by a Ministerial Conference meeting at least once every two years. A General Council oversees the operations of the agreement and Ministerial decisions on a regular basis. This General Council acts as a Dispute Settlement Body and a Trade Policy Review Mechanism, which concern themselves with full range of trade issues covered by the WTO, and has also established subsidiary bodies such as a Goods Council, a Services Council, and a TRIPs Council. The WTO framework ensures a "single undertaking approach" to the results of the Uruguay Round.

2 *General Agreement on Tariffs and Trade, 1994.* Texts on the interpretation of the following GATT articles were included in the Final Act: (a) Article II on schedules of concessions, (b) Article XVII on state trading enterprises, (c) balance of payments provisions, (d) Article XXIV on customs union and free trade areas, (e) Article XXV on

waivers of GATT discipline, (f) Article XXVIII on the modification or withdrawal of GATT schedules, and (g) Article XXXV on the non-application of the general agreement to an acceding country.

3 *Uruguay Round Protocol GATT, 1994.* The results of the market access negotiations in which participants have made a commitment to eliminate or reduce tariff rates and non-tariff measures applicable to trade in goods are recorded in national schedules of concessions annexed to the Uruguay Round Protocol that forms an integral part of the Final Act.

4 *Agreement on Agriculture.* The negotiations resulted in four principal parts of the Agreements: (a) the agreements on agriculture itself, (b) the concessions and commitments members are to undertake on market access, domestic support, and export subsidies, (c) the agreement on sanitary and phytosanitary measures, and (d) the Ministerial decision concerning least developed and net food-importing developing countries.

5 *Agreement on Sanitary and Phytosanitary Regulations.* This agreement concerns food safety and animal and plant health regulations. The agreement recognizes that such measures should not be applied arbitrarily or unjustifiably discriminate between members where identical or similar conditions prevail.

6 *Decision on Measures concerning the Possible Negative Effects of the Reform Program on Least Developed and Net Food-importing Developing Countries.* During the reform program least developed and net food-importing developing countries may experience negative effects. Therefore a special decision was taken to provide food aid, the provision of basic foodstuffs in full grant form, and aid for agricultural development.

7 *Agreement on Textiles and Clothing.* The objective of this negotiation was to secure the eventual integration of the textile and clothing sector – where much of the trade was subject to bilateral quotas negotiated under the Multifiber Arrangement (MFA) – into the GATT on the basis of strengthened GATT rules and disciplines. Integration of this sector into the GATT would take place according to an agreed schedule, beginning January 1995 and ending 2005. The agreement includes provision to cope with possible circumvention of commitments through transhipment, rerouting, false declaration concerning country or place of origin, and falsification of official documents.

8 *Agreement on Technical Barriers to Trade* sought to ensure that technical negotiations and standards, as well as testing and certification procedures, do not create unnecessary obstacles to trade.

9 *Agreement on Trade Related Investment Measures* provides that no contracting party shall apply any TRIM inconsistent with Article III (national treatment) and Article XI (prohibition of quantitative restrictions) of the GATT.

10 *Agreement on Implementation of Article VI (Antidumping).* Negotiations in the Uruguay Round resulted in a revision of this agreement. In the renewed form it addresses many areas in which the previous agreement lacked precision and detail.
11 *Agreement on Implementation of Article VII (Customs Valuation).* Customs administrations were given rights to request more information where they had reason to doubt the accuracy of the declared value of imported goods. They were also given rights to establish the value themselves, taking into account the provisions of the agreement.
12 *Agreement on Pre-shipment Inspection (PSI).* The agreement recognized that GATT principles and obligations apply to the activities of PSI agencies mandated by governments. However, a set of obligations has been placed on the PSI-user governments which includes non-discrimination, transparency, protection of confidential business, and avoidance of unreasonable delay.
13 *Agreement on Rules of Origin.* The agreement aimed at long-term harmonization of rules of origin, other than rules of origin relating to the granting of tariff preferences, and to ensure that such rules do not themselves create unnecessary obstacles to trade.
14 *Agreement on Import Licensing Procedures.* The revised agreement strengthened the discipline on the users of import licensing systems – which, in any event, are much less widely used now than in the past – and increased transparency and predictability.
15 *Agreement on Subsidies and Countervailing Measures.* It was intended to build on the agreement on interpretation and application of Articles VI, XVI, and XXIII which was negotiated in the Tokyo Round. Unlike its predecessor, the agreement contained a definition of subsidy and introduced the concept of a "specific" subsidy. For the most part, a subsidy is available only to an enterprise or industry or group of enterprises or industries within the jurisdiction of the authority granting the subsidy.
16 *Agreement on Safeguards (Article XIX).* Article XIX was a contentious one and the source of a great deal of friction. The agreement broke major ground in establishing a prohibition on so-called "gray area" measures and in setting a "sunset clause" on all safeguard actions. The agreement stipulated that members cannot seek, take, or maintain any voluntary export restraints, orderly marketing arrangements, or any other similar measures on the export or import side.
17 *General Agreement on Trade in Services (GATS).* The new agreement was part of the Final Act and has three principal elements. The first is a Framework Agreement containing basic obligations which apply to all member countries. The second concerns national schedules of commitments containing specific national commitments which are the subject of a continuous process of liberalization. The third is a number of annexes addressing the special situations of individual service sectors.

18 *Agreement on Trade Related Aspects of Intellectual Property Rights, including Trade in Counterfeit Goods (TRIPs).* The agreement recognized that widely varying standards in the protection and enforcement of intellectual property rights and the lack of a multilateral framework of principles, rules, and disciplines dealing with the international trade in counterfeit goods have been a growing source of tension in international economic relations. Rules and disciplines were needed to cope with such tension. To that end, the agreement addressed the applicability of basic GATT principles and of relevant international intellectual property agreements; the provision of adequate intellectual property rights; the provision of effective enforcement measures for those rights; multilateral dispute settlement; and transitional arrangements.

19 *Understanding on Rules and Procedures governing the Settlement of Disputes.* The dispute settlement provision of the GATT is generally considered to be one of the cornerstones of the multilateral trade order. As a result of reforms agreed following the Mid-term Review meeting held in December 1998 in Montreal, the system was strengthened and streamlined. The new rules include greater autonomy in decisions on the establishment, terms of reference, and composition of panels. These decisions are no longer dependent upon the consent of the parties to a dispute. The dispute settlement understanding (DSU) established an integrated system permitting WTO members to base their claims on any of the multilateral trade agreements included in the annexes to the Agreement establishing the WTO. To this end, a dispute settlement body (DSB) is to exercise the authority of the General Council. The DSU contains a number of provisions taking into account the specific interests of the developing and least developed countries.

20 *Trade Policy Review Mechanism.* This agreement confirmed the Trade Policy Review Mechanism (TPRM), introduced at the time of the Mid-term Review, and encouraged greater transparency in national trade policy making.

21 *Decision on Achieving Greater Coherence in Global Economic Policy Making.* This will set out concepts and proposals with respect to achieving greater coherence in global economic policy making. The text noted *inter alia* that greater exchange rate stability based on more orderly underlying economic and financial conditions should contribute to "the expansion of trade, sustainable growth and development, and the timely correction of external imbalances". The WTO was called upon to develop co-operative links with the international organizations responsible for monetary and financial matters. The Director General of the WTO was called upon to review with his opposite numbers in the International Monetary Fund and the World Bank the implications of WTO's future responsibilities in its co-operation with the two Bretton Woods institutions.

22   *Government Procurement.* The Final Act contains an agreement related to accession procedures to the Government Procurement Agreement which is designed to facilitate the membership of developing countries. It envisages consultation between the existing members and applicant governments. This agreement is not the same as the new Agreement on Government Procurement.

The WTO has an excellent website on these. Readers looking for greater depth are directed to it. Researchers seeking more detail should consult the *Legal Texts* of the WTO, as the above is no more than an outline.

3.3 Substance and implications

It is easy to see from the preceding section that the Uruguay Round spawned a complex array of agreements. These agreements resulted in a substantial strengthening of the rule-based multilateral trading system. In addition, existing discipline was tightened in a number of areas, including those involving the use of subsidies, countervailing and antidumping duties, and safeguard measures. While one cannot deny its limitations, it was no exaggeration when the Uruguay Round was described as "the biggest trade liberalization package in history".[4] The dispute settlement mechanism (DSM) is also a major element in strengthening the trade system.

Owing to these characteristics – achievements, if you like – of the Uruguay Round it was expected to have important implications for global trade, including that of the developing economies. The basis of the Uruguay Round agreement covering trade in goods was the GATT 1994, which is an updated version of GATT 1947, supplemented by understandings interpreting various provisions. In addition, there were agreements covering practices of relevance to GATT rules, agreements directed at liberalizing trade in agriculture, in textiles and clothing, and agreements governing the application of non-tariff barriers (WTO, 1994).

The major accomplishment of the agreement on agriculture is the creation of a "tariff only" regime. All NTBs had to be replaced by tariffs, plus agricultural tariffs have to be bound, that is, they are subject to agreed maximum rates. The principal outcome was improved market access through the reduction of barriers and the increase in the scope of bindings, a progressive reduction in trade-distorting measures of domestic support, and the lowering of subsidies to promote export competition. This process was expected to lay down the foundations for market-opening negotiations in the future. It must be immediately clarified that in practice this process turned out to be fairly "dirty" because the base tariff levels were not clearly defined. In the case of textiles and apparel, the reduction of restraints and the phasing out of the MFA over a period of ten years meant that a key export sector for many developing countries would be fully within the discipline of the multilateral trading system, although back-loading of implementation has slowed down market access for the exporting countries.

Rules governing the NTBs were clarified and updated. The so-called gray area measures, like voluntary export restraints (VERs) and orderly marketing arrangements (OMAs), had assumed nuisance proportions for the successful exporting economies, particularly the newly industrialized economies (NIEs). An agreement was reached that existing gray area measures should be eliminated or phased out by 1998. Of particular importance to developing countries is the application of antidumping and countervailing measures. Further clarifications were made in relation to determining whether a product is being dumped or subsidized, or whether dumped or subsidized imports are "causing injury" to a domestic industry. However, antidumping and countervailing measures continue to be a bugbear for the developing economies.

Trade in services was a wide and important area to which multilateral trading system was extended during the Uruguay Round. It was expected to provide the same advantages to developing countries as the rule-based multilateral trading system in merchandise trade. A number of areas of export interest to developing economies have already been committed to liberalization by major importing industrial economies, although according to a Services Council report there is a long way to go. In addition, GATS was unique in that it allowed WTO members, including developing country members, to negotiate the conditions under which foreign service suppliers may establish themselves in the importing countries. The terms and conditions to this effect are bound in the schedules of the members concerned. (Refer to Section 3.2.) The TRIPs Agreement offered potential benefits for developing countries by creating a framework conducive to technology transfer and foreign direct investment. Its main disciplines included non-discrimination, that is, most-favored-nation (MFN) and national treatment. Expansion of the coverage of the multilateral trading system to new areas has made the post-Uruguay Round system more meaningful to the developing economies – this is not to deny that implementation of some of the agreements is difficult. Although many developing economies were not able to take advantage of some of the improved market access opportunities immediately, they were expected to do so in the future as their domestic supply capacities increased. However, tightened discipline and wider coverage will prove to be effective and beneficial only if an efficient means of dispute settlement supports the system. The Uruguay Round has brought about a considerable improvement in the dispute settlement mechanism (DSM).

Many developing economies had begun undertaking trade liberalization measures since the mid-1980s. They did so either in an autonomous manner or as a part of wider programs of economic reform, and bound the

liberalization measures in the GATT system. For these developing economies the Uruguay Round proved to be timely. They were not only able to
participate more fully in the round but actively to promote and consolidate
their own economic reforms. When these developing countries adopted
binding commitments during the Uruguay Round, they were committing to
a transparent, open, and predictable trade regime. This represented an
important change in the relationship of many developing countries with the
multilateral trading system. For the first time, many of them were assuming
the same disciplines as their industrial country trading partners. To be sure,
there were some exceptions, and under certain circumstances developing
economies were allowed to use quantitative restrictions (QRs) and export
subsidies, which were not allowable to the industrial economies.

Although the Uruguay Round became instrumental in promoting integration of developing economies into the multilateral trading system, the
integration was far from uniform. A systematic review of the detailed information contained in sixty-one Trade Policy Reviews (TPRs) of forty-two
developing economies, which were prepared during the 1989–98 period,
revealed that integration of the developing economies into the multilateral
trading system has been impressive for a group of about twenty middle and
high-income developing economies, particularly those in East Asia and
Latin America. For many others, progress has been slow (Michalopoulos,
1999). The least developed countries fall in the latter category.

For the industrial economies, the main features of their market access
commitments in industrial products included (1) the expansion of bindings
to cover 99 percent of imports, (2) the expansion of duty-free access from
20 percent to 44 percent of total imports, and (3) a reduction of the trade-
weighted average tariff by 40 percent, that is, from the pre-Uruguay Round
6.2 percent to the post-Uruguay Round 3.7 percent. On the basis of data
available for twenty-six developing economies, the GATT secretariat identified the main features of their market access commitments. These included:
(1) the expansion of bindings to cover 61 percent of imports, compared with
a pre-Uruguay Round level of 13 percent, and (2) a reduction of ceiling rates
for tariffs leading to a decline of 30 percent in the trade-weighted average
tariff of developing economies. Large Latin American economies committed themselves to binding 100 percent of tariff lines at ceiling rates, which
provided an increase in the security of trade among developing countries.
Thus the Uruguay Round provided more secure and open markets for world
trade in industrial products. The proportion of total trade that was subject
to bound rates increased from 68 percent to 87 percent, largely as a result
of the substantial increase in the level of binding in developing economies. Markets were more open as a result of the reductions in average tariffs of developed economies (down 40 percent), developing economies
(down 30 percent), and transition economies (down 30 percent). The post-
Uruguay Round average tariff on industrial products was 6.3 percent, while
the pre-Uruguay Round average tariff was 9.9 percent (WTO, 1994).

As noted earlier in this section, increased market access for agricultural products included the "tariffication"[5] of all non-tariff border measures, with the exception of those products for which special treatment has been negotiated. It also included the binding of all tariffs on agricultural products. Consequently, the security of trade in agricultural products was for the first time greater than that of trade in industrial products. This was because of 100 percent binding of agricultural product tariff lines. Tariffs resulting from the "tariffication" process, together with the other tariffs on agricultural products, were to be reduced in a phased manner over a stipulated period. It was felt that these new market access opportunities for agricultural products would be of particular interest to developing economies exporting temperate zone food products.[6]

3.4 Negative consequences

Together, these measures were expected to improve multilateral trade discipline, open new markets, and promote global trade and GDP growth. However, Whalley and Hamilton (1996) disagreed and considered any such assessment optimism of the Pollyanna variety. According to them, liberalization in agriculture, textiles and apparel, and tariffs could prove less substantial than appeared at first glance. Many believed that agricultural liberalization was substantially weakened by "dirty tariffication", explained below in Section 3.5 (Ingco, 1996). The impact of systemic strengthening was difficult to judge, and impossible to quantify. The creation of a permanent trade body was expected to generate new momentum towards further liberalization but the new trade body at the outset merely repackaged previous GATT arrangements, with little immediate impact on the multilateral trading system. New antidumping regulations have been criticized as codifying practices rather than disciplining them. The new agreements in services, investment, and intellectual property were only the beginning of trade regulation in these areas. The process needed to be completed and much remained to be done in all these areas (Whalley and Hamilton, 1996).

As set out in Chapter 1, the Uruguay Round approach of a "single undertaking" served many developing countries poorly. Under this approach, developing economies had to accept the agreement on Trade Related Aspects of Intellectual Property Rights (TRIPs) in return for the dismantling of the Multifiber Arrangement (MFA). To be sure, dismantling of the MFA promises to remove distortions and improve global efficiency by freeing up trade in textiles and apparel. But this would happen in the long term, because most of the dismantling measures have been back-loaded, particularly by the US. As opposed to this the agreement on TRIPs is expected to reduce global efficiency by extending the monopoly power of patent holders in developing countries for twenty years. If anything, it is likely to result in a substantial redistribution of income from developing to developed economies.[7] Thus while developed economies benefited from the bargain on both counts, developing countries benefited on one count but lost on the other.

Tariffs on imports of manufactures into industrial countries were reduced from a trade-weighted average of 6.3 percent to 3.8 percent, with the reductions to be phased in over the 1994–99 period (Blackhurst *et al.*, 1996). Tariff reductions under the Uruguay Round were not uniform across commodities, but were the outcome of a series of bilateral negotiations during the round whose results were subsequently extended to all participants. The trade-weighted average of tariffs on manufactures of 3.8 percent given above conceals a stubborn protectionist reality. The majority of industrial-country imports enter other industrial countries tariff-free or at very low tariff rates, while a few politically favored sectors are sheltered from international competition by high tariffs. For developing countries high tariffs extend to a much larger range of sectors and products. Some revealing statistics in this regards are as follows. The proportion of industrial countries' imports of industrial products subject to bindings has risen from 94 percent to 99 percent, while that for the developing economies rose from 13 to 61 percent (WTO, 1998a). One explanation that is given for this dichotomy is that as developing and industrial economies export different manufactured products, the incidence of tariff cuts also varied between them.

Another empirical study shows that while industrial countries' tariffs on imports from other industrial countries were reduced by an average of 40 percent, those on imports from developing countries were reduced by 28 percent. In the developing economies, reductions of tariff rates on manufactures averaged 25 percent on products imported from industrial countries and 21 percent on products imported from developing countries (Abreu, 1996). To be sure, both industrial and developing economies made very substantial progress with their tariff bindings and reductions, but a great deal remains to be done.

As the Uruguay Round was the most comprehensive round so far, many developing countries have experienced institutional difficulties in implementing various recommendations. These difficulties have been faced not only by the world's poorest countries, the forty-eight UN-designated least developed countries, but also by countries like India and the Philippines. The least-developed country group is being provided with trade-related technical assistance by six international organizations, namely the International Trade Center (ITC), International Monetary Fund (IMF), United Nations Conference on Trade and Development (UNCTAD), United Nations Development Program (UNDP), the World Bank, and the WTO. These institutions are laying a great deal of emphasis on trade-related technical assistance, training, and capacity building in the least developed countries. Of the six international organizations involved, the World Bank would lead and co-ordinate the mainstream process, while the other five would participate actively. A trust fund of US$20 million has been created which would assist these forty-eight countries develop the necessary analytical and policy framework for mainstreaming trade into national development strategy. The UNDP will manage the trust fund (WTO, 2000c).

3.5 NTB regime: comprehending the profusion

If domestic and internal measures are taken, the range of NTBs is probably infinite. A broad definition of NTBs will have to include all non-tariff trade-distorting policies, public or private, that cause internationally traded goods and services, or resources devoted to the production of those goods and services, to be allocated in such a manner as to reduce potential real global income (Baldwin, 1970). In principle all barriers other than tariffs that in some manner impede trade or raise the cost of trading, which includes informal measures, should be included among non-tariff barriers. The range of NTBs has grown large. Given the enthusiasm of governments to protect domestic producers, it is likely to continue to expand. One operational definition capturing all the different kinds of NTBs is difficult.

The wide range of NTBs includes specific and general measures. The former applies to a product or to an industry, while the latter are all-encompassing, like an export subsidy. Other general NTBs work through monetary and fiscal policies. Thus the range is wide and unmanageable. Therefore, while dealing with NTBs it is prudent to narrow the scope to a realistic proportions. One of the first valiant attempts in this direction was made by Baldwin (1970), who set out twelve different groupings of NTBs. His twelve groups are (1) quotas and restrictive state-trading policies, (2) export subsidies and taxes, (3) discriminatory government and private procurement policies, (4) selective indirect taxes, (5) selective domestic subsidies, (6) restrictive customs procedures, (7) antidumping regulations, (8) restrictive administrative and technical regulations, (9) restrictive business practices, (10) controls over foreign investment, (11) restrictive immigration policies, and (12) selective monetary controls and discriminatory exchange rate policies.

The United Nations Conference on Trade and Development (UNCTAD) designed a different classification of NTBs during the early 1980s. This system breaks them down into seven major categories: (1) price control measures, (2) finance control measures, (3) automatic licensing measures, (4) quantity control measures, (5) monopolistic measures, (6) technical measures, (7) miscellaneous measures. Each of these broad groups is further subdivided into particular measures, as shown in Table 3.1. UNCTAD's classification, though broad, omits nearly half of the categories set out initially by Baldwin.

From among the broad list, UNCTAD also defines a set of core NTBs which are thought to be the most common and restrictive measures. These are also the measures for which it is relatively easy to find data. They

Table 3.1 The UNCTAD classification system for non-tariff barriers

1   Price control measures
   (a)   Administrative pricing
   (b)   Voluntary export price restraint
   (c)   Variable charges
   (d)   Antidumping measures
   (e)   Countervailing measures

2   Finance control measures
   (a)   Advance payment requirements
   (b)   Multiple exchange rates
   (c)   Restrictive official foreign exchange allocation
   (d)   Regulations concerning terms of payment for imports
   (e)   Transfer delays

3   Automatic licensing measures
   (a)   Automatic license
   (b)   Import monitoring
   (c)   Surrender requirement

4   Quantity control measures
   (a)   Non-automatic license
   (b)   Quotas
   (c)   Import prohibitions
   (d)   Export restraint arrangements
   (e)   Enterprise-specific restrictions

5   Monopolistic measures
   (a)   Single channel for imports
   (b)   Compulsory national services

6   Technical measures
   (a)   Technical regulations
   (b)   Pre-shipment formalities
   (c)   Special customs formalities
   (d)   Obligation to return used products

7   Miscellaneous measures for insensitive product categories
   (a)   Market permits
   (b)   Public procurement
   (c)   Voluntary instruments
   (d)   Product liability
   (e)   Subsidies

Note: Used in the UNCTAD TRAINS (1997) database; TRAINS stands for Trade Analysis and Information System.

comprise the majority of measures in categories 1, 2, and 4 in Table 3.1, and include (1) quantity control measures (excluding tariff quotas and enterprise-specific restrictions), (2) finance control measures (excluding regulations concerning terms of payment and transfer delays and queuing), and (3) price control measures.

Another classification of non-tariff barriers was developed by Alan Deardorff and Robert Stern at the University of Michigan.[8] Their typology includes a large variety of non-tariff barriers classified into five major categories: (1) quantitative restrictions, (2) non-tariff charges and related policies affecting imports, (3) government participation in trade, (4) customs procedures and administrative practices, and (5) technical barriers to trade. Like the UNCTAD classification, they further subdivided their classification into subparts (Deardorff and Stern, 1997; PECC, 2000).

Comparing the Deardorff and Stern (1997) and UNCTAD classifications, it is interesting to note that although two or three of the categories have similar labels in the two classifications (for example, quantity control measures and quantitative restrictions, or technical measures and technical barriers to trade), nonetheless the measures that have been included under the same category in each typology are quite different. This underlines the great difficulty, even among the most experienced economists, of deciding how to deal with these measures, and of agreeing on a categorization of even fairly obvious NTBs, such as those quantitative measures that affect the volume of trade.

Deardorff and Stern's typology is quite rationally set out, and has the advantage of isolating all potentially quantifiable (quantitative) measures into one category, separating trade remedy actions into another category, and placing most forms of government-initiated measures into still another category. However, the number and types of measures included in these two categories are extremely large, making them unwieldy for the purpose of data collection and analysis. Interestingly, the broad category labeled government participation in trade includes many of the measures identified earlier by Baldwin. However, these measures are of a nature which makes them almost impossible to quantify.

Even where particular types of measures are found in all three classifications, controversy may still rage over whether they should be included as NTBs at all. For example, all three include antidumping duties, and UNCTAD and Deardorff and Stern also include countervailing duties. The inclusion of these trade remedy measures has, however, been the subject of strong disagreement. Some countries argue that the measures represent legitimate policy tools under multilateral trade rules and should not be counted in the non-tariff category. This is another aspect of the difficulty of defining NTBs for purposes of analysis (PECC, 2000).

3.6 MFN schedule of the Quad economies

In examining the transformation in the global trade regime in general during the pre- and post-Uruguay Round period, it is necessary to focus on the Quad. The four members of this group are the largest trading entities and accounted for more than half (50.8 percent) of global merchandise exports in 1999 and more than two-thirds (68.2 percent) of service exports (WTO, 2000a). Tariffs and NTBs used by these large traders can have serious repercussions on their trading partners. Individual members of the

Quad are the largest, or the second largest, trading partners of the rest of the economies of the world. The use of tariffs and NTBs by major traders can therefore lead to welfare losses not just domestically, but on a global scale, provoking retaliation. The Quad also warrants special attention because these four trading entities played a leading role in liberalizing trade during the last half-century. In particular, the US has a history of championing the cause of free trade. The Quad looms large because of the sheer volume of their trade. Their participation in any round of the MTN is vitally important and has far reaching consequences. Notwithstanding the suspension of the Uruguay Round, it is hoped that they will do so in the future as well.

A comprehensive exercise was jointly attempted by the OECD, the UNCTAD, and the WTO to estimate the tariffs and NTBs of the Quad. The estimates were derived from a database constructed by the UNCTAD with the co-operation of the OECD and WTO (Daly and Kuwahara, 1998). The key findings of this exercise are reported in Table 3.2. First, when the implementation of the Uruguay Round recommendation is completed almost all tariff lines of the Quad will be bound. Second, specific duties[9] and mixed tariffs[10] compared with *ad valorem*[11] tariffs will decrease in all Quad members once the Uruguay Round is fully implemented. Despite the decline in the relative significance of specific duties, they continue to remain an important feature of Quad members' most-favored-nation (MFN) schedule. They are also likely to be there in the future, particularly on the agricultural items, and especially in the EU and the US. Specific duties tend to be biased against low-cost goods, although they are easier to operate. Specific duties also tend to distort domestic production patterns more than *ad valorem* tariffs.[12] They provide disparate levels of assistance for similar tariff line goods by taxing imports of cheaper products more heavily, in the process encouraging domestic firms to produce less expensive goods for which the level of protection against imports is proportionately greater.

As a consequence of the tariffication of agricultural NTBs in the Uruguay Round, tariff quotas[13] have increased in Canada, Japan, and the US. They were significantly high in the EU and would not rise as a consequence of the implementation of the Uruguay Round (Table 3.2). Also, as a consequence of the tariffication, protection for some broad categories of agricultural products will increase (Daly and Kuwahara, 1998). These product categories include live animals and meat products in Canada, the EU, and the US, and vegetable products, fats, and oils in the EU. In the case of the EU, the overall tariff rate of agricultural, forestry, and fishing products would rise substantially. All these increases are the consequence of the elimination of agricultural NTBs. Thus viewed, overall protection of these products will rise substantially when the recommendations of the Uruguay Round are implemented. The reason apparently is that the tariffs were set at substantially higher rates than the tariff equivalents of erstwhile agricultural NTBs.

Table 3.2 Structure of applied MFN tariffs[1] in the Quad (%)

Indicators	United States 1989	1993	URI[3]	European Union[2] 1988	1993	URI[3]	Japan 1988	1993	URI[3]	Canada 1988	1993	URI[3]
1 Bound tariff lines	98.1	98.1	100.0	91.8	92.7	100.0	89.8	90.5	98.8	98.4	98.6	99.6
2 Duty-free tariff lines	17.4	14.4	34.7	10.5	10.9	25.5	21.9	35.4	44.2	25.7	26.3	40.4
3 Specific and mixed tariffs/all tariffs	17.6	17.0	10.8	10.6	11.1	10.4	7.4	8.8	6.7	8.6	6.2	5.0
4 Tariff quotas/all tariffs	0.1	0.2	2.3	1.0	2.4	2.3	1.0	1.2	2.2	0.0	0.0	1.5
5 Tariffs with no *ad valorem* equivalent	1.3	1.6	0.0	8.4	8.1	1.6	1.0	0.4	0.6	0.5	0.1	0.0
6 Simple average bound tariff rate	6.3	6.5	4.0	7.5	7.6	7.2	8.2	8.5	4.9	9.3	9.3	5.6
7 Simple average applied tariff rate	6.2	6.4	4.0	7.4	7.6	7.2	6.9	7.0	4.8	9.1	8.8	5.0
8 Import-weighted average tariff rate[4]	4.0	4.0	2.5	6.0	6.2	5.1	3.8	3.6	2.8	6.9	6.7	3.9
9 Production-weighted average tariff rate[5]	4.4	4.7	2.7	8.2	8.4	5.6	4.2	3.6	2.4	8.7	8.4	6.9
10 Domestic tariff "spikes"[6]	4.5	4.0	6.4	2.2	2.3	5.5	5.3	5.7	6.9	0.5	0.3	5.5
11 International tariff "spikes"[7]	9.3	9.4	3.0	5.7	6.6	9.2	10.9	11.2	6.3	13.1	13.0	5.5
12 Overall standard deviation	7.7	8.6	5.8	6.1	6.1	15.9	8.9	12.7	9.2	8.8	8.4	12.9

Source: Daly and Kuwahara (1998).

Notes:

[1] Indicators 6–12 include *ad valorem* equivalents for specific and mixed duties insofar as such estimates are available.

[2] Indicators encompass sliding charges.

[3] After the implementation of the Uruguay Round recommendations.

[4] Constant OECD import weights.

[5] For the EU, German weights are used.

[6] Domestic tariff "spikes" are defined as those exceeding three times the overall simple average MFN rate.

[7] International tariff "spikes" are defined as those exceeding 15%.

This process, as noted in Section 3.3, was widely referred to as "dirty tariffication". It implies that the tariff rate adopted continued to provide the same, or a higher, level of protection than the quota did before the Uruguay Round. Francois and Martin (1995) provide numerous examples of tariff bindings set above the prevailing average rate of protection, substantially reducing the expected costs of protection to importing countries. Calculations of tariff equivalents for the EU and the US showed that excess tariff rates were 61 percent in excess for the EU and 44 percent for the US (Ingco, 1996). Although agricultural trade has come under multilateral trade discipline and market access has improved, substantial protection still continues to be present through dirty tariffication and a variety of controls and interventions.

The overall mean bound tariff rates in Quad were down to 5 percent. Going by simple import-weighted and production-weighted averages of applied MFN tariff lines, the overall level of tariff protection is considerably higher in Canada and the EU than in the US and Japan. It will stay in this manner even when the Uruguay Round recommendations are implemented. The deadweight losses associated with a country's tariff structure depend not just upon average tariff rates, but also on the dispersion of these rates across products. The higher the dispersion of tariff rates, particularly within groups of similar products, the greater the likelihood that consumers' and producers' decisions will be distorted by the tariff structure. A uniform nominal tariff, or a uniform restrictive NTB, minimizes the net welfare cost of such protection, if import demand elasticities are uniform across commodities.

Daly and Kuwahara (1998) also delved into NTBs in the Quad economies. They concluded that proportionately fewer imported products would be subject to "core" NTBs[14] after the Uruguay Round is fully implemented. Comparatively, the reduction in NTBs is much less in Japan than in other Quad members. The value of imports affected by NTBs would also drop considerably, albeit by much more in the EU, the US, and Canada than in Japan. This marked decline in the pervasiveness of NTBs is partly due to the elimination of voluntary export restraints (VERs) as well as to the phasing out of the MFA quotas. The product categories that continue to be affected by NTBs are live animals and products (in Japan), vegetable products and prepared food (in the EU), leather products (in the US), textiles (in the US and Japan), footwear (in the US and Canada), and base metals (in the US).

3.7 The tariff regime at the turn of the century

From an economic welfare perspective, tariffs are preferable to all other trade-inhibiting commercial policies. The reason is that they are transparent and their efficiency costs can be quantified easily. Estimating the level of tariff liberalization initiated by the Uruguay Round is a gigantic exercise, needing massive swathes of institutional time, energy, and resources. This exercise was attempted by the Organization for Economic Co-operation and Development (OECD) secretariat. It took two years (1997–99) of hard work by the Trade Committee working group to analyze the tariff liberalization in OECD member countries and major non-member countries. The exercise was limited to multilateral market access negotiations in merchandise trade. The project examined the tariff regimes of the Quad (Canada, the EU, Japan, and the US), non-Quad members of the OECD,[15] and thirteen major non-OECD members.[16] All these thirteen non-OECD members are developing economies that have established themselves as important traders and active members of the WTO community. The analysis took into account the full implementation of the Uruguay Round tariff commitments, irrespective of when they will come into force. Most cuts in bound tariffs were scheduled to take place in five equal annual reductions beginning January 1995, the date of entry into force of the WTO. In principle, the final offer rates were to be in effect no later than 1 January 1999; however, some countries have negotiated later deadlines in respect of some industrial goods.

The OECD (1999c) study drew information on tariffs from UNCTAD's Trade Control Measure Database (TCMD) as well as the WTO Integrated Database (IDB). TCMD is the most comprehensive database covering tariffs currently available. It covers all OECD-member countries as well as a good number of non-OECD-member countries. UNCTAD's data are recorded at the national tariff-line level using the Harmonized Commodity Description and Coding System (HS) as of 1992. The HS has been replacing the Standard International Trade Classification (SITC) over the decade of the 1990s. SITC Revision 3, comprising 4,346 products, was based on HS 1988. At present, all members make their foreign trade statistics available in the Harmonized System and most are also available in the SITC.

Another comprehensive exercise was conducted by the World Bank (Finger and Schuknecht, 1999). The most important findings of these two OECD and World Bank studies are reported below. For clarity they are divided into two distinct areas, tariffs and non-tariffs.

3.7.1 Tariff barriers

1. Much was achieved, and the tariff cuts compare well with the coverage and depth of cuts achieved during the Tokyo Round and the Kennedy Round before it. There has been minimal backsliding and minimal use of the special or general provisions for imposing new restrictions that the various WTO agreements included. The only exception in this regard was antidumping. Tariff cuts by developing countries were as broad and, at the same time, deeper than those conceded by the developed economies (Finger and Schuknecht, 1999).

However, in terms of the implementation of the Uruguay Round commitments, there is a clear dichotomy between developing and industrial economies. The majority of tariff cuts that developing economies *committed* themselves to were due in 1999 and 2000, while the majority of the tariff reductions and other commitments they *received* from the industrial economies are not deliverable until 2005, or are yet to be negotiated. What the developing economies committed themselves to – apart from the exchange of tariff reductions – was mainly acceptance of "codes" on major areas of domestic as well as import regulations, like intellectual property, technical and sanitary standards, customs valuation, and import licensing procedures. What the developing economies got in return from the industrial economies was MFA elimination, not due until 2005. The quota elimination under MFA was heavily back-loaded, most conspicuously by the US. The developing countries were also promised trade liberalization and a reduction of domestic support on agricultural products, negotiations on which are yet to be completed.

Implementation of the Uruguay Round agreement was far from uniform in the developing economies. A close scrutiny of sixty-one TPRs, for forty-two developing economies, revealed that protection through both tariff and non-tariff measures was greater in low-income developing economies than in middle and high-income developing economies (Michalopoulos, 1999b).

2 The flip side of the coin is that bound mean tariffs still exhibit wide-ranging variations, both across countries and across sectors within any one country. The overall mean bound rate in the Quad was 5 percent (see Section 3.5), in the non-Quad OECD countries it was 18 percent, and in the thirteen non-OECD-member countries examined the overall bound mean reached a high of 43 percent.

3 At the level of main sectors, the bound means of agricultural lines were 8 percent in the Quad, 42 percent in the non-Quad OECD countries, and 63 percent in the sampled thirteen non-OECD-member countries. The corresponding bound means of industrial lines were: 4 percent for the Quad; 14 percent for the non-Quad OECD; 39 percent for the thirteen non-OECD members.

4 Tariff spikes continued to affect a number of sectors, both in industry and in agriculture.[17] A recent empirical exercise showed that tariff spikes have risen or remained constant over the last ten years in Austria, the EU economies, Japan, Canada, New Zealand, Norway, Switzerland, and the US (Coppel and Durand, 1999). In OECD countries, high industrial spikes were found in such sectors as textiles, clothing, footwear, and motor vehicles. In the non-OECD countries, tariff spiked more often than not and spikes were characteristic of the majority of tariff lines, often spanning as much as three-quarters of

tariff lines. In both OECD and non-OECD countries, it was more often the case that the number of tariff lines with spikes was higher in agriculture than in industry.

5   Low tariffs, between 0.1 percent and 3 percent, affected a large number of lines, mainly in OECD countries. At the sectoral level, low bound rates in the industrial sector were concentrated in base metals and their products, mineral products, machinery, and instruments. In agriculture, they affected mainly some vegetable products and agricultural raw materials. The number of duty-free lines and those affected by low tariffs was practically zero in all of the non-OECD countries examined.

6   In the majority of cases, post-Uruguay Round bound tariff rates remained higher than those currently applied on an MFN basis, and the gap between the two rates remained large in many instances. In fact, this was the case in most of the thirteen non-OECD countries examined and in some non-Quad OECD countries, not just in terms of the overall difference between bound and applied rates, but also in each and every section of the tariff nomenclature.

7   The average trade-weighted MFN tariffs facing developing country exports of manufactures in the OECD markets, although small in absolute terms (3.4 percent), tend to be almost four times as high as those faced by the other OECD countries (Hertel and Martin, 1999b).

8   A high dispersion of tariffs still characterized the tariff schedules of many countries in 1999. In addition, and despite major achievements during the Uruguay Round, tariff escalation remained prevalent in many sectors.

9   The tariffication of agricultural non-tariff barriers following the Uruguay Round Agreement on Agriculture has led to the introduction of high outside-of-quota tariff rates.[18] In many instances, the same was true of inside-of-quota rates that were introduced to provide for minimum access. Even in the case of countries that did not introduce tariff quotas as part of the tariffication exercise, the agricultural negotiating modalities of the Uruguay Round still resulted in high agricultural tariffs. Recent calculations show that, in the OECD economies, protection of agriculture rose from 32 percent in 1997 to 37 percent in 1998 (OECD, 1999c).

10   In some countries, the agricultural sector and some non-agricultural sectors contained a large number of lines with non-*ad valorem* duties.

These findings indicate that tariffs continue to remain an important part of any future market access liberalization effort. The Cassandras were not mistaken. Notwithstanding the achievements of the Uruguay Round, the forthcoming round still has a good deal to work on.

3.7.2 Non-tariff and other barriers

Again, findings of the OECD and the World Bank Studies are reported below:

1   The Uruguay Round re-emphasized trade discipline regarding quanti-tative restrictions (QRs) and similar instruments, and made considerable progress towards that end. Regulations regarding QRs have been tightened and those QRs that fell outside this set of regula-tions were phased out; so too have the VERs been. The World Bank study provides evidence regarding these measures being on their way out. The new safeguard agreement (Article XIX) provides for notifica-tion of VERs by exporting as well as importing countries. All notified restrictions were to be eliminated by March 1999.[19]

As regards other NTBs, like restrictive import licensing procedures and price control measures, an OECD survey of members found such measures on a small percentage of tariff lines – 4 percent or lower for the OECD countries covered in the survey (OECD, 1997). A similar tabulation of NTB incidence for developing economies based on WTO Trade Policy Review indicates a wider range of NTB incidence among these countries in 1999. The tabulation exercise revealed that Hong Kong and Singapore had virtually no NTBs, while Brazil, India, and Indonesia had a large number of them. The tabulation also indicated that Latin American economies, particularly Argentina and Chile, have reduced NTBs significantly over the last ten years. However, some NTBs persist. The ones related to the protection of human, animal, and plant health, to the application of industrial standards, and to the trade in arms and ammunition are considered WTO-legal.

2   The MFA and accompanying QRs have to be eliminated under the post-Uruguay Round system. In addition, the industrial economies agreed to tariff cuts on textiles deeper than those on industrial prod-ucts. However, this agreement has two glaring limitations. First, the agreement is written in such a manner that the industrial economies can (and do) legally put off the elimination of MFA restrictions until 2005. Although the provision of four "stages" suggested that 33 percent of the agreed liberalization should have been in place by the end of 1997, the US has eliminated only 1 percent of its MFA quotas and the EU 7 percent. Second, industrial economies' tariffs on textiles and clothing remain two to three times higher than their tariffs on other industrial goods (Finger and Schuknecht, 1999).

3   There was less of substance in the agriculture liberalization agreement than had been expected. Although the further use of NTBs was banned, the conversion formulas for setting tariffs "equivalent" to the NTBs they represented were negotiated guidelines, not legal obligations. Similarly, the often cited 36 percent cut by industrial economies and 24 percent cut

by developing economies were guidelines, not legal obligations. The guidelines could be rendered meaningless for tariffed products by setting inflated tariff equivalents. Soon many examples of these inflated tariff equivalents appeared. Consequently, the post-Uruguay Round tariff rates were lower than the tariff equivalent of pre-Uruguay Round protection for only 14 percent of products that underwent tariffication.

4   Around 1990, antidumping became the most popular tool of governments seeking a GATT-legal means of accommodating a domestic industry that could not face import competition and was clamoring for protection. With the significant strides made towards liberalization during the Uruguay Round, there was apprehension that the application of antidumping measures would become more rampant. The traditional users of antidumping measures, Australia, Canada, the EU, and the US, have not gone on applying them with abandon.

This scenario has changed and several developing economies have now become major users of antidumping measures. Argentina, Brazil, India, and Mexico became major users, with the number of cases per US dollar of imports considerably higher than the ratios for traditional users. China has become the biggest target country. The US was the next biggest target of antidumping action. Measured per dollar of exports, antidumping initiatives against an economy are much higher against developing economies than against industrial economies. Although developing economies employ antidumping measures, such measures are disproportionately used *against* them. Where antidumping measures were applied, they provided a degree of protection that was usually much higher than what was taken away by the Uruguay Round tariff reduction. Antidumping duties of 40 percent to 50 percent were common and higher levels were easy to find. Paradoxically such high levels of antidumping duties were applied in product areas where the Uruguay Round tariff reductions were in the range of 2 percent to 4 percent.

5   Following the Uruguay Round agreement the number of countervailing duty cases fell sharply. However, since 1997 they have been rising and their 1998 level was the same as their pre-1995 level. The US is the largest user of countervailing duties, accounting for over 40 percent of such duties in the recent period. Among the developing economies, Brazil, Chile, and Mexico are the most frequent users.

6   The safeguard agreement has successfully curtailed protection outside the multilateral framework. Since the phasing out of the VERs there have been no complaints of the imposition of any gray area measures. After the Uruguay Round agreement it was believed that, by lifting the compensation requirement on time-bound and regressive safeguard measures, the agreement has made safeguard measures more user friendly. Therefore a shift was expected from antidumping measures to safeguard measures. No such shift ever came about. During the

1995–98 period, when there were 900 antidumping actions, only nineteen safeguard investigations were initiated. Of these nineteen safeguard initiations, fourteen initiations were by developing countries (Finger and Schuknecht, 1999).
7   The significance of bringing the whole service sector under the multilateral trade discipline cannot be overestimated. In most countries at least half of the GDP generated is in this sector. However, the Uruguay Round agreement did not result in far-reaching liberalization in the sector. To be sure, the GATS can be a notable step towards opening global markets in services.

3.8 The global trading environment in 2000

Several developing economies had expressed their difficulties in implementing the recommendations of the Uruguay Round. The WTO secretariat established a mechanism to consider implementation-related issues during 2000. Second, mandated negotiations on agriculture and services started on schedule. Third, the WTO attempted in a proactive manner to integrate the developing and least developed country members into the global trading system so that they can secure the benefits to be derived therefrom. Fourth, as an institution the WTO continued to explore, at the political and technical levels, the possibility of reaching a consensus on a broad negotiating agenda for the new round (WTO, 2000e).

That the members had confidence in the five-year-old institution was apparent from its growing membership, which had risen to 140 by December 2000. Jordan, Georgia, Albania, Oman, and Croatia, in that order, acceded during the course of the year. Lithuania was poised to accede and twenty-eight accession negotiations were in progress. China, the largest developing-country trader, and the ninth largest exporter, had reached the last stage of its accession negotiations. Although each accession is significant in its own right, both for the new WTO member concerned and for the organization, China's accession to the WTO is momentous. China's eagerness to accede is evident from the fact that it has continued to negotiate for fourteen years, the longest ever for any WTO member. Opening its markets to foreign trade and investment would make China more prosperous, and committing China to global trade regulation would foster and consolidate its ongoing market-based reforms. Conversely, the WTO members stand to gain by better access to an economy of 1.3 billion consumers which is growing at an average rate of 8 percent per annum.

Another sign of confidence in the global trading system was that WTO members constantly had recourse to the dispute settlement mechanism. Up to the end of 2000, over 200 complaints had been lodged by a broad cross-section of WTO members, developing and industrial, small and large. Members' commitments open the channels of commerce, which stay open out of respect for the global trade regulations. If a breach of the regulations is alleged, the dispute settlement mechanism is available to the members. It allows a member to obtain an authoritative ruling, which is binding.

The recent emerging market crises have demonstrated that the global trading system can prevent protectionist solutions of domestic crises. The crisis economies and the global economy recovered much more quickly than had been anticipated. One of the reasons behind such rapid recovery was that these WTO members kept their markets open, notwithstanding a crisis situation. Owing to the implementation of the recommendations of the Uruguay Round and new GATS initiatives in the liberalization of services and information technology, those markets were more open than ever before.

The 2000 telecoms agreement succeeded in introducing competition to a sector which was once the preserve of government-owned monopolies. This agreement expanded the variety of communication services, brought prices down, and gave connection to the Internet a major boost. The latter rose sharply in 2000. The Internet is also central to the emergence of the "new economy" on a global basis. The telecoms agreement has spurred the development of wireless communication services and the advent of the "mobile information society" (WTO, 2000e).

3.9 Summing up

The most significant upshot is that, despite delays, contretemps, and obstructions, the Uruguay Round turned out to be a noteworthy success; it was also the most significant round of MTNs from the perspective of developing countries. However, much remains to be done to improve the global trading regime. The forthcoming round needs to build upon the achievements of the Uruguay Round. Although, when it was launched in 1986, developing countries' support was hesitant, as it progressed the mind set of the policy mandarins changed and developing-country support began to build up. Their participation in the Uruguay Round was far greater than in the preceding rounds. A complex array of elements were made to address long-standing sectoral problems, created a permanent trade body, strengthened dispute settlement procedures, and provided new trade or trade-related arrangements in services and intellectual property. It resulted in a substantial strengthening of the rule-based multilateral trading system, and was extended to new areas of trade.

Notwithstanding these strengths, the Uruguay Round agreement has several weak spots. In addition the "single undertaking" has not served many developing countries well, although the alternatives could be worse. It suffers from several serious problems, including "dirty tariffication", tariff spikes in manufactures, and the MFA. Several large exercises in estimating the level of tariff using different databases have been undertaken.

The results show the tariff cuts have been reported and compared with those in the preceding rounds. In terms of implementation of the Uruguay Round, there was a clear dichotomy between developing and industrial economies. Also, a review of sixty-one TPRs revealed that protection through both tariffs and NTBs was greater in low-income developing economies than in the middle and high-income developing economies.

4 An action agenda

A post-Seattle perspective

4.1 Striking a balance

To eliminate the likelihood of another Seattle, the agenda of any new round of multilateral trade negotiations (MTNs) must strike a balance between the interests of the industrial and developing economies. Although the four members of the Quad[1] are the largest traders and overwhelmingly dominate global trade, developing economies dominate the membership of the World Trade Organization (WTO) in terms of number. Striking a balance includes agenda, process, and outcomes. A lack of balance will not only imperil the forthcoming round but also any future MTNs. A new round, therefore, must not only focus on those sectors in which industrial economies have a special advantage, like financial services and information technology, but also those in which developing economies have a special interest, like agriculture, construction, and maritime services. It must not only include the protection of intellectual property rights, of interest to the industrial economies, but must also address issues of current or potential concern to developing economies, such as property rights to knowledge embedded in traditional medicines, or the pricing of pharmaceuticals in developing economies (Stiglitz, 1999a).

In approaching the upcoming negotiations, the member delegations must take into account the marked institutional disadvantage that developing economies have in participating meaningfully in negotiations. For instance, while nineteen of the forty-two African WTO members are not even represented at the WTO headquarters in Geneva, the average number of trade officials from each of the OECD economies is seven. In addition, the upcoming negotiations must not be looked at in isolation, but in their proper historical context. Other than the differences in the levels of economic growth, Stiglitz correctly draws attention to the "suspicions born of a legacy of past power imbalances". The developing and industrial economies play on an uneven playing field. It is tilted against the former. Developing countries face greater volatility; under certain circumstances trade liberalization can also create volatility. They find it relatively more difficult to deal with economic adjustments which are a consequence of trade liberalization. A related factor is that developing economies either do not have social safety nets or have only weak ones. Unemployment has been a persistent problem in the majority of them. Thus regulations and liberalization measures that *prima facie* look even and fair to both the country groups may have very different and unequal consequences for them. The power imbalances at the bargaining table are exacerbated by the imbalance of consequences.

The Uruguay Round, and the ones before it, focused on liberalizing tariff and non-tariff barriers (NTBs) to manufactures. A 1997 joint study by the United Nations Conference on Trade and Development (UNCTAD) and the WTO concluded that the manufacturing sectors with the highest levels of tariff escalation and tariff spikes were textiles and apparel, footwear, leather goods, and travel goods. All of these sectors are of special interest to exporters in developing economies, especially clothing and textiles, which are often subject to tariff rates of 12–30 percent in the OECD economies (UNCTAD/WTO, 1997). Issues like these need to be considered for reopening if a sufficient number of developing economies have rational and well founded concerns.

The seven rounds of MTNs before the Uruguay Round did little to address barriers to agricultural trade, a sector of immense interest to many developing economies because they have a comparative advantage in it. When it was addressed during the Uruguay Round, despite some healthy progress, it fell victim to "dirty tariffication". As seen in Chapter 3 (Section 3.4), tariffs on agriculture continue to be very high even after the implementation of the Uruguay Round Agreement on Agriculture. Recent calculations show that in industrial economies, the production-weighted average nominal rate of trade assistance to agriculture was 33 percent, compared with 2 percent for the other primary and manufacturing industries (Anderson *et al.*, 1999). The agricultural liberalization that occurred was driven by the interests of industrial-country exporters like Australia, Canada, the US, and developing countries that are part of the Cairns Group.[2] Exporters of tropical products did not play an active role in the design of the agricultural liberalization agenda (Stiglitz, 1999b).

4.2 Crafting an action agenda

The dexterity and foresight with which an agenda for the next MTN is crafted will determine the rhythm of world trade in the twenty-first century. As seen in the preceding section, two of its indispensable qualities will have to be fairness and inclusiveness (Stiglitz, 1999a). The basic challenge facing WTO members is to craft an agenda for the next round of global trade negotiations that provides opportunities for the broadest participation and the greatest potential for agreement on significant new trade reforms. This agenda should also include some of the old problematic issues like trade in textiles and apparel or the Agreement on Textiles and Clothing

(ATC). Given the diverse and divergent trading interests of the participants, formulating the agenda will take some effort.

As evident from Chapter 3, not only the interests but also the impact of any new round will necessarily be asymmetric over the participating economies. In addition, while some trade issues can be broken down on North–South or regional lines, others do not clearly break down along such lines. In the post-Seattle world, it is disturbingly obvious that the constituencies driving the new trade issues are diverse, and span the different regions of the globe. For instance, it is obvious that the small economies of the world[3] have little in common with the larger ones like Brazil, the People's Republic of China, or India. Again, the latter country group finds economies like the newly industrialized economies (NIEs) to be competitors as often as allies during the MTNs (Das, 1999).

Crafting an agenda is indubitably a non-trivial exercise because all the participating economies in the MTNs pay a good deal of attention to their individual accomplishments. Without exception each one of them attempts to "take home" some of their negotiating priorities – some of which may well be far-fetched – otherwise they perceive the round as a failure from their perspective. Therefore the new agenda should have something of value for every participating member. This is essential because without it participating economies may be able neither to attract enough domestic political support to be able to participate in the MTNs nor to reform their own trade regimes. This makes the process of crafting an agenda an arduous and onerous one at best, and as we saw in Seattle an impossible one at worst.

To begin with, developing economies must devise a clear-headed pragmatic strategy before crafting – and joining the multilateral endeavors to craft – an agenda. Few of the developing economies study in a methodical manner the desirable contents or the implications of a multilateral trade agreement in an area of interest to them. They leave such work to multilateral institutions and think-tanks in the industrial countries. The Uruguay Round, its recommendations, and the problems associated with their implementation show that many developing economies, particularly the low-income ones, are not able to participate fully and effectively in the WTO process because of inadequate human and institutional capabilities. Oyejide (2000) thinks that in some cases they allocate this capacity suboptimally. There are three distinct, albeit interrelated, dimensions of participation in the WTO process. First is active involvement in designing the rules governing multilateral trade, or the systemic implications of multilateral trade. Second, there is the exchange of concessions during the negotiations. The process is to first identify interests, construct "concessions" around those interests, and exchange them during the MTNs. The third dimension of participation consists of the effective use of established systems and institutional mechanisms to ensure that each member country's rights are enforced and its obligations are met (Oyejide, 2000). Together, these dimensions of WTO participation are a considerable challenge for many developing economies.

Little wonder that many developing countries lack negotiating capacity for a round with an extended agenda that extends for a long period, although there are some exceptions. Countries like Brazil, India, and the larger members of the Association of Southeast Asian Nations (ASEAN) have shown in the recent past they have skillful negotiators who can play the game of negotiation as well as their industrial country counterparts. However, this asymmetry in experience had a detrimental impact on the outcome of the Uruguay Round and may again have a similar impact over the forthcoming round. Developing economies need to make up for this gap in institutional capability in the near future. While they do so, they should make the best use of the resources available from the multilateral organizations.

To use the oft-cited bicycle analogy, if we need the next round to keep the momentum of MTNs going, we should not load the bicycle with so much baggage that it collapses from excess weight. Bigger need not be better (*Economist*, 2000). Having a relatively small number of topics to negotiate on or around would be a pragmatic and functional idea. In the present circumstances, "small and steady movement" will indeed be a worthwhile strategy for the forthcoming round. After the debacle in Seattle, not even the WTO's bureaucrats were able to muster enough enthusiasm for a massive new round (ibid.). They preferred the idea of a small, briskly rolling new round to a large "compromise-laden jumbo package". Their logic was that a large number of negotiating issues were sure to severely tax countries' negotiating and institutional capacity and could not be concluded in a reasonable time span. The time period of the new round should be fixed at three years; only under exceptional circumstances should it be extended to four. The Uruguay Round provides a worthy lesson in this regard. It not only overshot the originally determined time limit, it kept on transgressing the ones that were subsequently set.

There are strong political economy arguments supporting a round involving a "single undertaking".[4] The single undertaking is a major innovation of the Uruguay Round. It stands for the universal application of obligations. It is a meaningful strategy because when negotiators deal with a wide range of topics within a single undertaking they can make trade-offs that are not easily made in a series of disconnected negotiations.[5] For instance, liberalization in agriculture and the implementation of ATC on predetermined lines are of interest to developing countries. Other than that, it will be in their interest to push for further reductions in peak tariffs and tariff escalation on industrial goods, to seek a modification of TRIPs, as well as liberalization of some specific service sectors and modes of supply. Conversely, industrial countries will be looking for additional developing country commitments in the form of more bindings and reductions in the bound and applied tariff rates of industrial products as well as some additional commitments in the services sector. One way of overcoming the opposition of entrenched protectionism in industrial economies

– in sectors like agriculture, or maritime services, or textiles – is to take advantage of the pressure that export interests in the industrial economies will bring to bear on their own governments to negotiate in order to open up developing country markets (Krueger, 1999a).

Non-trade agenda items, like labor-related issues and environment standards, must be banished permanently. The EU and the US are expected to renew efforts to add labor and environmental issues on to the multilateral agenda with the objective of "harmonizing" the labor and environmental laws of WTO members. This thicket must be avoided. A substantial body of academic research is now available that persuasively argues against the inclusion of these items in any round of MTNs in the present or the future. Some scholars of international trade consider them an "intrusion" in trade affairs and trade policy (Anderson, 1996). Developing economies need to take a concerted stand and oppose this intrusion in unison. Similarly, competition or antitrust-related issues should have a lower priority on the agenda, given the WTO's unsuitability to monitor and police the domestic activities of private sector companies. Thus viewed, labor, the environment, and competition-related issues are incompatible with the WTO, given its mandate, and would not help the new round to take off. Beyond the built-in agenda and ATC only carefully selected areas should be included in the agenda. WTO members should seek an "early harvest" of realizable or deliverable agreements if progress stalls – always a likely possibility – in more contentious areas.

Other than the concern regarding the appropriate agenda, it is vitally important for the developing economies to take a pragmatic stand while deciding on broad negotiating items. While entering the negotiations, the criteria developing countries can profitably employ in deciding their negotiating position should include the following considerations: (1) the net benefits they should expect to obtain for their economies both through their own liberalization and through improved access to the markets of others, (2) the net benefits that would result from setting new rules and/or changing the existing ones, and (3) the institutional capacity needed to implement whatever new agreements are reached. The last criterion is important because of the problems many developing economies have encountered in implementing the Uruguay Round agreement (Michalopoulos, 1999a).

Lindsey *et al.* (1999) have suggested their own formula for the forthcoming round. The principal strands of their suggestion are as follows. First, during the negotiations participating members need to abandon the traditional exports good/imports bad mind set. Instead their mind set should be that trade liberalization is its own reward. Second, special attention must be paid to slashing agricultural tariffs, particularly the highest tariff rates. All agricultural tariffs below 5 percent should also be eliminated (Section 4.5.3). Export subsidies and production-distorting domestic subsidies must be eliminated. Third, the commitment of the industrial economies to implement the ATC fully by 31 December 2004 must be reconfirmed. Fourth, although it is has been difficult, attempts must again be made to liberalize trade in services through a "negative list" which assumes all service sectors will be liberalized unless specifically excluded. Fifth, the Dispute Settlement Understanding should be reformed to make additional liberalization possible. Sixth, the antidumping code must be tightened so that domestic "fair trade" laws do not intervene and cannot be used as a tool of protectionism. Seventh, participating members need to seek full compliance with the existing Agreement on Trade Related Aspects of Intellectual Property Rights (TRIPs). Developing economies are seeking renegotiation in the following three areas: geographical indicators, traditional knowledge, and medicaments. Finally, Lindsey *et al.* also agree that the enforcement of labor and environmental standards through trade sanctions must be rejected. These are pragmatic, if somewhat ambitious proposals, and targeting them during the forthcoming round would certainly have far-reaching implications. In addition, the new round should have the provision for a mid-term review, like the Uruguay Round. The review must be at a high – preferably ministerial – level. It must not refrain from mid-course correction, that is, if it feels the need for it.

4.3 Built-in agenda

The Marrakesh Agreement had a "built-in agenda" for the next round of MTNs, which includes further negotiations over agriculture and services. Although the breadth and depth of these two sets of issues provide the next round with a certain scope, and going by the experience of the Uruguay Round these issues can potentially keep the negotiators busy for a while, they cannot comprise a round. The reason is that for a round of MTNs to be launched a "critical mass of issues" is needed. That said, these two areas do provide the next round with a starting point. MTNs are generally wide ranging, as was the Uruguay Round. In wide-ranging MTNs the negotiating countries can exchange cross-sector concessions, necessary for a successful round of MTNs. A critical mass of issues is needed for a round to be fruitful. Had the scope of the Uruguay Round not been extended to agriculture, textiles, services, and intellectual property, its results would have been limited and its achievements would not have been so highly rated.

The agreements on (1) information technology products, (2) basic telecommunications services, and (3) financial services, were also a part of the built-in agenda of the Uruguay Round and were finally completed on schedule as noted in Chapter 2. Other than these three, many of the substantive agreements that were arrived at during the round have "general review provisions" after stipulated periods of varying length. These reviews could create fresh areas for negotiations on that or related subjects. The Uruguay Round Agreement on Agriculture and the General Agreement on Trade in Services (GATS) share an important characteristic, that is, they go further and call specifically for negotiations to carry forward the process of liberalization embarked upon during the Uruguay Round. This was expressly noted in these two agreements because negotiators were aware of their being incomplete.

It was well known that what was achieved during the round was merely a beginning and that the two agreements needed to be broadened. When they are broadened in scope in the forthcoming round, the agreements are expected to affect the major trade interests of most countries either as exporters or importers. Each one of the two agreements provided a framework of principles, rules, and procedures of practical significance largely related to the specific liberalization of commitments made by individual WTO members. It was recommended that the rules and procedures be followed at the time of further negotiations, although some of the rules may need to be re-examined (Anderson, 1998; Das, 1998).

4.3.1 Agricultural negotiations

The GATT treated the agriculture sector differently from the industrial sector. After 1950, a great deal of growth in agriculture protection occurred in the industrial economies and subsequently in the NIEs. The protectionist trend accelerated in the early 1980s, and trade in agriculture remains subject to costly distortions. The widespread use of export subsidies was perhaps the most disruptive element in the operation of world agricultural markets. That it was a contentious issue is proved by the fact that it became the largest stumbling block during the Uruguay Round owing to disagreement between the EU and the US on almost all aspects of the draft agreement. It delayed the conclusion of the round by two years. The EU worked hard to defend the Common Agricultural Policy (CAP), which was essentially designed to be a price support scheme on certain agricultural products (like wheat) to protect EU farmers.[6]

The principal beneficial impact on the Uruguay Round was that a foundation for reversing the trend in growth in agricultural protection was laid. The Uruguay Round Agreement on Agriculture irreversibly changed the climate of farm policy making in both advanced and developing countries, albeit it has not resulted in large cuts in agricultural protection. Agricultural tariffs were bound for the first time. Article XX of this agreement relates to commitment to negotiations on trade in agriculture. The practice of subsidizing exports of agricultural products has been constrained by the Uruguay Round, but most of the subsidies are allowed to continue in a reduced form.

Agriculture has played an important role in the economic growth and development prospects of a large number of developing economies. This sector still employs half, or more, of the labor force in many developing economies. In the OECD countries the corresponding proportion is small and declining. African countries derive 15 percent of their export income from agricultural products, the Latin American economies 20 percent. In contrast, for the EU economies the proportion was 4.2 percent in 1999, for the US 4.9, and for Japan a paltry 0.1 percent (OECD, 2000a). The agricultural trade performance of the developing economies has been evolving over the years. International trade in agriculture is increasingly a trade in processed and other higher-value products.

There are considerable differences between the market access conditions applying to agricultural products and those applying to other products. These differences include the high and disparate levels of border and other forms of market access protection as well as special agricultural safeguard provisions. Distorted world markets for agricultural products penalize countries that have liberalized and discourage countries from implementing further liberalization. Countries that have liberalized cannot compete against heavily subsidized producers in other countries. High levels of export and trade-distorting subsidies, and market access barriers, affect both domestic competitiveness and access to export markets, particularly for developing countries. For a long time the developing and other exporting economies have asked for improvement in access to world markets for their agricultural exports, and for more equitable conditions of competition. The interests of the developing economies lie in further reductions in and the eventual elimination of export subsidies, and more effective disciplines on other forms of export subsidization. Therefore, their interest in the current agricultural trade negotiations is immense. Concessions on agricultural raw materials and other bulk commodities, which many industrial economies have to import anyway, cover only part of the spectrum of developing economies' export interests. Concessions on temperate zone products, efficiently produced by developing economies, as well as on processed agricultural products, are likely to figure prominently in the negotiating process when it starts to get into the specifics. As the largest incidence of poverty in the developing economies is generally on farmers, it is important that the most be made of the opportunities offered by the built-in agenda during the next round, so that this group benefits as much as possible. Liberalizing trade in agriculture would increase the role of market discipline in the allocation of resources in the agricultural sector. Market access negotiations should be given their due priority because the potential welfare gains from liberalizing access to agricultural markets is huge (Anderson *et al.*, 1999).

During 2000 four special sessions of the Committee on Agriculture took place in the months of March, June, September, and November. In total forty-five members, or almost one-third of the WTO's entire membership, had submitted proposals. Negotiations on trade in agriculture have come to follow a certain pattern. It is likely that this pattern will, with some variations, be repeated during the future round. What can be reasonably expected is that the US and the Cairns Group will again push for further trade liberalization, and for the total elimination of export subsidies. The Cairns Group members have been asking for "fundamental reform which will put trade in agricultural products on the same basis as trade in other goods".[7] At the end of 2000 the principal proposals that were tabled during the special sessions and were being debated among the WTO members included the one by the Cairns Group. It proposed deep cuts in all tariffs using a formula approach which could deliver greater reductions on higher-level tariffs, including tariff peaks, and eliminate tariff escalation, and the establishment of maximum levels for all tariffs. They proposed tariff reduction commitments on the basis of final bound tariffs. They also asked the following measures to be considered: (1) provisions to make tariff regimes simpler and more transparent, (2) no bound duties, (3) tariff commitments expressed in *ad valorem* terms, and (4) a substantial increase in tariff quotas. The Cairns Group of countries wanted the complete elimination of access to the special agricultural safeguard mechanism contained in Article 5 of the Agreement on Agriculture. As the Cairns Group comprises the exporting countries, their demand in this respect is the most ambitious.

The proposal from eleven newly acceded transitional economies of Central and Eastern Europe and the Baltic States is for cautious market opening. Given the difficulties faced by their economies during the ongoing process of structural reform and increases in domestic prices, these countries have proposed that a flexibility provision be included in the future tariff reduction modalities. This country group expects such a provision to exempt low agricultural tariffs from further reduction commitments. A larger group of these countries, thirteen, have asked on behalf of their "capital deficit" farmers for provision for investment subsidies, input subsidies, and interest subsidies, to reduce the costs of financing. Individual countries could invoke this provision only while the agricultural sector suffered from problems of a dramatic decline in production.

The EU proposal takes a very different line. During the Uruguay Round negotiations on agriculture a parallelism with traffic lights was established. Support for agriculture was classified in three parts: red or unauthorized, amber or the one needing disciplining, and green or freely granted. The idea was to classify domestic measures *only* according to their trade impact. This framework was refined during the negotiations. The assumption was that the reduction commitments should be based on price and/or the volume of output support, which might lead to a significant trade impact. Thus support that could significantly impact trade, and therefore should be subject to a reduction commitment, was named the "amber box" measure, and support that could be considered as having no or minimal trade distortive effects was named the "green box" measure. Under the Uruguay Round Agreement on Agriculture, only the amber box measures should be subject to reduction commitments, while the other measures even if linked with a certain degree of production could go on unhindered.

During the last stages of the Uruguay Round negotiations, following the Blair House agreement, a new category of support measures was introduced. It was named the "blue box" measure and entailed direct payment linked to factors of production. It was not linked to price or volume of output. The color chosen for this category did not specifically intend to identify the degree of impact on trade, because blue box measures were new at that point in time and their effects on production and trade were not known. The EU believes that blue box direct payments have been useful in reforming domestic policies, in the direction set by the WTO. The 1992 reform of the CAP has been translated into a shift from market price support to blue box payments. These payments have ensured transparency among the support policies and allowed market balance to be restored. The decision-making process of EU farmers is much more market oriented now than ever before. The EU also asserts that the latest CAP reform, the so-called Agenda 2000, has further improved the possibility of farmers reacting to market signals. Therefore, the EU wishes continuance of the blue box direct payments.

The final post-Uruguay Round tariff bindings for the major agricultural products are on average high in both the developed and the developing economies (see Chapter 3), but they are higher in the former. Thus there is a pressing need to negotiate these bound tariffs down in the forthcoming round. Laird (1999) suggests that in the forthcoming round the bound rates should be brought down to the actual rates to begin with. Having achieved that, further liberalization should begin. It could best be achieved by adopting a logical and effective formula similar to the one used in the Tokyo round for industrial products. According to this formula, the higher tariffs should be reduced more and lower tariffs should be reduced less. At present tariff spikes are high or extremely high in the following products and product groups: major agricultural staple food products such as meat, sugar, milk, and cereals; cotton and tobacco; fruit and vegetables; processed food products (canned meat, fruit juices, etc.) (UNCTAD/WTO, 1997). As many of the tariff spikes in the industrial economies are extremely high, this formula will make negotiations efficient. It also makes sense on mercantilist strategic grounds. Secondly, tariff escalation in line with successive stages of processing is another characteristic of tariff barriers in agriculture. The above formula will also help reduce effective protection more than simple radial reduction.

The consultations, debate, and discussion of different proposals that took place until December 2000 were lively. They were *inter alia* focused on (1) the provisions for net food importing countries, and (2) the development of internationally agreed disciplines to govern the provision of export credit.

4.3.2 *Tariff rate quota*

The pervasiveness of "dirty tariffication" has also been discussed in Chapter 3 and the Agreement on Agriculture recognizes that it could result in reduced market access for agricultural products imports, some of which were permitted in the past through non-tariff barriers, like voluntary export restraints (VERs). The Agreement on Agriculture provided for the introduction of tariff quota rate[8] (TQR) to raise the share of imports to at least 5 percent of domestic consumption of that agricultural product for which imports were reduced to a negligible level before the Uruguay Round.[9] A two-tier tariff structure was stipulated to achieve the 5 percent market share target by 2000. The TQR provision was applied at bilateral and global levels, with the former allocated to traditional export suppliers on the basis of historical market shares, and the latter available in principle on a most-favored-nation (MFN) basis.

The problem with TQR was that the bilateral arrangements kept the new, more efficient, suppliers out of the market. The global quota had several serious administrative problems. How the global quota should be allocated turned out to be a rancorous issue. The WTO members had negotiated importing countries to incorporate their preferential trading arrangements into the market access opportunities, which further complicated the issue. Consequently the 5 percent market share level could not be reached in many cases. Besides, in some cases, imports were charged higher outside-of-quota tariff rates. The forthcoming round will have to address these issues and resolve them, bearing in mind the efficiency considerations. Global efficiency will be best served by first unifying the bound tariff rates and the rate applicable to the TQR to the level that will ensure the minimum import requirement. The next step should be to bring the tariff rates down gradually (Panagariya, 2000). Developing economies must also negotiate for increasing access under tariff quotas significantly above the current 5 percent of consumption level.

In the consultations that took place during 2000, the WTO members suggested that the administration of TQR should be made more transparent, equitable, and non-discriminatory. They suggested that this might be achieved by ensuring that notifications submitted to the Agriculture Committee include detailed guidelines and procedures for the allotment of TQRs.

4.3.3 Export subsidy

Although the Agreement on Agriculture forbids any new subsidies, it tolerates the existing ones. Both industrial and developing economies were to slash budget outlays on export subsidies. The proportions of cuts were large for the industrial economies (36 percent) and relatively smaller for developing countries (24 percent). Likewise, the volume of subsidies for exports was to be reduced in both the country groups, according to a predetermined schedule, between 1995 and 2004. The magnitude of subsidy is far larger in the industrial economies than in the developing ones. The former accounted for 80 percent of the global volume of agricultural subsidy in 1995, and they are concentrated in a small number of products, namely cheese, butter, wheat, and beef. Therefore the task of agricultural subsidy reduction has to be disproportionately focused on the industrial economies. Nothing less than a ban on farm export subsidies is needed to bring agriculture into line with non-farm products under the WTO (Binswanger and Lutz, 2000). Such a ban will benefit many potential developing country exporters. The other subsidy that needs to be drastically reduced is the domestic producer subsidy. This will entail binding aggregate support levels as well as support for individual commodities, outlawing carryovers of "savings" from year to year, and cutting high subsidy spikes.

Deliberations during 2000 were limited to Article IX of the WTO Agreement, and interpretation of Annex VII. The proposal was that developing member countries be allowed an eight-year transition period for the phase-out of export subsidies. It was proposed that Annex VII could include the countries that have not reached GNP *per capita* levels of US$1,000 in constant 1990 US dollars for three consecutive years. The threshold level of US$1,000 and other issues were going to be taken up in further discussions.

4.3.4 Sanitary and phytosanitary measures

These measures are designed and intended to ensure the maintenance of public health. With the liberalization of agricultural exports into industrial economies, sanitary and phytosanitary (SPS) measures are assuming increasing importance. This is a problem area for the developing economies because the majority of them are not technologically well equipped to cope with them. Another area is lack of information about SPS measures in the developing economies. While the agreement on SPS does acknowledge this and encourages industrial economies to provide them with technological assistance, it leaves provision to the donor country's discretion. The agreement in the next round should take this further and a formal mechanism for ensuring the implementation of the agreement should be laid down. Also, during the next round all the member economies should guard against the use of existing and new SPS measures for protectionist purposes.

4.4 Furthering trade in services

4.4.1 General Agreement on Trade in Services

The General Agreement on Trade in Services (GATS) was a first step towards a comprehensive framework to regulate trade in services. The WTO secretariat classified them into eleven broad categories: business services; communication services; construction and other related services; distribution services; educational services; environmental services; health care services; tourism and related services; recreational services; cultural and sporting services; and transport services. The obligations of individual countries under the GATS were specified in their "schedule of specific commitments" to market access, which also provided a list of exceptions. These schedules are an integral part of the agreement. As the Uruguay Round was not able to conclude all sectors and it was felt that there was enormous room for improvements, it was decided to continue negotiations immediately after the entry into force of the GATS.

Many key obligations in the GATS apply only to those services for which the country concerned may have made liberalization commitments in its "schedule of specific commitments". In the next round negotiations on trade in services will certainly focus attention on improvements in the rules, but their primary emphasis is likely to be on extending the reach of the present rules by adding to the coverage of WTO members' services schedules (Anderson, 1998; Das, 1998). Negotiations should strive for progressively higher levels of liberalization of trade in services. In essence, success in the forthcoming round of negotiations will depend upon the extent to which member countries are able to improve their "schedules of specific commitments" in terms of the increased coverage in sectors and degree of liberalization. Several scholars (e.g. Snape, 1998; Warren and Findlay, 1999) have observed that the GATS is too general in its attempt to cover all kinds of service delivery and all forms of barriers to access, yet at the same time not general enough in terms of obligations on countries making liberalization commitments. Snape and others have argued that GATS, like WTO, must embrace MFN and national treatment principles, and the current practice of countries taking MFN and national treatment exceptions must be abandoned.

Strengthening Article VI of the GATS, which provides the basic framework for minimizing trade distortions created by domestic regulations, should be one of the important objectives of the forthcoming round. This article states that "in sectors where specific commitments are undertaken, each member shall ensure that all measures of general application affecting trade in services are administered in a reasonable, objective and impartial manner". A strengthened version of this article, and a clearer interpretation, could go a long way in facilitating market access liberalization by committing member countries to the reform of regulations that impede competition. Under the amended version of Article VI, member countries should be asked to establish procedures for the review of regulations at the request of the exporters of services.

The forthcoming negotiations need to ensure that the amended version of Article VI is based on objective and transparent criteria which are not more burdensome than necessary to ensure the quality of the service that is being exported. Transparency can be achieved by asking the member countries to state explicitly the objectives served by a restrictive policy regulation. Such a statement will facilitate and expedite any examination of whether the regulation is "more burdensome than necessary to ensure the quality of the service". This article can be further improved in a fundamental manner. For instance, it can define the "quality of services" by including reliability, safety, integrity of network, and service to under-served regions and population segments.

As stated earlier in this section, the GATS was only the beginning of trade regulations in services. It is indeed possible to make significant improvements in it during the forthcoming round of MTNs (Whalley and Hamilton, 1996). Article XIX(1) of GATS aims at "achieving a progressively higher level of liberalization" and mandates the development of new rules. There is also a need for an explicit mandate for work on improving the clarity of the agreement. According to Low and Mattoo (1999), there are several obvious ambiguities of a fundamental nature in the GATS in its present form. The areas that need immediate clarification and attention include:

1   Relationship between market access and national treatment in order to specify precisely the scope of existing and future national treatment commitments.
2   Relationship among modes of supply with respect to commitments on a given service activity, for instance if a service is delivered under different modes it should be considered a "like" service regardless of the modal distinction made in the schedule.
3   Confirmation of the principle of technological neutrality within modes, that is, within a mode of supply a service is regarded as "like" independently of the means by which it is delivered. This should confirm that existing commitments cover electronic delivery of the service in question. At this point, this is no longer seriously questioned.
4   Removing interpretative confusion regarding the true scope of bound market access and national treatment.
5   Development of a detailed nomenclature for general application to trade in services. The classification system so far is not problem-free.

Article XIX can potentially provide more assistance and guidance on the content of, and preparation for, negotiations. It says that the negotiations are to be directed in such a manner that the final outcome is "the reduction or elimination of the adverse effects on trade in services" (GATS, 1994).[10] It emphasizes that the liberalization of trade in services should take place "with due respect for national policy objectives and the level of development of individual members [of the GATS], both overall and individual sectors". This provision can be profitably utilized by the developing economies. It further suggests "appropriate flexibility for individual developing country members for opening fewer sectors, liberalizing the types of transactions". To provide a better knowledge and understanding of trade in services, Article XIX of GATS called on the WTO's Council for Trade in Services to carry out an assessment of trade in services, in overall terms and on a sectoral basis, before the launching of the next round of the MTNs. The WTO has responded by conducting various scholarly studies of trade in services.

One of the conspicuous weak spots of the GATS is that it has ignored subsidies. Just as with trade in goods, they have a distorting effect on trade in services, and there should be useful policy discussions on this issue in the new round. Some, not all, middle and low-income developing countries need flexibility in the use of subsidies to develop their service sector. This should be allowed to them. As opposed to this, industrial economies that have robust service sectors should be subjected to stricter discipline in this regard, identical to the regulation on subsidies of trade in goods.

Article XIX(1) of the GATS has provided a future negotiating agenda and called on the WTO's Council for Trade in Services for broad-based negotiations on services, "beginning not later than" January 2000. Accordingly, these negotiations started on schedule. They are expected to provide an opportunity to get more countries to make commitments in more service sectors, and to eliminate – or at least narrow down – some of the exceptions and exemptions set out in the current schedules.

Some of the areas of special interest to developing economies are liberalization involving the movement of natural persons, particularly in construction services. Several developing economies, particularly those in Asia, have developed large capacities in exporting construction services over the last two decades because they have a comparative advantage in this area. Maritime services are another major area of interest to developing economies. Shipping conferences, which are veritable cartels, set prices and pursue other collusive activities in 85 percent or more of maritime services. These cartels are often exempt from antitrust law in the industrial countries. Negotiations on this issue were started in 1995, but they were inconclusive. When they were suspended, it was decided that they would be re-started in 2000 in a wider context. The issue has enormous significance for the developing economies.

The current GATS negotiations would do well to give fresh impetus to negotiations on numerous rules-related issues which were left unattended in the past and over which a good deal of disagreement persists among the members of the GATS. For instance, there is little agreement on how to handle subsidies and safeguard actions in the services area. Members still hold widely divergent views, and negotiators are still struggling to clarify basic concepts. Not all members believe that rules are needed in this area. Second, the GATS provided for multilateral negotiations on government purchases, but they have not got off the ground. Some progress might be made in this area. Third, negotiations on the recognition of professional qualifications could be started so that service professionals like architects and lawyers can enter new markets.

The new services negotiations started in January 2000 and the Council for Trade in Services met in May, July, and October 2000. Delegations undertook a heavy and intensive program of work in the Services Council. Deliberations on issues like MFN exemptions continued. The purpose of reviewing the MFN exemption was to examine whether the conditions that had created the need for exemptions continued to prevail. The ASEAN concept paper on safeguard and the EU presentation of subsidies were discussed. On government procurement, the European Union put forward an informal paper highlighting possible areas of discussion. The EU proposed to focus on the application of non-discrimination and transparency principles to government procurement of services. However, differences of view among delegations have persisted. Some members emphasize the need to create new classifications like environmental services and energy services.

During 2000 the work was concentrated on rule-making issues. Most of the discussions and negotiations focused on the establishment of guidelines and procedures, which were mandated by the GATS. The guidelines were expected to form a framework within which future negotiations would take place. A concerted attempt was made to establish the fundamental principles which should guide future GATS negotiations, their scope, and the negotiating modalities. The Working Party on GATS Rules sought to develop disciplines, which the GATS lacks, on emergency safeguard measures, subsidies, and government procurement services. The Working Party on Domestic Regulations was developing disciplines for qualifications, technical standards, and licensing. The Committee on Specific Commitments was working on the classification of services and on revising the guidelines for the scheduling of commitments. Pending agreement on the guidelines, members agreed on a 'road map' in late 2000. In December the secretariat was tasked with consolidating the members' numerous written and oral contributions and producing a first draft of the guidelines. The draft was scheduled to be approved by March 2001.

4.4.2 Electronic commerce

The impact of the information revolution in lowering communication and computing costs is adding a whole new dimension to global economic integration. During the 1980s, the globalization of merchandise trade and investment altered the entire manufacturing scene. In the 1990s, the digital revolution, aided by deregulation and the transferring of many services from the public to the private sector, transformed the services sector, particularly knowledge-based, or ideas-based, industries. Previously non-traded services have now become highly traded ones. Their tradability has become so high that in some products national borders are becoming irrelevant. The digital revolution has made information one of the key factors of production. Unlike land, labor, and physical capital, information is highly mobile internationally. Financial capital was already internationally mobile (WTO, 1998b).

In 1991 the Internet had less than 3 million global users and its application to e-commerce was non-existent. In 1999 an estimated 250 million users accessed the Internet, a quarter of them making purchases on-line

(OECD, 2000b). Until 1999 electronic trade or e-commerce was small (US$26 billion) but it is growing dynamically and may approach US$1 trillion by 2004 (OECD, 1999b). E-commerce is the newest subject to dawn on the horizon of MTNs. E-commerce offers unprecedented opportunities for both industrial and developing economies. In the short run the benefits are likely to be concentrated in the former, but over the long haul the latter may have more to gain. Given its explosive growth in recent years, it is going to be an important area of negotiation in the next round. The explosive growth so far has occurred in a legal vacuum, with few accepted rules and disciplines. The cross-border nature of the transactions has made the issue of legal jurisdiction unclear. But there is little doubt that before it is too late a framework of global rules for transactions through the Internet will have to be established.

The WTO has done a substantial amount of work with regard to e-commerce, but the cross-cutting and rapidly evolving environment of e-commerce posed a challenge both to the organizing structure of the WTO and the operational methods of its members. The crucial issue was whether e-commerce and digitalized products should be classified into WTO, GATS, both, or neither. The EU asserted that "all electronic transmissions consisted of services" and therefore such products should be classified under the purview of GATS (WTO, 1999b). Most countries agree that services delivered over the Internet are covered by GATS, but other products are more like goods or are a hybrid between goods and services – electronic books are a good example. The US, therefore, argues that more time should be allowed to elapse and the evolution of e-commerce should be monitored before a decision regarding final classification is taken.

E-commerce was first discussed in the context of the Geneva Ministerial conference in May 1998. It was proposed that the member countries should not impose any tariff barriers on electronic transmissions. As e-commerce was growing rapidly, the US proposed that the WTO should demonstrate support for its continuing expansion and that no precedent should be set for taxation or regulation of the sector. A standstill was agreed and WTO members consented to "continue their current practice of not imposing customs duties on electronic transactions" (WTO, 1998c).

The WTO members need to establish a predictable environment in which e-commerce can thrive, so this new form of international trade benefits all consumers in all countries. The original US proposal was intended to become a multilateral agreement that would permanently exempt electronic transmissions from tariffs. Many developing country members were put off by the proposal because they felt that it had not been sufficiently discussed and explored. They were not willing to pledge themselves regarding never to impose any tariff or taxes on it – not without thoroughly studying the fiscal and revenue implications of such a commitment. Several developing economies, including India and Pakistan, have raised questions regarding related issues, including the risk of discrimination in favor of e-commerce over traditional forms of trade, potential loss of revenue, and the issue of the proper recording of transactions. In May 1998, WTO Ministers formally agreed that the WTO should conduct a comprehensive study of all trade-related issues relating to global e-commerce. The study was also to take into account the economic, financial, and development needs of developing economies. Its mandate was to draw up a list of recommendations for the third Ministerial Conference to be held in November–December 1999 in Seattle.

Although a near-consensus exists regarding the application of all GATS provisions to e-commerce, and that the "technological neutrality" of GATS means that electronic supply of services is permitted unless specifically excluded, there are many moot points and uncertainties. Some of the unanswered questions are: how to classify Internet access and services, whether certain products when they are electronically transmitted should be classified as goods, how to link this arrangement with the Telecommunications Agreement, how to ensure the privacy of transactions and how to value encrypted data, and the like (WTO, 1999c). Concern on the part of the developing economies regarding loss of tariff revenue seems somewhat exaggerated, because most countries provide many and large-scale exemptions to their existing tariff schedules. The choice before the developing countries is clear and the stakes are enormous. The WTO members can and need to establish a predictable environment in which e-commerce can thrive, allowing the benefits of this new form of international trade to be realized by all member economies, developing and industrial. The information technology (IT) sector contributes almost 8 percent of GDP in the US, where e-commerce has its strongest hold. The remarkable growth in IT-related industries, especially those that are directly linked with e-commerce, have helped create the longest period of economic growth with low inflation in US history. This kind of gain is available to all countries, not merely to first users like the US and the EU. Developing countries should see that liberalization via e-commerce is not a zero-sum game (Mann, 2000).

During the last summer meetings of 2000, the General Council agreed to reinvigorate the work of the WTO on electronic commerce on a practical basis and invited four subsidiary bodies to pick up the thread from where they left off their work in this area. These four bodies were the Councils on Goods and Services, the TRIPs Council, and the Committee on Trade and Development. These four bodies were charged with the task of examining all trade-related issues with respect to global electronic commerce; they reported their findings to the General Council on their progress in December 2000.

4.5 Beyond the built-in agenda: potential issues

Beyond these two major, and already agreed, areas which could help initiate the forthcoming round of MTNs, there are several significant areas and issues waiting to be taken up as agenda items. First, consultations were going on about the rules of origin during 1999 and 2000. Second, some WTO members had suggested the inclusion of the environment, competition, and investment during the last two Ministerial Conferences, although so far there is no consensus on them.[11] Third, suggestions were made regarding the inclusion of trade facilitation and electronic commerce. Although the WTO secretariat started work on these issues, there are again divergent views as to whether they should be included in the new round. Fourth, some subjects involved "general review provisions" (Section 4.3) mandated under the Marrakesh Agreement. According to the schedule, these general reviews were expected to start in 2000. Some of them could be folded into the new round. Trade Related Aspects of Intellectual Property Rights (TRIPs) and Trade Related Investment Measures (TRIMs) were two important areas of this kind. Finally, there are subjects like industrial tariffs and labor standards that have not been agreed for any kind of consideration, but have been suggested by some WTO members repeatedly.

The above subject areas have a vast array of agenda items for multilateral negotiations to choose from. In some subjects developing economies have not evolved a stand. TRIPs is one such important subject. It is not yet decided whether to include it in the wider array of issues for the next round. On other issues, the developing economies have a choice of whether to support multilateral negotiations on the subject or not. They also have to choose whether to do so in a separate and parallel negotiation or combine the negotiations in a "single undertaking". It is natural that, based on the net benefits criteria, different countries and country groups will certainly have asymmetric and varying degrees of interest and commitment in these topics. For the forthcoming round of MTNs to start, it is necessary to reach some consensus among the members of the WTO regarding the desirability of negotiations in each of these areas.

I have chosen and analyzed some of the most important areas for discussion below. As mentioned in Section 4.2, too many issues will severely tax the negotiating skills and institutional capacity of the developing economies, I have kept the number of proposed issues to a manageably low level. To be sure the number of issues should be meaningfully small, but there should be a critical mass to justify a full round of MTNs. Only the vitally important ones are being proposed for the forthcoming WTO round.

4.5.1 *The WTO and system strengthening*

Although the creation of the WTO was not visualized when the Uruguay Round was launched, the possibility of its creation emerged later during the negotiations. It was a system-strengthening measure. Its establishment has generated some controversies. They range from concern about national sovereignty (particularly in India and the US) to concern about whether the WTO can integrate international trade disciplines on goods, services, and intellectual property, given the possibility of cross-retaliation with the new dispute settlement procedures agreed to under the Uruguay Round.

The "single undertaking" clause or all-or-nothing approach (noted in Section 4.2) adopted to implement the decisions of the Uruguay Round, in which countries must accept the results of the round without exception, is a strong discipline-strengthening approach. It was very different from – almost the antithesis of – the approach adopted during the Tokyo Round, which was menu-driven. The approach had some soft spots because it allowed countries to accede to some codes but not to others (Whalley, 1996). Long before the creation of the WTO Jackson (1989) had posited his strong and oft-cited thesis on restructuring and strengthening the global trading system. The structure of the WTO agreed under the Uruguay Round came remarkably close to the one posited by him. He *inter alia* proposed a new draft charter for a global trade institution that imposed few substantive obligations but would apply them on a definitive, rather than provisional, basis. Jackson believed that the major benefit from pursuing such an arrangement was the coherence that would be embodied by the organization under its constitution, clear mandate, and orderly rules for its secretariat.

Globalization is one of the key forces that are pushing for a further expansion of the WTO mandate, particularly in the policy coverage dimension. A growing share of GDP is being traded by an increasing number of economies. This endeavor involves not only transnational corporations (TNCs) but also medium-sized corporations and sometimes small firms in both industrial and developing economies. These enterprises are increasingly spreading activities like sourcing, marketing, and investment across national boundaries. It is widely felt that the WTO discipline reflects these and other modern commercial realities. In addition, as globalization progresses and economies become more intertwined, there is an increased risk that trading partners will be affected by spillovers from ostensibly domestic policies. This makes it imperative to strengthen and expand the WTO's mandate.

The mandate given to the WTO is expanded in Article III of the WTO agreement, which spells out all the functions of the WTO: (1) administer and implement the multilateral and plurilateral trade agreements that together make up the WTO; (2) act as a forum for multilateral trade negotiations; (3) administer arrangements for the settlement of disputes; (4) review national trade policies; and (5) co-operate with the International Monetary Fund and the World Bank with a view to achieving greater coherence in global economic policy making. A strengthened and extended dispute settlement provision, the system of regular trade policy reviews, and co-operation with the other supranational bodies were three of the most significant innovations of the Uruguay Round. The three have resulted in a much strengthened WTO, which in turn can be taken as the principal institutional innovation of the Uruguay Round.

The members of the WTO are there because the existing balance of their rights and obligations is it seems by and large satisfactory to them. Changing this balance may seem disturbing to some of the members. The very process of changing it may take them into negotiations in areas that may be quite outside those under discussion. There is no apparent and pressing need for substantial institutional improvements in the WTO at this stage. None of the WTO members has sought any fundamental change in the young institution. However, the US and Canadian delegations proposed an initiative to "consider how to improve the transparency of WTO operations", which cannot be called a fundamental change. The transparency these two countries have asked for is beyond Article X of the GATT, which requires transparency related to trade-related policies and the practices of governments. It further implies notifying the WTO regarding developments in environmental and labor policies. Criticism has also been expressed on such issues as the slow-moving procedures for accession to the WTO, lack of substance in the role of the Council for Trade in Goods, and the level of minimum budget contribution payable by countries with a small share of world trade. To be sure, some of these problems could be overcome by appropriate administrative changes (Blackhurst, 1998; Croome, 1998).

4.5.2 Restraining dumping abuses

By far the most controversial and problem-ridden Uruguay Round agreement was on antidumping measures. Lindsey *et al.* (1999) consider it "the major flaw in the WTO". Antidumping rules became one of the central issues of the Tokyo Round and subsequently of the Uruguay Round, and lack of agreement among countries on antidumping reforms threatened the success of the round. At present it is possible for countries to block "dumped" imports in an entirely WTO-consistent manner even when the foreign producers whose goods are targeted are engaged in perfectly normal business practices that do not meet any plausible definition of "unfair trade". Lindsey (1999) presents numerous examples of ways in which antidumping laws in industrial economies punish normal business practices. All the WTO members, except the US, agree that there is a need to discuss antidumping further.

Antidumping abuses are becoming an increasingly serious problem for the global trading system. The recent alarming increase in the number of antidumping actions pursued by both industrial and developing economies has caused considerable concern among economists, trade reformers, and policy makers. The Uruguay Round Antidumping Agreement (URAA) lays down regulations regarding how governments, which use antidumping measures, should establish the existence of dumping, and the damage, or threat of damage, to domestic producers. It goes further and prescribes procedures for antidumping investigations and for the imposition or termination of antidumping duties. As the Antidumping Agreement was finalized somewhat hastily during the dying days of the Uruguay Round a number of concessions were made to the views of the industrial economies. However, the agreement is fully in effect for all the WTO members and there is no provision for its general review.

So-called "screwdriver plants" and their output are a chestnut in this regard. Industrial economies agree that when such plants carry out the final assembly in the importing country or a third country, to circumvent tariffs, the importing country should be allowed antidumping action against their products. While it was agreed that universally accepted rules on "anti-circumvention" action were desirable and that discussion should continue in the Antidumping Committee, no time frame was set for it (Clarida, 1996). Even the first Ministerial Conference in Singapore set no work program for antidumping apart from an effort to improve notification. The anti-circumvention issue may be raised in the Millennium Round by the industrial economies.

Croome (1998) pointed out that the pattern or use of antidumping action has shifted significantly in the recent past. The Antidumping Agreement was negotiated when almost all antidumping measures were imposed by the industrial economies. In the past it was the "sin" of the industrial countries, in particular of Canada, the EU, and the US. There has been a striking change in this trend. Of late, developing economies have taken to imposing antidumping measures. During 1996–97 developing countries accounted for seventeen out of twenty-three notifications of antidumping actions to the WTO. The list of users was a roll call of the developing countries most active in the WTO. It included Argentina, Brazil, Chile, Colombia, India, Indonesia, Korea, Malaysia, Mexico, Peru, the Philippines, Singapore, Thailand, and Venezuela. Several of the actions taken were against suppliers in other developing countries. An interesting turn of events in this regard is that at present US corporations are divided over the antidumping issue. While some corporations (particularly large steel producers) still prefer rules that would allow easier introduction of antidumping measures, corporations having a strong export interest (as well as performance) are aware that weaker rules might expose them to greater risk in their export markets. Another new element in the situation is that the WTO is now discussing competition issues, and may one day negotiate on them. Hong Kong, China, and Korea have pointed out that effective rules could make antidumping action superfluous. All these new elements are bound to affect the outlook for any future multilateral negotiations on the antidumping rules.

During the third Ministerial in Seattle, the US delegation was dead set against any rationalization of WTO antidumping rules. Among other things, it ignored the interests of its own exporters, who were being injured by foreign antidumping action in their markets. The experience of the last five years shows that antidumping measures have enormous potential for abuse and non-transparency. In the forthcoming round an overhaul of the

WTO antidumping code is called for and the imposition of meaningful restrictions on protectionist abuse is badly needed. An important measure in this regard is to redefine "dumping" so that antidumping duties are imposed *only* when market-distorting practices like trade barriers or subsidies in the exporting markets are clearly identified. WTO discipline must be tightened in this area. To be sure, such tightening holds out the promise of improving market access conditions in both developed and developing countries.

4.5.3 Market access and tariffs

From an economic welfare perspective, tariffs are generally to be preferred to other trade-inhibiting commercial policies owing to their transparency and readily quantifiable efficiency costs. In broad terms, the distorting impact of a tariff depends upon the price elasticitiy of demand of the product on which the tariff has been levied. It rises disproportionately with the level of the tariff. Thus low tariff rates cannot be ignored as insignificant. A low tariff rate could disguise significant efficiency losses if the dispersion of tariff rates was high.

One of the fundamental rationales of all trade negotiations was – and continues to be – to improve market access by bringing down tariff barriers and bind them. These objectives were the *raison d'être* of all the MTNs since the inception of the GATT/WTO system half a century ago down to the Uruguay Round. In the first Ministerial Conference in Singapore in 1996, Ministers renewed their commitment to the "progressive liberalization and elimination of tariffs and non-tariff barriers to trade in goods", but did not include tariff reduction in the long list of subjects on which they agreed to start working. Perhaps the reduction of tariffs on industrial products, agreed upon during the Uruguay Round, was being brought into force, making it unnecessary to add it to the list. The MFN tariff reduction process entailed reduction in five equal annual installments, the last of which was to be on 1 January 1999. Again, as a result of the three recent sectoral agreements, the MFN tariff is being brought down in many countries. This is particularly applicable to the Information Technology Agreement reached in July 1997.

Some sectoral negotiations, of both the regional and the global variety, were also in progress. For instance, the APEC economies, committed to their brand of "open regionalism", had identified fifteen product categories as candidates for early voluntary trade liberalization. Of these, nine were considered priority areas for commencing liberalization. At the same time tariffs were being scaled down in Europe. This was being done under bilateral agreements between the EU economies on the one side and the transition economies of Europe on the other. The EU economies were also undertaking a similar exercise with the economies of the Association of Southeast Asian Nations (ASEAN). This is certainly not an exhaustive enumeration of tariff reduction endeavors that were in progress during this period.

With the contemporary regional, subregional, and sectoral initiatives on tariff reduction one may be seized by the futility of any such future exercise. This impression is incorrect because, first, most observers concur that a broad-based and balanced round of MTNs cannot possibly ignore tariff reduction. Even after the Uruguay Round agreements are implemented, by which time tariffs on manufactured goods will be down to very low levels, there will be sufficient scope for tariff reduction on manufactured and non-manufactured goods. High tariffs still impede trade, and tariff spikes continue to affect a number of sectors both in industry and in agriculture. High tariff lines with spikes are to be found in both industrial and developing economies. In the industrial country markets numerous tariff spikes are present in products of interest to developing country exporters. The number of tariff lines with spikes was higher in agriculture than in industry. Before the launch of the Seattle Ministerial, during the preparatory phase, both developing and industrial members of the WTO called for new negotiations on market access and tariffs.

As noted above, low tariff rates cannot be ignored because they could disguise significant efficiency losses if the dispersion of tariff rates is high. Low tariffs, such as those below 3 percent, also create an unwarranted nuisance to trade. Nuisance tariffs are not likely to provide any significant protection for domestic industries but have high domestic administrative costs. Sometimes these costs are higher than the revenue generated. They are known to generate lengthy administrative procedures and costs, and are a burden to traders. Government administrations incur high monitoring costs. They hamper efficient trade flows. Removal of these nuisance tariffs could be expected to provide several benefits. Industries that use inputs having nuisance tariffs would benefit from lower costs. They include export industries that are not located near the metropolitan centers. Consumers should ultimately benefit from the lower costs and from direct price reductions and improved choices flowing from reductions of general tariffs on consumer goods. This assessment is supported by estimates by the Australian Productivity Commission (APC) (2000). Unilateral tariff removal in this manner would not reduce negotiating strength, it might even increase it. Credit has been given for unilateral reductions in tariffs during the MTNs. There is no doubt that this practice would continue in the new round of MTNs. In addition to focusing on tariff slashing, the next round may devote its energy to harmonization that would reduce tariff spikes and escalation.

Many developing economies, particularly those in Latin America, have managed to keep a large gap between applied and bound tariffs. The latter are much higher than the former. If this gap is reduced – even better, eliminated – it will contribute to improving the predictability of market access.

In addition, bringing the bound tariffs down would provide the developing economies with some bargaining chips, without any loss of revenue or domestic protection. The forthcoming round could also be useful from the perspective of domestic trade policy. Developing economies might use it as leverage against domestic interest groups that resist tariff reduction.

The average trade-weighted MFN tariffs facing developing country exports of manufactures in the OECD markets, although small in absolute terms (3.4 percent), tend to be almost four times as high as those faced by the other OECD countries (Hertel and Martin, 1999a). As industrial products make up almost three-quarters of exports of developing countries and are of importance to practically all of them except sub-Saharan countries, advancing negotiations in this area during the forthcoming round would offer an opportunity to slash tariffs, particularly to address the continuing problem of tariff spikes.

In order to have tariffs slashed in the industrial country markets on products of interest to developing country exporters, developing economies would need to improve access to their own markets. Their own applied tariffs are not only higher than those in the industrial country markets but also have a greater degree of dispersion. The newest trend in the direction of trade is that developing country exports of manufactures to other developing countries are on the rise. Except for Latin American economies, developing economies have not bound a significant proportion of their industrial tariffs. Even those that have bound them have opted for "ceiling bindings", with bound rates much higher than applied rates. The ideal approach for tariff slashing in the new round would be to adopt a greater proportional reduction for higher bound tariff rates in both developing and industrial economies (Section 4.3.1). High tariff spikes exist not only in agricultural product groups (Section 4.3.1) but also in textiles and clothing, footwear and leather products, and some automotive and transport equipment products (UNCTAD/WTO, 1997). These products and product groups are of great significance to exporters in several developing economies.

A mutually beneficial approach could be adopted in which developing and industrial countries exchange tariff concessions. On their part, developing countries may reduce ceiling bindings and some applied tariffs, while industrial economies may further slash tariffs on industrial products from developing country products and bring about a significant reduction in the spike tariff rates. This line of negotiations is doubly beneficial to the developing economies, and would result in welfare gains of a high order. It would liberalize the trade regimes of the developing economies, and stabilize their trade regimes through binding more products. In addition, they would benefit from increased market access in the industrial economies (Michalopoulos, 1999a).

4.5.4 Textiles and apparel

The inclusion of trade in textiles and apparel within the ambit of the WTO regime is widely considered a major achievement of the Uruguay Round. This is an important area for the developing economies in general and Asian economies in particular. The transitional Agreement on Textiles and Clothing (1994) reached during the Uruguay Round did not promise a great deal in absolute terms, but it did achieve a lot relative to the past. The Multifiber Arrangement (MFA) was considered "the mother of all GATT-inconsistent measures" (Martin and Winters, 1996). Under the 1994 Agreement on Textiles and Clothing (ATC) all WTO members agreed that, come December 2004, the MFA, which dates back to 1974,[12] will cease to operate. The ten-year period between 1994 and 2004 was divided into subperiods during which growth rates in quota were to be elevated, and products were to be progressively taken out of the coverage of the ATC. It is because of this schedule that trade in textiles and apparel has adopted a low profile as an issue for the forthcoming round.

There are six key elements in the ATC: (1) the product coverage, set out in the Annex to the ATC, which basically includes most textile and clothing products from the first stage of manufacturing, (2) the program for integrating the products covered by the ATC fully into WTO rules and disciplines, (3) the progressive liberalization of the quotas carried over from the former MFA through improved growth rates until they are eliminated, (4) the treatment of QRs other than MFA quotas, (5) the transitional safeguard mechanism to deal with further cases of serious harm or the actual threat thereof, and (6) the supervision, monitoring, and reporting on the implementation process by the Textiles Monitoring Body. The central element of the ATC is the process of integrating all textile and clothing products listed in its Annex into the full application of WTO rules and disciplines. A significant achievement of the transitional ATC is that it adopted the goal of tariff-only restraint on trade.

The first stage (1995–97) in the transitional process of the ATC has been completed and 1998 saw the beginning of the second stage (1998–2001). The agreed rate for the integration of products in the first stage was not less than 16 percent of the total volume of each country's imports in 1990, which was applied on 1 January 1995. A further 17 percent was integrated on 1 January 1998 to begin the second stage. Thus, at present, one-third of all textile and clothing products have been integrated fully into WTO rules. At the beginning of the third stage, on 1 January 2002, a further 18 percent of products will be integrated. The process will be complete on 31 December 2004 with the integration of all remaining products. At each of these stages, members shall include products from the following four groups: tops and yarns, fabrics, made-up textile products, and clothing. As in the Uruguay Round Agreement on Agriculture, the implementation of this agreement needs careful monitoring. The three-yearly review of 1998 showed that very little progress was achieved in dismantling protection (Anderson, 1999). Even more effort is required to minimize further slippage – particularly when China joins in.

The integration programs of the major importing members have begun with the shift to WTO rules of the least sensitive textile and clothing products and, consequently, with the removal of few quotas. In the third stage it is anticipated that more products of export interest to developing countries will be integrated, with some additional quotas removed. It is apparent that most of the quotas will be maintained, though with increasing growth rates, up to the end of the transition period. Norway, however, is an exception because it has removed all quotas unilaterally, outside of the integration process. The retention of quotas to the end of the process – or back loading – could lead to serious problems in their total elimination after 2004.

There were some built-in problems with the ATC, which did not surface until the implementation began. If one examines the fine print of the ATC, tariffs are not going to be the key constraint on trade fast enough to make quotas redundant by the end of the transition decade. Hertel *et al.* (1996) calculated that by 2005 the quotas would have increased by about half the amount necessary for them to become redundant. If so, tariffication would require the other half of the increase to occur at the end of the ten-year transition period, that is, on 31 December 2004. This raises questions about the political commitment to implementation. So far there is no indication that the major importing countries are willing to liberalize their quotas in a reasonable manner in the next tranche, which is scheduled for 31 December 2002. Doing so would prove decisively helpful in meeting the Agreement goals in 2004 (Spinanger, 1999). Besides, the transitional Agreement on Textiles and Clothing specifies nothing about what may or may not happen beyond 2004. Textiles and apparel as a sector are going to return to the WTO discipline, which need not mean that free trade will prevail in the future. Developing countries are apprehensive that textiles and apparel will become open to dumping action by industrial countries (Whalley, 1999).

The transitional ATC reached during the Uruguay Round has nothing in its text to give rise to new negotiations in the immediate future but it does have a provision for review before the end of each of the three stages of implementation of the agreement. The first such review, which was completed in 1998, showed that very little progress had been made by then. The developing countries felt that the importing countries, in particular Canada, the EU, and the US, had completely disregarded the spirit of the Agreement by applying its letter in ways that have brought about little or no liberalization so far. Some industrial economies, including the above-named ones, have supplemented the effects of repealed quotas by unjustified antidumping actions as well as restrictive rules of origin (Croome, 1998). Textile and apparel exporting countries are concerned that so much of the agreed liberalization measures have been left for the final years of the transition period that full integration of the trade in textiles and apparel into the WTO regime may never be achieved. However, the importing industrial economies disagree with the exporting economies on these issues. They are sure about meeting the deadlines by 1 January 2005. On their part, the industrial countries complain of the level of tariff and non-tariff barriers against imports of textiles and apparel maintained in the developing economies, particularly the Asian economies.

The ATC is one area in which the opinions of developing economies are in complete unison in the WTO. Twenty-three exporting economies are members of the International Textiles and Clothing Bureau, a body through which they co-ordinated their position in the textile negotiations during the Uruguay Round. During the last review of the agreement in the WTO Council for Goods, the Bureau presented a cogent unified case. Representatives of Colombia, Hong Kong, China, and Pakistan made forceful statements on behalf of the exporters. This show of solidarity is indispensable for the exporting developing countries. An additional apprehension the exporting countries have is that the importing countries may increasingly resort to changes in rules of origin (Section 4.5.11), antidumping action, and measures supposedly introduced to protect the environment and labor standards as substitutes for present quantitative restrictions.

Since the ATC covers a wide range of products (cotton, synthetic fibers, wool, silk, and ramie) and a large number of countries, one can expect the impact of dismantling it to be large. Importing countries will benefit from lower import prices due to the abolition of quota rent. After ATC is dismantled, importers can source from the most efficient exporters. Import competition will also improve resource allocation. The exporting countries that have a comparative advantage in textiles and apparel will benefit because they will be able to expand their exports. The quotas will no longer restrict the exports of competitive producers. At the same time the less competitive exporters, that were able to export only thanks to their ATC quotas, will soon lose their market shares. It should, however, be noted that exporting countries will face lower prices after the dismantling of the ATC (Croome, 1998). Thus viewed, eliminating the ATC would lead to an enhancement of global welfare.

Two recent developments have buttressed the case for broaching ATC-related issues and renegotiating and broadening the transitional ATC in the next round. Since its signing in 1994 several important transformations have occurred in the pattern of trade in textiles and apparel. Two of the most important ones are: first, there has been a tremendous growth of regional trade in textiles and apparel, particularly among the major importers, the EU, and the US. Much of this trade is free of quota restraints, which is the characteristic of the ATC. There has been a rapid growth in imports in the US from Mexico under the North American Free Trade Agreement (NAFTA), which was according to the NAFTA rules but not according to the ATC quotas. Textiles and apparel imports have also grown from Jamaica and the Dominican Republic under the Caribbean Basin Initiative under transformation rules. Likewise, the Central European countries (the Czech Republic, Hungary, Poland, Romania, Slovakia) have increased their textile and apparel exports to the EU economies. This trade is also free of quota restraints and has grown rapidly. This regional trade growth has built a constituency among a subset of exporting countries which now find themselves more favorable to the ATC. Expansion of regional trade has also weakened the general opposition to the ATC from the exporting developing economies.

The second material transformation has been in the pattern and direction of the trade in textiles and apparel. Some two decades ago, Korea, Taiwan, and Hong Kong accounted for almost 60 percent of all developing country exports of such products. Their exports were growing rapidly and they were tightly constrained by the MFA in the past. Consequently, quota-hopping foreign investment took place in ASEAN economies, which also began to face the tight quota constraints over time. These two country groups were the most dynamic exporters of textiles and apparel and were the source of strong pressure to dismantle the MFA. The scenario in the 1990s was markedly different. By late 1990s, it was China that accounted for 60 percent of total exports of textiles and apparel from the developing economies. China was not a member of the WTO. The exporting developing economies resent ATC quotas in the important OECD countries less now because they provide them with selected markets. Besides, the most dynamic exporters of the past are now left with unused and unfilled quotas because many of them have moved up the technology and growth ladder, and textiles and apparel are not as important an item of export as they were in the past. Their comparative advantage now is in electronics and higher-technology products. This has reduced the pressure for a dismantling of the quotas from the former dynamic exporters of textiles and apparel (Whalley, 1999).

By 2000, South Asia had become a large exporter of textiles and apparel. India became the second largest shipper after China, and Pakistan and Bangladesh had significant exports in this product category. Pressure for full implementation of the ATC now comes from these countries. Of these countries, Bangladesh falls in the category of least developed countries, and therefore is free from quota restraints in the EU. This made Canada and the US the principal focus of exporting countries' efforts to implement the transitional Agreement on Textiles and Clothing. Yet another reason why textiles and clothing are assuming a low profile for the forthcoming round is the recent conflicts among the exporting developing countries. Of late, there have been complaints from some exporting countries about China and India subsidizing exports and production, respectively. These two large exporters are providing subsidies through the pricing of petrochemicals and synthetics, respectively. There have also been disputes among the exporting developing countries over access to each other's markets. All this is breaking down the old unity of stance among the developing economies on textiles and apparel exports.

Why textiles and apparel have assumed a low profile as an issue to be raised during the forthcoming round has been adequately explained. In addition, many industrial economies, including the US, may not be prepared to negotiate their tariff rates until 2004, although the EU has announced[13] that it has no intention of excluding the issue of textiles and apparel from the forthcoming round. Therefore, efforts should be made by developing economies to raise ATC-related issues. In order to improve global efficiency in this sector of trade, some of the pressing issues that they should still try to open negotiations on are: (1) accelerating the pace of integration, (2) expanding the base of negotiations, making it more comprehensive and speeding up the dismantling process, and (3) slashing the higher average tariffs in this category as well as tariff spikes.

4.5.5 Trade Related Aspects of Intellectual Property Rights

Many industrial economies, in particular the US, have lobbied for stronger protection of intellectual property rights (IPRs) through bilateral, regional, and multilateral action. The US has been concerned about the international infringement of IPRs since the early 1980s. This concern reflected the strong competitive position of American knowledge-based industries (USIA, 1998). As opposed to this, developing economies believe that such protection would result in reduced welfare for them and for the global economy as a whole. Developing countries, particularly the low-income ones, see in TRIPs a clear case of multilateral agreement that has been smuggled into the WTO framework and away from the legitimate mandate of another international organization (the World Intellectual Property Organization, or WIPO). It has been done to take advantage of the more effective enforcement mechanism of the WTO.

Developing economies, including several Asian economies, believe that as a public good, innovations have crucial characteristics, namely "non-rivalry in consumption and non-exclusion" (Panagariya, 1999). The former implies that the use of an innovation by yet another individual does not reduce its availability to the existing users. That is, the marginal social cost of an innovation is zero. Non-exclusion implies that once an innovation has been made, we cannot prevent others from using it. As innovations have costs, no one wants to reinvent the wheel. It is this public good thinking that is behind the opposition of the developing economies to certain facets of trade-related intellectual property measures (TRIPs). In addition, the standard of intellectual property protection in a given country is largely explained by its level of economic development. Low-income developing economies have a limited ability to create much intellectual property and thus little to gain from its protection. If these low-income economies maintained a strong intellectual property protection regime, it would amount to granting monopolies to foreign patentees at considerable cost to themselves. What is worse is that strong intellectual property protection rights tend to restrict the diffusion of knowledge and information so badly needed for the development of low-income countries (Primo Braga *et al.*, 1999).

Despite resistance from some developing members of the WTO, the US was able to multilateralize the IPR issue during the Uruguay Round. It succeeded in doing so because it was clear that having some kind of IPR regime for the US was a deal breaker for the whole round. Also, the WTO members knew that without an agreement on IPRs the US would increase the application of "Special 301" to sanction IPR-infringing countries (Taylor, 1997). Developing country members believed that the Agreement on Trade Related Aspects of Intellectual Property Rights (TRIPs) would work as a deterrent to the use of "Special 301" by the US.

The successful conclusion of the Agreement on TRIPs was heralded by many trade analysts as a triumph of the Uruguay Round. It is also considered the most comprehensive and best international agreement on intellectual property to date. It is comprehensive in that it has clear provisions on MFN and national treatment clauses, as well as on transparency. These are the three important cornerstones protecting the rights of intellectual property holders (Otten and Wager, 1996). The TRIPs agreement extends patent protection for industries critically dependent on strong IPR regimes. One of the most important examples is the pharmaceutical industry. Before the agreement was signed in 1994, some twenty-five developing countries did not respect patent protection for pharmaceutical products.

The TRIPs agreement included trade in counterfeit goods. Although TRIPs did not promote a globally applicable standard of IPR protection immediately, it did lay the foundation of future convergence towards higher standards of protection on a global scale. Constantly emerging new technologies have led to the continuous adaptation of IPR protection instruments. For example, the evolution of IPR protection for biotechnology and its implications for agriculture and the pharmaceutical industry represent an important new area with high relevance for developing economies. Computer software and digital environments like the Internet are other important examples. The IPR regime is still in a state of flux in all these areas, although some inchoate trends are emerging. They are being ratified by new international agreements with minimum standards of protection. They pose new challenges for the legal systems of the developing economies as well as for institutions that have played a prominent role in the international diffusion of knowledge. Therefore, the TRIPs agreement provided for a review in 2000 to "examine relevant new developments which might warrant modifications or amendment of the Agreement".

The TRIPs agreement, as noted above, will require WTO members to observe minimum standards of IPR protection. Maskus (1998) called it a "complex legal system which so far has been uncharted territory" for trade policy officials. The advantage of its inclusion in WTO regulations is that it is equipped with binding dispute settlement procedures. Although the TRIPS obligations were applied to the industrial economies, the developing economies were given a transition period. The Uruguay Round agreement gave developing economies until January 2000 to apply TRIPs rules, and the patent rules will not be applicable until January 2005 to products that are not patentable at present. Policy makers in the developing countries should pay greater attention to strengthening the TRIPs legislation because recent economic data indicate that stronger IPR protection tends to have positive long-term economic benefits for the developing economies (Maskus, 1998).

Developing economies are obliged to extend MFN treatment and national treatment to other WTO members in their protection of intellectual property. While they can decide not to support patent protection for pharmaceuticals or agricultural chemicals, they do have to allow the registration of patent applications. India failed to do so and invited a formal dispute case against it in the WTO dispute settlement mechanism. Anecdotal evidence shows that a significant number of developing countries have not been able to adapt their legislation to the agreement's minimum standards yet. During 1997 and 1998, the TRIPs Council was engaged in research and inquiries as well as negotiations on some specific IPR issues. It has also reviewed the intellectual property legislation of the industrial economies and has plans to conduct similar reviews of the developing economies. TRIPs-related research, deliberations, and negotiations are sure to continue in the future. A country-by-country review of the TRIPs legislation was being undertaken by the TRIPs Council at the time of writing this book.

Several developing and transitional economies have recently asked for an extension of the time period for the implementation of TRIPs obligations. Canada and the EU did not disagree with their demand. India asked for the revision of the TRIPs agreement because the Indian government feels that it does not reflect the original objective of the agreement with respect to the transfer of technology. Several African nations are asking for a comprehensive change in the TRIPs agreement. A formal review of the TRIPs agreement was mandated for 2000.

The expression "mandated negotiations" did not refer to agriculture and services. One negotiation and several reviews took place during 2000 in the TRIPs Council. The council also reviewed provisions dealing with the protection of biotechnology inventions and a few plant varieties. The discussions ranged from a number of specific issues relating to the way in which these provisions are being implemented to the meaning of the specific terms contained in them. As mandated, the entire TRIPs agreement was reviewed during 2000.

4.5.6 Subsidies and countervailing measures

Among the Uruguay Round agreements, one whose provisions are less stringent for the developing countries than for the industrial economies, is the Agreement on Subsidies and Countervailing Measures. Under the agreement subsidies intended to improve export performance are "actionable" but if their motive is to promote R&D or help a disadvantaged region they are permissible. The old dictum of a subsidy "threatening and causing injury" to producers in the importing country being punishable by countervailing measures stays (Feketekuty, 1998). Industrial economies can no longer subsidize their exports. But developing economies with *per capita* income below US$1,000 are allowed to maintain their subsidies for an indefinite period. All the other developing countries have to phase the subsidies out by January 2004. Two important rules of this agreement were scheduled to be reviewed in late 1999. They related to subsidies that amount to more than 5 percent of the value of the product, or are given to cover an industry's operating losses, and the "green" subsidies.[14] It was strongly felt that these subsidies have trade-distorting effects and must be dismantled (Feketekuty, 1998). Clarification of the rules on measures, and pricing policies that are disguised as export subsidies, are two of the important outstanding issues that need to be addressed in the new round. Although several glaring deficiencies continue to exist in the subsidization calculations in anti-subsidy proceedings, WTO members have not evinced any interest in new negotiations. They are more concerned with the implementation of the agreement because a large majority of them have provided little implementation-related information.

A subsidy-related issue that was left unresolved during the Uruguay Round was the use of export credits. After long-drawn-out negotiations, it was not brought under export subsidy constraints. The OECD countries had negotiated a code for non-agricultural export credits which put limits on export credit terms and the length of credit extension. Agricultural exports have not been included in this agreement despite an URAA undertaking to work towards internationally agreed disciplines. Thus this issue is a natural candidate for inclusion in the forthcoming round. WTO members need to negotiate on the allowable terms for export credit, and hence to calculate the magnitude of the subsidy that is involved if and when softer credit terms are offered. Subsidy equivalent calculations have not been easy. One way of resolving them is, having calculated the subsidy equivalent, charge it against the export subsidy limits in the agreed schedule for the exporting country.

Export subsidies in agriculture (Section 4.3.3) are largely the policy of developed countries, particularly the EU. A push to rein in export subsidies will be high on the agenda of the Cairns Group. The US, which holds significant "rights" to export subsidies in the WTO, has made cautious use of subsidies recently. It will be strongly inclined to reduce, if not eliminate, export subsidies in the forthcoming round. Only ten developing economies committed themselves to slash export subsidies. This does not mean that they and others will go on subsidizing without limit. If anything, it implies that they must not subsidize their exports at all. The only export subsidies that are temporarily allowed are those that reduce the cost of marketing exports and international freight charges on export shipments. Thus the majority of developing economies stand to gain by having export subsidies further reduced in the forthcoming round. Cuts in subsidies will improve their competitive situation in international trade without imposing any further constraints on them.

4.5.7 Safeguards

Article XIX of the GATT was on safeguards and, for nearly two decades, it was considered ineffective. There was a serious need for its thorough revision. The Uruguay Round Agreement on Safeguards aims at facilitating structural adjustment and to enhance rather than limit competition in global markets. Its basic rationale was to address the lack of control over "legitimate" safeguard measures and the excessive and non-transparent use of distorting gray area measures. If the agreement only succeeds in controlling such measures it will amount to an improvement in the safeguards area from the point of view of competition policy. In the new agreement a considerable amount of procedural and substantive detail has been introduced, where formerly there was only a GATT article containing the basic requirements for applying a safeguard measure in a single paragraph, namely "serious injury or threat thereof" caused by increased imports. There was no procedural requirement of an investigation to determine the existence of "serious injury or threat thereof". Procedural rules for such an investigation have also been determined. In the absence of such a requirement, there was a tendency to apply safeguard measures where they were not substantively warranted.

The so-called gray area measures have been banished from the WTO regime. The agreement represents a trade-off that outlaws the gray area measures and installs a special mechanism which allows departure from the general MFN rule with particularly tight restrictions on the most dynamic suppliers. This provision is known as "quota modulation" and can only be applied easily and less provocatively. The Agreement on Safeguards is fully in force, with one exception. A special provision allowed the EU to continue to restrict imports of Japanese cars until the end of 1999. Although no member governments are at present seeking changes in the agreement, developing economies, including Asian economies, will continue to keep a close watch on how it is applied (Croome, 1998; Morgan, 1999). Therefore this issue does not have a high priority for the next round.

4.5.8 Trade Related Investment Measures

During the latter half of the 1990s, the value of sales by foreign affiliates of transnational corporations (TNCs) exceeded global exports of goods and services (UNCTAD, 2000b). In the context of worldwide trade liberalization and the growth and integration of international markets for traded goods and services, foreign direct investment (FDI) has grown at a rapid clip. Falling costs of communication have eased the constraints on global rationalization of production, leading to ever greater geographical specialization and international splicing of the value chain. FDI has become as important as trade in the conduct of international economic relations. Annual flows of FDI have been growing faster than world trade. In 1999, new FDI flows exceeded US$850 billion (UNCTAD, 2000b). FDI not only brings long-term foreign capital into the economy but also a bundle of productive assets, particularly entrepreneurship, technology, and managerial and export marketing knowhow. Increasingly, therefore, a need for multilateral rules on investment was widely felt. Having a set of common rules that are not product-specific but activity-specific would be good for the global economy.

The OECD responded by launching the Multilateral Agreement on Investment (MAI) in 1995, but it failed to take off, largely because of disagreements among the twenty-nine members of the OECD. MAI negotiations not only covered FDI but also technical knowhow and portfolio investment. Therefore many negotiating delegations felt that the MAI would restrict their ability to regulate the flow of portfolio investment. The MAI also faced popular opposition from the non-governmental organizations (NGOs) on the grounds that it sought excessive power for TNCs. Subsequently, efforts were made to have an MAI-like agreement under the WTO. Polemicists charge that any WTO agreement on investment that resembles MAI would erode the power of national governments to regulate commercial activities within their own borders. A popular target of criticism is a clause in the MAI that would allow private businesses to "sue" national governments in the WTO Dispute Settlement Body for damage caused by national policies that reduced the value of their products.

FDI was a major issue during the Uruguay Round negotiations, although the developing economies have historically shown reluctance to provide a right of establishment to foreign investors. They consider investment policies a part of their economic development policies and prefer to maintain flexibility in this regard. Conversely, the US took a considerable initiative in the negotiations on Trade Related Investment Measures (TRIMs) during the Uruguay Round. TRIMs became a contentious issue and the forthcoming round negotiations may not yield a great deal. The US objective has been to establish a new set of regulations prohibiting governments from attaching potentially trade-distorting conditions on FDI. Although five trade-distorting measures were identified, the final outcome of the US endeavors was modest. Industrial economies were required to eliminate these trade-distorting measures by January 1997, developing economies by January 2000, and the least developed countries by January 2002 (Croome, 1998).

The TRIMs agreement is essentially based on Articles III and XI of the GATT and states that WTO members shall not apply measures which require investors or producers to purchase their inputs locally to the exclusion of competing imported products (typically called the local content requirement), or to sell their output domestically rather than exporting it (typically called domestic sales requirements). In both the cases the objective is to discipline measures which restrict or distort trade flows.

The proposals made in Seattle for the negotiation of a WTO framework agreement on FDI had the following basic features: (1) WTO rules would *not* apply to government policies designed to manage short-term or other potentially volatile foreign capital inflows, (2) provisions were designed to ensure the transparency of member governments' FDI-related policies, (3) applying the traditional WTO principle of non-discrimination in this area, (4) like GATS, allowing members to make commitments on industries and sectors in which they would allow foreign investment to operate, (5) provisions to address the use of investment incentives and of post-establishment policies, such as performance requirements, and (6) provisions for the settlement of state-to-state disputes that would *not* apply to investor–state arbitration. No consensus on these proposals was reached in Seattle. Some members opined that, to the extent that international rule making for FDI is needed at all, Bilateral Investment Treaties (BITs) and regional arrangements are the more attractive and development-friendly way of proceeding.

This is a valuable negotiating chip for developing countries, as the industrial economies are the "demandeurs" in this area of negotiations. Some scholars (Hoekman and Saggi, 1999) point to the possibility of a "grand bargain" for the developing economies. Although there may be significant scope for a large benefit as a *quid pro quo*, a broad investment agreement should be approached carefully by developing economies. A broader agenda would indeed benefit those developing economies that face domestic resistance in adopting better FDI policies; however, there is a definite down side. Attempts to broaden the agenda may allow some special groups to seek cross-issue linkages in areas such as the environment and labor standards, which are not the core issues for the WTO and bear no relation to its objective of expanding international trade. However, there was some relenting in the attitude of industrial economies after the Seattle debacle and the TRIMs agreement was reviewed in the Council for Trade in Goods during 2000, as mandated in Article IX of the agreement. More work is to be done in the WTO Working Group on the relationship between Trade and Investment. Discussions among members have continued on this subject and will continue until the fourth Ministerial Conference in November 2001.

4.5.9 Regional Trading Agreements

New developments in trade and in the institutional structure of global economic relations over the last decade have led to the re-emergence of regional trading agreements (RTAs). Regionalism, as a force in world trade, is growing very rapidly. Around 170 RTAs are in force. The majority of them were concluded after 1990. This has happened despite general recognition that RTAs are second best and that multilateral trade liberalization is the preferred approach to the globalization of world trade. Approximately seventy more RTAs are likely to be finalized by 2005.

With the completion of the Uruguay Round and the birth of the WTO, the global trading system has been extended to new subjects and strengthened. In some regions, the share of intraregional trade has increased substantially. The number of formal regional organizations has increased at an unprecedented rate, with new groups emerging and old ones reviving. Many RTAs have shown a commitment to other forms of co-operation in parallel with the extension of the coverage of trade. The present revival of interest in RTAs can be dated back to the beginning of the EU's move towards a Single European Market (SEM), which started in 1985 and was completed in January 1993. The SEM was reinforced by the moves to monetary union and co-ordinated foreign relations. The EU acts as a single unit in some cases, rather than as a group of members having common interests, albeit EU members still act separately in other circumstances. Many other RTAs are trying to follow the EU's example. The multilateral organizations and non-members of the RTAs are having to adapt to new links among their members and to new counterparts. The global trade structure has become more diverse, with a mix of countries and groups at various stages or degrees of integration (Page, 2000).

During the Uruguay Round, the question of regionalism being an alternative to multilateralism was continuously raised. It became increasingly relevant when the round failed, before finally succeeding. The query never left us, even after the Uruguay Round's successful conclusion. Perhaps it is more appropriate to ask now whether the two trends, regionalism and multilateralism, can be reconciled and balanced. Although the current re-emergence of interest in RTAs is the "second wave" of regionalism, the effect of RTAs on trade and welfare is still being debated.

What are the welfare effects of RTAs? Under what conditions are RTAs more or less conducive to improvement of the welfare of members of the RTA, and of those that are outside the RTA? There is considerable disagreement on these issues. Some economists have concluded that preferential trading agreements threaten the open multilateral trading system and should be severely circumscribed, if not proscribed, under the WTO (Bhagwati, 1995). Others argue that such agreements are a step towards multilateral liberalization and inherently strengthen the WTO and the global trading system (Bhagwati *et al.*, 1998). For instance, it is less time-consuming and less complicated to work out mutually agreeable arrangements with a few neighbors than with the full membership of the WTO. In addition, regional groupings are demonstrably willing to proceed much more boldly. Many of them have decided to adopt free trade, whereas none of the global conclaves has even considered such an ambitious goal. The rapid growth in the membership of the WTO, whose predecessor GATT had close to fifty members during the first few rounds of the MTNs, has added to this change in perspective.

Regional and global initiatives have interacted creatively in the past and have mutually reinforced each other. Bergsten (1996) believes that the political economy of competitive liberalization over the last two decades has played itself out in the dynamic interaction between regional and global initiatives to reduce trade barriers. To a greater or lesser degree, this creative tension was present throughout the post-war period. For instance, the US initiated the Kennedy Round (1964–67) to counter the discrimination inherent in the creation of the European Common Market (ECM) and the Tokyo Round (1973–79) to counter the additional discrimination from the ECM's expansion to include the United Kingdom. The Europeans co-operated in both ventures and thus enabled the regional and global efforts to "ratchet up" the scope and pace of liberalization. This kind of positive interaction has also extended to subregional level. US President George Bush's 1991 offer to extend NAFTA throughout the western hemisphere led to an explosion of bilateral and plurilateral agreements across South and Central America as countries sought to prepare themselves for free trade with North America. In Asia, the Asian Free Trade Area (AFTA) accelerated its timetable and substantially broadened its coverage to stay ahead of the APEC forum. Australia and New Zealand have been discussing a possible formation of AFTA–CER or AFTA Close Economic Relations.

Regionalism sometimes raises fears of trading blocs that potentially could eliminate access by outsiders. In addition, gravitation towards large regional blocs may lead to increased apprehensions about retaliation and trade conflicts. Casual empiricism shows that there has been little increase in protectionism on the part of the major RTAs, like the Asia Pacific Economic Co-operation (APEC) forum, the EU, or NAFTA. The development of RTAs has progressed alongside an expansion of trade with non-members. To be sure, global leadership needs to ensure that conflicts between regionalism and globalism are avoided (Bergsten, 1996). This requires the maintenance of effective global trade rules to provide a framework to deter conflict between the regional arrangements, including global rules that apply to the regional arrangements themselves. A global institution like the WTO is needed to enforce such rules.

There is considerable evidence that RTAs have increased intraregional trade among their members. Trade creation greatly exceeds trade diversion in virtually all RTAs. Therefore, in general, the welfare of all members increases. Furthermore, welfare for old members increases as new members join the RTA, suggesting that there are gains from expanding the RTA. Domestic policy reforms in conjunction with an RTA provide additional welfare gains. These encouraging findings are based on computable general equilibrium models (Krueger, 1999b; Robinson and Thierfelder, 1999).

During the post-Uruguay Round period, RTAs have taken on greater significance than before. An important point of focus during the first Ministerial Conference in Singapore in 1996 was the fact that RTAs have expanded vastly in number, scope, and coverage. More than half of world trade is now carried out within RTAs and almost all WTO members are parties to one or more RTAs. This is a clear manifestation of the fact that RTAs have become important and have become an integral part of the multilateral trading system. Recent experience shows that RTAs have contributed to a great extent to the growth of world trade by expanding the production of, and trade in, goods and services, both between parties to the agreements and, in most cases, also with third parties (WTO, 1999a). RTAs have also contributed to a greater degree of transparency and predictability in world trade. The Singapore communiqué stated that such agreements can promote further liberalization and may assist least developed, developing, and transition economies in integrating into the multilateral trading system (Vamvakidis, 1999; Soloaga and Winters, 1999). RTAs can often supplement the process of trade liberalization and globalization. Neighboring countries may find that agreements between them are easier to achieve than those with all the countries in the world. This in turn can potentially work towards a faster pace of liberalization in a regional context than in a global context.

Trade regulation in relation to the RTAs (Article XXIV of the GATT) has had well known areas of ambiguity. Consequently a good number of RTAs came into being even though almost none of the agreements has been formally found totally compatible with the article. The Enabling Clause, adopted in 1997, accorded differential and more favorable treatment to the developing economies. It also provided further flexibility for such agreements among developing countries.

Although during the Uruguay Round a minor interpretative understanding was reached on Article XXIV, it cleared up a number of largely technical points. It fell far short of the ambitions of some governments that are not members of the major regional agreements and believe that Article XXIV has been cited as a cover for discrimination against non-members. In 1996 a new WTO Committee of Regional Trade Agreements was set up to provide a single body to review new or enlarged arrangements, to improve examination and reporting procedures, and "to consider the systematic implications of the regionalism/multilateral relationships". In its first task, the committee appears to have been successful, except to the extent that progress is held hostage to the disagreements on systemic issues, and there is no suggestion that a change is needed. On reporting procedures, the committee agreed in February 1998 on three sets of recommendations covering (1) obligations under GATT Article XXIV, (2) the Enabling Clause, and (3) GATS Article V (Croome, 1998). However, these recommendations are regarded by some countries as less binding than they should be. The EU and Canada, in particular, believe that the provision of trade statistics should be obligatory rather than just "desirable" (Frankel, 1997). During the first Ministerial Conference in Singapore Trade Ministers had agreed that it was important to analyze whether the system of WTO rights and obligations, as it relates to RTAs, needs to be further clarified, both from the substantial and from the procedural point of view. The issue of "the systemic implications of the regionalism/multilateral relationship" may well contain the seeds of future negotiations.

4.5.10 State trading

While Article XVII of the GATT stipulates the right of members to grant special rights to a limited number of governmental and non-governmental enterprises, it also reminds members that state trading enterprises can erect significant non-tariff barriers to trade. State trading importers can reduce market access below the levels agreed in the Uruguay Round negotiations, and state trading exporters can use "hidden" export subsidies to increase market share. State trading exporters and importers are also known to exploit their monopoly or monopsony power (Das, 1991). The potential for trade distortion and the likelihood of the application of non-tariff barriers (NTBs) is highest when state trading enterprises benefit from monopoly import or export rights.

Governments, through their special rights or privileges, can create trade distortions by favoring particular exporters, and by fixing prices. The decision-making process of these enterprises is influenced by government objectives that are not solely in accordance with commercial considerations. The present rules applying to state trading are not adequate. Unlike many other provisions of the WTO that constitute exceptions to general rules, they not only lack the necessary precision that would ensure that their enforcement is feasible but also do not take into account the implications of new disciplines introduced during the last round of MTNs. During the Uruguay Round there was an attempt to address the shortcomings of Article XVII, but the Understanding on the Interpretation of Article XVII of GATT appears to have fallen short of making the necessary clarifications.

To establish the nature and extent of trade distortion due to state trading, a working party was set up in April 1998 under the Uruguay Round Understanding. This working party examined notifications by WTO members of enterprises covered by a newly designed questionnaire for the trade distortion notifications. The findings were to be analyzed during 1999 and 2000 by the working party. Based on these findings, the working group is to recommend how to ensure MFN and national treatment in state trading as well as consider ways of tightening the disciplines spelled out in Article XVII.

The use of state trading, albeit declining, is still to be found in the developing economies. They use this instrument for controlling domestic markets and to regulate trade. Any change in Article XVII in the forthcoming round will have a direct impact on these developing economies. Asking for an exemption from strict regulation in this regard is questionable because it is not in the long-term interest of the developing economies. Long-term adoption of state trading is detrimental to growth. It adds to distortions of incentives and sharply reduces the efficiency of resource allocation (Das, 1991). As a short-term measure governments can seek "special and differential treatment" under the provisions of the WTO, but in the medium term it is better to take the initiative in dismantling their state trading enterprises, and adopt the WTO discipline in this regard.

4.5.11 Dispute settlement provision

The central institutional feature of the WTO is its dispute settlement process. At the end of the WTO dispute settlement procedures, if all else fails, lie multilaterally approved trade sanctions. The Dispute Settlement Understanding (DSU)[15] is a binding treaty. This is a welcome move towards a more rule-oriented system that is expected to allow better adjustment of friction between nation states as well as greater predictability and reliability for traders. However, it has come under criticism from various quarters. Some of its rules and procedures have been castigated by the member countries (Cameron and Campbell, 1997).

Over the 1995–99 period the number of consultations sought by the members quadrupled. These consultations played a central role in dispute settlement. Of the 138 consultation requests made up to 30 June 1998, seventy-two were not brought before the panel. Thus more than half the cases were settled through consultation (Panagariya, 2000). Developing countries were active participants in this process. They brought cases not only against industrial economies but also against other developing economies. In addition, the rate of compliance has been high. This applies to both cases against developing countries and cases against industrial economies.

Although there has been a dramatic increase in the number of consultations, developing economies feel themselves at a disadvantage in dispute settlement proceedings, particularly if the opposing party is the US or the EU. The developing economies feel at a disadvantage because of the technical nature of disputes. They are able neither to present their case forcefully nor to defend themselves adequately. The industrial economies are far better equipped, both legally and technically. They can not only call on an array of legal experts but also the technical support of corporations often involved in the disputes.

A decision was taken at the end of the Uruguay Round, in April 1994, regarding a complete review of the DSU. A meeting of the Dispute

Settlement Body (DSB) in March 1998 also agreed that WTO members should submit written suggestions regarding the issues and rules that should be taken up for negotiations. The DSU review identified five issues: (1) the operation of the surveillance function, (2) the professionalization of dispute settlement panels, (3) the problem of developing-country member participation in the system, (4) transparency and accession issues, and (5) the adequacy of resources available to the WTO for processing disputes. These issues can be taken up for negotiations in the forthcoming round.

4.5.12 Rules of origin

This has introduced an element of uncertainty in international trade. Therefore several guiding principles were agreed upon by the WTO members regarding the rules of origin during the Uruguay Round. Even small trading members are interested in establishing harmonized rules of origin because they will successfully eliminate a favored instrument of protectionist action. Developing country exporters recognize that they have substantial trade interests at stake, therefore they prefer to have a definitive set of rules of origin. As alluded to in Section 4.5.4, these rules are of particular interest to the textile and apparel exporters, who frequently face problems on this count. Imprecision in these rules can be used as a substitute for the quantitative restrictions that are being phased out under the Agreement on Textiles and Clothing (Croome, 1998).

As regards the guiding principles, a consensus was arrived at regarding these rules being objective, predictable, coherent, and based on positive standards. An export product should be considered as originating from a country where it was wholly produced; or, if more than one country was associated with its production, where it was last substantially produced. As this appeared somewhat simplistic, the development and adoption of a single set of harmonized rules of origin were considered necessary. This work was being done by the Technical Committee on Rules of Origin of the World Customs Organization. This was under way for some time and may or may not be completed before the next round starts. Developing countries need to request a relaxation of the stringent rule of origin applied to the textiles and apparel sector. Many of them find rules of origin being used as a hidden NTB in this sector. Many industrial economies tend to impose stringent process requirements in their national rules of origin laws.

4.6 Ongoing issues

As a follow-up of the Uruguay Round, work was started in the following four subject areas in the WTO: (1) trade and environment, (2) trade and competition, (3) trade and investment or FDI, and (4) trade facilitation. None of these areas is at present being covered by multilateral trade negotiations in a substantive manner. The first two issues are virtual intruders into the trade arena and therefore developing economies should ignore them. Three working groups were established during 2000 to study (1) the relationship between trade and investment, (2) the interaction between trade and competition policy, and (3) transparency in government policy. Several papers were presented by members on these issues and the future course of action in these areas was discussed.

4.7 Passing the "Green Room"

The WTO operates by consensus[16] but the consensus-building process has broken down. This problem had taken a large dimension before the failure at Seattle. The "Green Room" process of evolving consensus has been much maligned because many consider it the biggest contributing factor behind the failure at Seattle. The "Green Room" process was functional and worthwhile when GATT was a small organization, but it is unsuitable for the WTO, given its current dimensions, diversity, and mandate. The WTO is a much larger organization, and the "Green Room" has been left behind by the rapid expansion of the global trade. It should, therefore, be abandoned.

Although during the GATT period the "Green Room" process did work, some hold the view that its operation was far from democratic (Sampson, 2000). They point to the fact that frequently there were informal consultative meetings with limited participation. Their argument is reinforced by the lack of participation by many small developing country delegations in Seattle Ministerial meetings. In such closed meetings, "non-papers" were discussed which many delegations never got to see. According to this view, some countries, particularly developing ones, were systematically denied access to information and "excluded" from what were on occasion important negotiations (Khan, 1998).

While dealing with the above charge of the GATT–WTO system being undemocratic, one must draw a dividing line between lack of participation in meetings and exclusion on purpose from the negotiation process. Delegations do meet informally from time to time, particularly while drafting texts. Limited participation in many respects contributes to efficiency and swift progress towards the desired objective. After reaching an agreement among a smaller group of countries which are directly involved in the issue, the agreement can be extended to other, less directly involved countries. Absence from such small country group meetings may involve both industrial and developing economies. If this was the process of "exclusion" the charge of GATT–WTO system being undemocratic does not stand up.

What was, and continues to be, crucial in such meetings is representativeness. In any informal consultative meeting of the kind described above, the chairperson must ensure the representation of all member countries that have an interest in the issues under discussion. If it is not ensured, the consultative meeting will become dysfunctional because the unrepresented member could block the decision at a later stage when a consensus is being sought. If a country delegation with an interest in the issue is unable to attend the informal consultative meeting, another delegation with a similar interest should represent it. One of the ways to ensure that an informal consultative group decision will not be blocked later by a member that was not present is to keep the other interested, but absent, members informed. This responsibility should go to the interested and participating member and to the chairperson. The success or failure of this process would depend upon the deftness with which a chairperson handled a meeting, no matter how big or small.

Although representativeness is indispensable, developing country delegations were and continue to be absent from many important consultative meetings. The same applies to formal GATT–WTO meetings. This non-participation is the consequence of a broader problem, namely lack of resources as well as lack of expertise to service the negotiation process. This process is increasingly complex and resource-intensive. To deal with various trade agreements, over seventy different councils, committees, working parties, and other bodies meet at the WTO headquarters in Geneva. The same country delegations, in collaboration with the WTO secretariat, service these agreements and functions. A high degree of professional expertise is built into these delegations and the WTO secretariat. Many developing countries, particularly those from Africa, do not have representative offices in Geneva, which makes even partial participation in the WTO process almost impossible. Many developing economies need to strengthen their human and institutional ability to participate in a meaningful and profitable manner (Sampson, 2000).

Schott and Watal (2000), among others, have suggested replacing the "Green Room" process with a small informal steering committee. Each suggestion of this kind has its own favorite number. Such a committee could comprise twenty members without being unwieldy and might be called the SC-20, or merely C-20. This steering committee should be charged with developing consensus on trade issues among the member countries. This group would not be seen by the WTO members as undercutting existing WTO rights and obligations because members themselves would create it. This steering committee would contribute to inclusive, efficient, and transparent decision making, although each member would retain the ultimate decision to accept or reject such a pact.

Membership of this steering committee should be based on the broad participation among the WTO members. Clear, simple, and objective criteria should determine it. According to Schott and Watal (2000), the two guiding principles could be:

1   The absolute value of foreign trade (defined as exports plus imports).
2   Global geographical representation (with at least two participants from each region).

Given the above criteria, the four members of the Quad (Canada, the EU, Japan, and the US) would be the most significant members of the C-20. The other possible members would be chosen from Hong Kong, the Republic of Korea, Singapore, Switzerland, Mexico, Malaysia, Australia, Thailand, Brazil, Norway, Indonesia, India, Turkey, Poland, South Africa, the Czech Republic, the Philippines, and Argentina. Indeed, the People's Republic of China would be added to this list after it becomes a member of the WTO.

Schott and Watal (2000) suggested that groups of countries, based on present regional arrangements or formed on an *ad hoc* basis, would be encouraged to pool resources and share representation. The Nordic countries followed this practice during the GATT regime. Several developing country groupings also work on these lines. The Mercosur and the Caribbean Regional Negotiating Machinery are two good examples. These groups will be voluntary and would select their representative for participating in the negotiations on their behalf. An arrangement like this would in no way preclude issue-based alliances among different groups. For instance, the Cairns Group on agriculture might find support among a sizeable share of the C-20 delegates. The idea of a group of countries represented by one of them in an international organization is an old one. The International Monetary Fund, the World Bank, and regional development banks have all followed it successfully for decades.

That said, would a C-20 be acceptable? Would a C-20 work? Hardly. The WTO members do not support such a C-20. To call a spade a spade, the members do not trust each other. What then could be the solution? The General Council chairman should hold independent open-ended consultations with members in groups as well as individually. It is a long and painful, but indispensable, process. This is the only way to ensure the inclusion of all members and all interests. In fact, since the debacle at Seattle open-ended discussions have already been initiated by the General Council chairman. There is a down side to this process. The discussions can be highly time-consuming and inefficient, particularly when the level of disagreement rises.

4.8 Opacity and the WTO

GATT was often and correctly criticized for its lack of transparency. Almost all GATT documents were listed as restricted, regardless of content. As recently as October 1994 the US government complained that the balance between the need for confidentiality surrounding the discussions of GATT contracting parties and the need for public awareness was not being achieved (Adamantopoulos, 1997). The US government also expressed apprehension regarding the WTO procedures which were to be based on those of the GATT. Regrettably, this apprehension proved to be well founded. All information relating to discussions and decisions taken at the

Ministerial Conference of the WTO, in the General Council, and trade councils and committee are classified as restricted unless there is a consensus to release the material.

Although the GATT had a blasé attitude towards the allegation of opacity, the WTO needs to become transparent. This need took on urgency after the Seattle Ministerial. The organization does not deal with any secret matters. All its rules and regulations are in the public domain. There may be some documents that need to be restricted to protect national interests, but certainly only a minuscule number of them fall into that category. The WTO secretariat is attempting to (1) raise the level of general awareness regarding the organization and its operations, (2) establish channels of co-operation with the non-governmental organizations (NGOs) and other multilateral organizations, and (3) accelerate the formal process of derestricting its documents and making them available to interested people and organizations.

The earlier view was that it is the task of the national governments to disseminate information regarding the role and activities of the WTO. The national governments did so for the other multilateral organizations, WTO could not be an exception. Apparently the national governments did an inadequate job of dissemination, the WTO secretariat had to take up the gauntlet, and launched several initiatives. As we shall see below, concern regarding transparency in the WTO was not new. However, new initiatives were taken. The WTO website was the most important such initiative. The first homepage was poor and unattractive, but the second one has turned out to be much better. In July 2000, the website was receiving over 200,000 hits a month. Visitors to the website most often consulted the links that provided access to WTO documents. In addition, the WTO secretariat has organized joint symposia involving WTO members, representatives of multilateral organizations, and NGOs (Marceau and Pedersen, 1999). The Articles of Agreement of the WTO provide for close contact between the WTO and NGOs. Article V(2) says that the "General Council may make appropriate arrangements for consultation and co-operation with non-governmental organizations on matters related to the WTO" (GATT, 1994). The WTO needs to continue such symposia so that general awareness regarding its activities attains a high level.

Well ahead of the third Ministerial Conference in Seattle, in July 1996, the General Council adopted *WTO Guidelines for Arrangements on Relations with Non-governmental Organizations*. During the first Ministerial Conference in May 1998, the conviction of seeking closer ties with the public, NGOs, and civil society was further reinforced. The WTO members "recognized the importance of enhancing public understanding of the benefits of the multilateral trading system in order to build support for it and agree to work towards this end". They had declared that "In this context we will consider how to improve the transparency of the WTO operations."

In Seattle, NGOs accused the WTO of being oblivious of concerns of society, and of not being accountable and responsive to the needs of society at large. Their position is that involving NGOs in the WTO consultations and negotiations would enrich the deliberations of the WTO because of their unique experience and exposure. However, those who disagree counter-argue that it is the task of national governments that are represented in the WTO to keep the intergovernmental body fully posted of the ground realities. Member governments need to present dispassionate and accurate views of the ground reality during deliberations and negotiations. It is widely believed that it will not be possible for NGOs to be directly involved in the WTO negotiations. Should one more constituency be added in an organization that is heavily loaded with a large number of members? It is difficult to be reasonable and answer this rhetorical query in the affirmative.

Attitudinal flexibility in the stance of the WTO as an institution is essential and periodic exchanges of views with representative – preferably predetermined – NGOs should be part of the WTO annual schedule of meetings and consultations. NGO observers, from a predetermined set of NGOs, should also be invited to attend the annual meetings of the WTO. The Director General should have the right to consult NGOs with special competence in a particular subject area. Communication with the NGOs must be a two-way street. On their part, the selected NGOs should communicate their concerns to the Director General, who in turn should publicize the documents widely among the WTO members. To maintain a high order of credibility on the global fora, NGOs must take their responsibility seriously. While providing inputs they must ensure that they do not get carried away by emotional issues and take an analytical, pragmatic, and balanced stand on issues under deliberation. In addition, they must keep themselves confined to "soft" issues, and shun an "us versus them" attitude.

Many WTO members are averse to the proposal of accepting NGOs as observers in the WTO meetings. Many of them consider it inappropriate. Even if the proposition is accepted, it is not clear what criteria to apply for admission. To make their mark in the international fora, including the WTO, it is vitally important for the NGOs to have access to their national governments.

4.9 Summing up

The dexterity and farsightedness with which an agenda for the forthcoming WTO round of MTNs is crafted will determine the rhythm of world trade in the twenty-first century. There is an imperative need for it to be a balanced agenda, squarely reflecting the interests and concerns of the industrial and developing countries. While the Quad countries dominate global trade, the developing economies dominate the WTO in terms of sheer numbers. Therefore a lack of balance will not only imperil the forth-coming round but also any future MTNs. The time period of the round should be fixed at three years and it should take up a relatively small number of issues so that it does not severely tax the negotiating and insti-tutional capacity of the developing economies. To take stock of progress, there is a need for a mid-term review. Non-trade agenda items, like labor and environment standards, must be banished permanently from the MTNs. Similarly, competition or antitrust-related issues must not be allowed on to the agenda. Developing economies need to take a pragmatic stand while deciding on broad negotiating items. They need to approach the issue with a new mind set. Beyond the built-in agenda and built-in problems with the ATC, only carefully selected items should be included on the agenda.

Agriculture, being a large area and a contentious issue, is again sure to take a good deal of time, energy, and resources. The same applies to multilateral negotiations on services, because so much has yet to be done. An agreement on e-commerce should be deferred some way into the near future. There is little felt need among the WTO members for substantial institutional improvement in the WTO. There is a need to learn from the post-Uruguay Round experience, reopen the issue of antidumping mea-sures, and rationalize them. A broad-based and balanced round of MTNs cannot possibly ignore tariff reduction. High tariff lines with spikes are to be found in both industrial and developing economies. In the industrial country markets numerous tariff spikes affect products of interest to devel-oping economies. The number of tariff lines with spikes is higher in agri-culture than in manufactures. The gap between applied and bound tariffs, generally to be found in the developing countries, needs to be removed. Industrial and developing economies need to adopt a mutually beneficial approach. Developing economies could use the forthcoming round to make domestic trade policy adjustments by using it as leverage against domestic interest groups that resist tariff reduction.

Efforts are required to minimize, if not arrest, slippage in the imple-mentation of the Agreement on Textiles and Clothing. Although the importance of this agreement is declining owing to structural changes in trade in textiles and apparel, some aspects of it need to be discussed to improve the global efficiency of this sector. Several developing economies have reported problems in implementing the TRIPs agreement. Many of them have asked for more time for implementation and India has asked for a revision of the TRIPs agreement. These issues need to addressed in the forthcoming round. Some subsidy-related issues were left unresolved during the Uruguay Round. This issue is of considerable significance to the developing economies. On their part, developing economies need to slash subsidies in their trade structures. Working group consultations were going on in the area of state trading. The safeguards issue and TRIMs are low priority areas for the new round, although some developing economies consider the application of TRIMs an important issue. Some unresolved issues in the area of dispute settlement can be raised, although it is not a pressing issue. Clarifications are needed of certain aspects of rules of origin "guiding principles".

As the "Green Room" process has failed to serve the MTNs, a functional alternative needs to be devised. One possibility could be a steering committee of twenty, based on broad participation among the WTO members. However, there is considerable distrust among members and it is unlikely to work. A more inclusive consultative approach by the WTO is the ultimate answer.

5 Implications of the forthcoming round

Trade liberalization in a dynamic setting

5.1 Dynamic path of adjustment

A multilateral round of trade negotiations ultimately results in the liberalization of trade barriers, which include tariffs, non-tariffs, and regulatory. Barriers to trade in services are of the third kind, that is, they are typically regulatory barriers, rather than taxes. (Refer to Section 5.5.) Barriers to market access are often designed to protect incumbent firms from any new entry, which could be domestic or foreign. Trade liberalization, tariff slashing, and the dismantling of restrictive regulatory barriers increase returns to capital in three ways. First, by increasing the return to capital in some sectors and stimulating overall investment in the economy. Second, some sectors would gain directly from the removal of tariffs that act as an implicit tax on their inputs. Third, the wealth effect would surely raise demand in the liberalizing economy for a large range of products, which should raise the return to capital in the short term. Higher investment can be financed out of domestic savings. But it is likely that a rise in the savings level would be delayed because consumers prefer not to reduce current consumption significantly to benefit from the higher returns to capital. If so, international financial capital, which has been highly mobile in recent decades, would fill the gap. Higher returns can rapidly attract capital inflows. The result would be to generate additional GDP. However, domestic consumption gains might not show up directly because foreign capital owners would repatriate returns from higher production. Thus when foreign capital flows are brisk, it is important to evaluate trade liberalization in terms of (1) income gains and (2) consumption gains, rather than by change in GDP.

When trade liberalization measures are being implemented, an economy also gains from liberalization in its trading partner economies. The gains can be transmitted through various channels. A typical dynamic path of adjustment is as follows. Lowering tariff barriers and non-tariff barriers (NTBs) *ceteris paribus* stimulates the demand for exports of the home economy, raising income. Second, when trade liberalization spurs domestic investors to invest in the liberalizing economy, additional gains result if those investments realize a higher rate of return than they would in the home economy. In addition, the role of expectations can be important when a trade reform is phased in, because financial markets would rapidly factor in expected changes in rates of return while evaluating asset prices. Most economies have sticky labor markets, and capital reallocation also does not occur smoothly. These rigidities need to be included in the model. In addition, asset prices adjust rapidly in response to international capital movements, while the exchange rate has a tendency to overshoot during the adjustment period.

It is important to know how multinational corporations behave under a liberalizing regime. As the new round undertakes various liberalization measures, including the liberalization of services and investment regulations, MNC behavior is affected. Section 5.6 attempts to quantify this dimension of the new round.

5.2 Mechanisms of CGE models

This chapter requires a little more knowledge of economics, particularly computable general equilibrium (CGE) modeling. Those new to this area can consult an elementary textbook. Two suggestions are Gilli (1996) and Buehrer and Di Mauro (1994). In this chapter we explore the impact of the new WTO round, using CGE models. Such models are popular because they have a comparative advantage in analyzing long-run resource allocation issues in a general equilibrium framework as well as estimating the welfare implications of various policy adjustment measures. They are a useful tool for estimating the various direct and indirect effects of trade liberalization and have provided a range of profitable insights. Multi-country macroeconometric models are an alternative to CGE models. However, they are not ideally suited to the purpose of estimating the impact of trade liberalization. Their suitability comes into question because of the so-called "single-good" assumption they make. The single-good assumption assumes away relative price adjustment, which is the key to resource allocation issues within an economy. Bryant *et al.* (1993) provide an informative survey of these models. Although dynamic adjustment to trade liberalization is not an extensively researched area, some studies by noted scholars have estimated the consequences for long-term resource allocation of reducing barriers to international trade (Martin and Winters, 1995a; Hertel, 1997). There are other scholarly studies that focus on the short-run dynamics of individual country groups (Koupparitsas, 1997) or the quantified gains from sectoral liberalization (McKibbin, 1997). A specially constructed version of the CGE model was used by Brown *et al.* (1996) to estimate the economic effects of the tariff reductions on industrial products during the Uruguay Round.

The kinds of mechanisms that CGE models capture are simple and rational. When trade is liberalized unilaterally, import prices plummet, which has a wealth effect in that it raises the purchasing power of consumers. The change in relative prices induces firms to reallocate resources away from protected sectors towards other more efficient activities, which tends to raise efficiency in the economy. The increased level of economic efficiency should be reflected in the aggregate productivity growth of the economy, although total factor productivity (TFP) growth at the sectoral or disaggregated level may or may not change. If TFP growth at the sectoral level does show signs of improvement, it could be due to more efficient resource allocation due to trade liberalization. It could also be due to the direct effect on TFP growth. The strength of CGE models lies in calculating how great the efficiency gains will be and how much consumption will rise as a result of the aforementioned implications of trade liberalization (McKibbin, 1999). Computable general equilibrium modeling proves to be a highly useful technique for this purpose. Once dynamic elements are incorporated into the analysis, a rich mixture of results generally emerges. For instance, from a political economy point of view, CGE models help explain how resources made redundant in one sector can be used in others.

A useful version of the CGE model is the Michigan Model of World Production and Trade, originally developed by Alan Deardorff in the mid-1970s at the University of Michigan. It initially included eighteen industrial economies but was soon extended to thirty-four countries. The model provides measures for individual countries and regions of the effects of liberalization on the trade, output, and employment for the goods and for the service sectors (Deardorff and Stern, 1990). It was used to analyze the results of the Tokyo Round and the Uruguay Round. More recently it was used for the computational analysis of the accession of Chile to the North American Free Trade Agreement (NAFTA) and for an economic assessment of the integration of the Czech Republic, Hungary, and Poland into the European Union (EU).

There is a certain degree of interdependence between countries and sectors. Therefore estimating the impact of trade liberalization in a dynamic setting requires a global economy-wide framework which incorporates both the links between sectors of production in each economy and the links among economies. Two of the leading global economic models which have been widely used by academics and policy makers alike to examine the implications of trade reforms are: (1) the Global Trade Analysis Project (GTAP) and (2) the Asia–Pacific G-cubed (APG-cubed) framework. Of the two, GTAP is a static CGE model, while APG-cubed is a dynamic CGE model.

GTAP is a modeling framework which is designed to facilitate quantitative analysis of policy issues. Developed from the Global Trade Analysis Project established in 1992, it has been widely used to examine such issues as the impact of the Uruguay Round, trade liberalization in the Asia Pacific Economic Co-operation (APEC) forum, and future patterns of global trade. GTAP captures linkages within economies and among them by modeling the economic behavior and interactions of producers, consumers, and governments. It is, therefore, possible to trace the implications of a policy change like tariff cuts to other parts of the economy, as well as to other regions and economies in the model. Within GTAP, consumers are assumed to maximize utility and producers to maximize profits. Markets are assumed to be perfectly competitive. There are constant returns to scale. Different regions and economies are linked in the model through trade. Some of these assumptions mean that the gains from trade liberalization will typically be understated. One such assumption is constant returns to scale.

The APG-cubed framework is a global economy-wide model accounting for interactions between sectors and between regions. As it is a dynamic model, it incorporates considerable macroeconomic detail, including both real sector and financial sector interactions. Countries and regions in this model are linked both temporally and intertemporally through trade and financial markets. As it is a dynamic model, it allows the user to implement the trade reform in a particular calendar year or years. It explicitly describes the time path of liberalization and its effect. With its macroeconomic detail and integrated real and financial markets, APG-cubed can account for the effects of liberalization on interest rates, exchange rates, and international capital movements. It also accounts for the effects of different fiscal and monetary responses to liberalization and the way in which future policy changes can affect economic activity in the early stages of implementation (ADFAT, 1999). What is even better is that APG-cubed takes into account adjustment costs associated with the reallocation of labor and capital when tariff and non-tariff barriers (NTBs) plummet. It is a global model with substantial regional disaggregation and sectoral detail. It contains a strong foundation for the analysis of both short-run macroeconomic policy analysis and long-run growth consideration of alternative macroeconomic policies. A caveat that is needed here is that these additional characteristics – dynamic and financial market features – come at the cost of country and commodity details. APG-cubed divides the global economy into eighteen regions and six sectors.

These two leading economic models are quite different from each other. APG-cubed captures some dynamic effects which GTAP cannot. The former also takes into account adjustment costs that emerge from the reallocation of labor and capital when trade barriers fall. It is possible to see the effect of varying the rate of liberalization over any stipulated time period, five or ten years. It is a good idea to use the models together so that the advantages of both can be exploited, that is, more country and commodity details from the GTAP model and more information about the macroeconomy, financial flows, and time paths from the APG-cubed model. The Australian Department of Foreign Affairs and Trade (ADFAT) did exactly that. We shall see the results in Sections 5.3 and 5.4.

5.3 The APG-cubed model

This model was based on the G-cubed model developed by McKibbin and Wilcoxen (1999), which in turn was a synthesis of two previously constructed models. McKibbin (1999) estimated the results of trade liberalization in each country on the assumption that the forthcoming round would reduce tariffs from 2000 to 2010 by one-third of the initial tariff in 2000. A large number of results for each country and regional groupings were calculated. Only a subset of these results is presented to illustrate various key points about the dynamic adjustment story (Section 5.2).

Three groups of countries were selected by McKibbin (1999). The first was Australia, Japan, New Zealand, and the US. The second included Indonesia, Malaysia, the Philippines, Singapore, Thailand, China, Taiwan, Korea, Hong Kong, and India. The third group comprised all the rest of the OECD countries. Empirical estimates by McKibbin of the long-run gains, and short-run adjustments, of the new WTO round show that by 2020 all the economies in the sample – that is, all the three groups – have higher GDP than would have been the case without the new WTO round. For the individual OECD economies the gains range from 0.4 percent to 0.68 percent. For the non-OECD economies the gains were higher, ranging from 0.4 percent to 2.5 percent. Overall, this version of the modeling of a new round would lead to higher GDP and consumption levels for all the countries. In the short run, countries that undertake the most liberalization experience an increase in the aggregate return to capital, which attracts foreign capital, which leads to appreciation of their exchange rate and worsen their current account and trade balance. They also experience larger falls in employment in the short run because of larger falls in goods prices with sticky wages. Over time they also begin to experience larger gains than economies with less liberalization to undertake.

The Australian Department of Foreign Affairs and Trade also used the APG-cubed model to conclude that *ceteris paribus* investment would rise under early trade liberalization in the crisis-affected Asian economies[1] (ADFAT, 1999). Trade liberalization would lead to additional investment of 5 percent a year until 2005 in Indonesia and Thailand, and 4 percent a year in Korea, Malaysia, and the Philippines. Trade liberalization would also lead to substantial increases in output and welfare for these economies. Thus trade liberalization could have led to a brisker recovery. As regards the aggregate gains of trade liberalization, Figures 5.1 and 5.2, based on APG-cubed modeling, indicate that removing protection over the five years from 2004 would result in additional welfare gains of more than US$600 billion as early as 2008. These results also take into account adjustment costs associated with the reallocation of labor and capital when trade barriers fall.

Trade liberalization generates significant increases in exports above those that would otherwise have occurred. The results from APG-cubed for

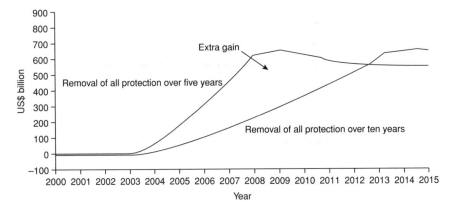

Figure 5.1 Comparison of benefits from five-year and ten-year reform: world welfare (real consumption).

Source: Simulations with the APG-cubed model (ADFAT, 1999)

a 50 percent cut in tariff barriers are shown in Figure 5.3. They show increases in exports by 2015 of over 14 percent a year for India, over 7 percent a year for China, almost 6 percent a year for the United States, 5 percent for Korea, and over 4 percent for Australia. Other than these, Indonesia, Japan, Malaysia, the Philippines, and Thailand all show increases of 3 percent or more.

The APG-cubed model can also be used to measure broad effects going beyond the traditional static effects of trade liberalization. Trade liberalization and economic growth reduce the risk premiums applied to lending

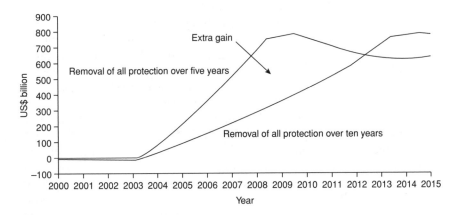

Figure 5.2 Comparison of benefits from five-year and ten-year reform: world GDP.

Source: Simulations with the APG-cubed model (ADFAT, 1999)

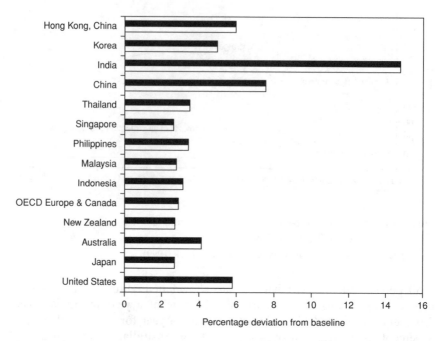

Figure 5.3 Annual percentage change in exports by 2015: all barriers cut by 50 percent.

Source: Simulations with the APG-cubed model (ADFAT, 1999)

by financial markets, which feed back into increased investment opportunities in an economy. Also, estimates of dynamic gains from capital accumulation and endogenous productivity growth, which means technological improvements and increasing skill levels, can be made. Stoeckel *et al.* (2000) estimated the effects of liberalization using an intertemporal APG-cubed model developed by Warwick McKibbin of the Australian National University and the Brookings Institution and Peter Wilcoxen of the University of Texas and the Brookings Institution (McKibbin and Wilcoxen, 1998). The results from the model are generated by, first, projecting a baseline from 1996 to 2020 based on a range of assumptions concerning tariff rates, population growth, and sectoral productivity. Once the baseline has been generated, each simulation is run and the results are reported as a percentage deviation from it.

As the purpose of economic activity is consumption, not production, Stoeckel *et al.* (2000) reported estimates for the deviations from the baseline in real consumption. All countries and regions reported in the model were found to experience a gain in real consumption, which is a good proxy for real welfare. In terms of percentage change, the ASEAN countries, China, and Taiwan gained the most, since that is where the barriers to trade were the greatest, making the largest gains possible. For Malaysia and Thailand, liberalization raised real consumption in 2009 by 11 percent and 16 percent, respectively, above what it might otherwise have been. For Europe and other OECD countries, real consumption was around 2 percent higher in 2010, after the full implementation of liberalization. For the US, real consumption was found to be only 1 percent above the baseline by 2010. These smaller effects can be explained as follows. First, less liberalization is to take place in these economies because the barriers are already low. Second, investment in Asia, particularly in the ASEAN economies, is more attractive, which would lead to capital being reallocated to these countries. This in turn would leave smaller increases in income for labor relative to the higher income achieved by capital that was relocated.

In this simulation analysis, to see how the liberalization mechanisms work, one economy, the Philippines, was selected. The effects of full trade liberalization starting in 2000 and finishing in 2010 on key macro variables were estimated. Cutting tariffs had the effect of increasing the return on capital in different sectors, depending on the capital intensity of the sector involved and the extent of tariff reduction. The result was that for the Philippines economy as a whole there was an increase in real investment of 4.4 percent above the baseline in 2009. Part of this additional investment was financed by foreign capital and, therefore, these capital inflows caused a deterioration in the current account. The current account expressed as a percentage of baseline GDP falls by 2.5 percentage points by 2009. With the removal of protection, consumers gain and real consumption rises. Rising real consumption and appreciation of the real exchange rate, which lowers the price of imports, cause imports to be 8 percent above the baseline by 2010. Exports initially fall and cause a deterioration in the trade balance sufficient to mirror the increase in the current account deficit. By 2004, exports start to increase and eventually rise above imports. This causes the trade balance to move towards surplus in order to service the foreign capital inflows. Extra investment and consumption lead to a rise in real GDP, which generates extra tax revenue.

Simulations with ATP-cubed undertaken by Stoeckel (2000) show that lack of liberalization and reforms has high stakes. Full liberalization throughout the world phased in from 2000 to 2010 was simulated, although that outcome is unlikely. This analysis shows the opportunity cost, or what the countries of the world are forgoing by not reducing barriers to trade. Stoeckel's (2000) results include the effects of reducing barriers to trade in services, which often involve, for example, denial of the right to establish themselves in another country rather than a formal barrier to trade. If the barriers to trade were eliminated globally, real consumption for most economies would rise by US$630 billion in the year 2010.[2] Resource allocative gains, terms of trade effects, and dynamic gains from capital accumulation would coalesce to real consumption gains of this order. The annual gains to Asian countries would be among the biggest in proportion to their GDPs, because they experience some of the greatest barriers to trade and so the reductions in their risk premiums are also the greatest in this simulation exercise.

5.4 The GTAP model

Hertel *et al.* (2000) simulated an applied version of the GTAP model of global trade. They took into account the dramatic changes in the pattern of trade since the lead-up to the Uruguay Round. Furthermore, they developed projections of the global economy to the year 2005, when the Uruguay Round is to be fully implemented. They also took into account the sharp increase in trade between developing economies as a consequence of continued growth and liberalization under the Uruguay Round. They consider across-the-board 40 percent cuts in estimated 2005 agriculture protection, services protection, as well as mining and manufacturing tariffs. To be sure, more liberalization and greater welfare gains could be achieved by cuts that go deeper, or which focus more on spikes.

They reported that agricultural liberalization in the forthcoming round could yield substantial welfare gains for the global economy in 2005. The total gains amount to US$70 billion for 40 percent cuts in both market price support and domestic subsidies. These gains shrink to US$60 billion if domestic subsidies are left unaltered. In the case of agricultural liberalization, the rates of protection are the highest in the industrial economies and they are the ones to capture the majority of the absolute gains from the liberalization of farm markets. In the case of manufacturing tariff cuts, in this simulation exercise, the developing economies make the biggest cuts in protection because their initial tariffs are higher than those of the industrial economies. The developing economies also enjoy the lion's share of the gains.

Results from GTAP simulation by ADFAT (1999) show that Japan and Korea make the biggest welfare gains from a tariff reduction. Other Asian economies, particularly ASEAN, also stand to gain substantially in absolute terms, reflecting gains in all the major sectors, that is, agriculture, services, and manufactures. A 50 percent reduction in tariff barriers in the agricultural sector is projected to increase net global economic welfare by US$90 billion annually. The absolute annual welfare gains are large for the US (US$6.0 billion), the ASEAN economies (US$3.3 billion), China (US$1.2 billion), India (US$1.1 billion), and Australia (US$1.3 billion). A more meaningful measure, however, is to express the gains as a percentage of GDP. Expressed this way, the results show that New Zealand gains the most, followed by Japan, ASEAN, and Korea. The strong result for New Zealand reflects the significance of agriculture for the New Zealand economy and the high protection against some of its key agricultural exports.

Results from simulations of cuts in protection for manufacturing suggest an annual global welfare gain of US$66 billion from a 50 percent tariff cut in manufactures. For many developing economies a major proportion of the gains would derive from the textile, clothing, and footwear (TCF) sectors alone. China would receive the largest welfare gains, totaling US$16 billion per year, half of which would accrue from TCF reforms. Economies with the most substantial interest in TCF reforms are ASEAN; over 90 percent of their welfare gains would come from these sectors. As a proportion of GDP, however, economies projected to gain the most from tariff liberalization in manufactures are China and India. Korea, large ASEAN economies, and Latin America also stand to gain significantly. While manufacturing contributes less than 20 percent to the gain to global GDP under a 50 percent reduction scenario, its projected contribution to world trade growth is a massive 80 percent, reflecting mainly its dominant position in world trade. Trade in manufactures tends to be more responsive to changes in relative prices and incomes than trade in agricultural produce.

Simulation of the global services sector throws up somewhat surprisingly optimistic results. Liberalization results in large welfare gains because of the substantial scope for productivity improvements in services. The results indicate a huge annual gain in world welfare of US$250 billion from a 50 percent reduction of distortions globally in the provision of services. In this case, the largest gains accrue to the large industrial economies, the EU, the US, and Japan, in that order. It is, however, notable that all economies stand to gain and, in proportion to the size of GDP, the gains would be spread fairly evenly. The projected trade gains are not large. In this area the modeling significantly understates the dynamic effects of service sector reforms.

5.5 The FTAP model and the elimination of barriers to trade in services

The FTAP model was used by Dee and Hanslow (2000) to estimate gains from the elimination of barriers to trade in services (see also Dee, 2000). This model is a version of GTAP (Hertel, 1997), or GTAP with foreign direct investment (FDI). Hence it is known as FTAP. It also incorporates increasing returns to scale and large-group monopolistic competition in all sectors. FTAP makes provision for capital accumulation and international borrowing and lending and is implemented using the Gempack software suite (Harrison and Pearson, 1996).

This framework distinguishes barriers to commercial presence (largely through FDI) from those affecting other modes of service delivery (cross-border supply, consumption abroad, and the presence of natural persons). It also distinguishes non-discriminatory barriers to market access from discriminatory restrictions on national treatment, the first of a comprehensive new set of estimates of barriers to services trade. It makes use of estimates of the barriers to trade in banking and telecommunications services. The global economy was projected to be better off by this simulation analysis as a result of eliminating all post-Uruguay Round trade barriers. Of these benefits, US$130 billion per annum would come from trade liberalization in the services sector.

Dee and Hanslow (2000) noted that because the structure of trade barriers in services was relatively complex, addressing partial liberalization in this sector was a difficult proposition. Their results showed that it was difficult to find Pareto improvement from partial liberalization when it involves removing only one type of barrier. The different types of barriers include barriers to market access, restrictions on national treatment, on commercial presence, or on other modes of service delivery. This suggests that a better strategy could be to negotiate gradual reductions in all types of barriers simultaneously. They also stressed the return to market access over national treatment. The ongoing GATS negotiations can benefit from this strategy.

5.6 The Michigan CGE model

The Michigan Model of World Production and Trade is another useful CGE model (Section 5.2). The simulations will be based on two versions of the Michigan CGE Model of World Production and Trade.[3] Version I comprises sixteen sectors and twenty countries/regions. It is similar to what was used in recent years for modeling trade policies, as for example in Brown *et al.* (2000). Version II has been designed explicitly for the purpose of analyzing the economic effects of reducing barriers to trade and foreign direct investment (FDI) in services. As stated in Brown and Stern (1999), it is distinguished from Version I insofar as it incorporates the activities of multinational corporations and allows for international capital movements in the form of FDI in response to changes in rates of return induced by service liberalization. Since the services–FDI model is still very much work in progress, and because of computational constraints, we include only three aggregated sectors – agriculture, manufacturing, and services – together with eighteen countries/regions. In both model versions, the Asian countries are individually modeled, although because of data limitations the coverage differs somewhat at present. The computational experiments consist of simulating the reductions of tariffs and non-tariff barriers on bilateral trade in agricultural products, manufactures, and services in the respective rounds of trade negotiations under consideration.

5.6.1 Version I of the Michigan CGE model

The distinguishing feature of our Version I model is that it incorporates some aspects of the New Trade Theory, including increasing returns to scale, monopolistic competition, and product heterogeneity. Some details follow. A more complete description of the formal structure and equations of the model can be found on www.spp.umich.edu/rsie/model/. However,

Version I is not very relevant to this chapter because it essentially dwells on what the global economy could be expected to look like in 2005 if the Uruguay Round negotiations had not taken place. This book is futuristic and our principal concern here is the new round.

5.6.2 *Version II of the Michigan CGE model*

Unlike the various computational studies that have been done previously using Version I of the Michigan CGE model, Version II focuses on the behavior of multinational firms. In what follows, we use the Version II model to address trade in services, FDI, and the associated barriers. The Version II model draws on the structure developed by Petri (1997) and Markusen *et al.* (1999). The equations of the Version II model and a list of variables are available from the authors on request.

In the Version II model, each multinational corporation (MNC) produces a differentiated product and allocates production to its various host-country locations. Each location has different characteristics of production. Therefore, the outputs supplied by a multinational from the various locations are imperfect substitutes. Consumers use a three-stage budgeting procedure. Two somewhat different demand structures have been employed in the literature. Petri (1997) assumes that consumers first allocate expenditure between an aggregate of the output of a representative firm headquartered domestically and an aggregate of the output of firms headquartered in other countries. At the second stage, expenditure on the import aggregate is allocated across the varieties produced by representative firms headquartered in each of the foreign countries. At the third stage, expenditure on the output of each representative firm is allocated across the various plant locations.

Dee and Hanslow (2000) and Dee (2000) have produced a variation of the Petri (1997) model. Like Petri, they assume that consumers follow a three-stage budgeting procedure. However, in the first stage, consumers allocate expenditure between goods produced domestically and varieties imported. At the first stage, consumers are concerned not with the nationality of each firm's headquarters but with the nationality of the plant location. At the second stage, consumers allocate imports across goods produced by each trade partner. At the third stage, imports from each national source and domestically produced goods are allocated across the national firms. Dee and Hanslow also incorporate imperfect competition. Firms are assumed to set an optimal markup over marginal cost, and entry and exit may not occur, so that firm profits may not be zero.

For the purposes of this study we will adopt the demand structure of Dee and Hanslow. However, as in the Version I model, we assume free entry. Each MNC's profits over all locations consequently sum to zero.

Turning to firm behavior, in order to undertake production, each MNC must employ capital and labor to engage in product development at its headquarters location. This expenditure generates a fixed cost of labor and capital at home. The MNC then faces a fixed set-up cost of capital and labor in each host-country location. Production itself requires capital, labor, and intermediate inputs. Intermediate inputs are both produced locally and imported. They are then used in fixed proportion with the primary inputs.

Firms set a price for the output of each plant with an optimal markup of price over marginal cost. The elasticity of demand is derived assuming that each stage of the consumer's utility function is constant elasticity of substitution, with an elasticity of substitution equal to 3. However, the elasticity of substitution among various MNC products is taken to be 4.

Labor is taken to be freely mobile between sectors but not across borders. Therefore, there is a single equilibrium wage for each country. Capital, however, is mobile internationally, though not perfectly mobile. New firms that enter a market must purchase capital on international markets for installation in the host country. The degree of international capital mobility can be set exogenously. The rate of return paid for capital depends on the international interest rate plus a risk premium, with the premium paid by capital importers in a country depending on the overall change in its capital stock. In the results presented below, we assume that a 1 percent increase in a country's capital stock due to capital imports will generate a 0.5 percentage point increase in the interest rate.

A host country's barriers to FDI can be modeled in one of two ways. That is, the barriers to foreign firms may take the form of an increased fixed cost of locating in a host country. Alternatively, the barriers may take the form of a tax on installed capital. In what follows, we have selected the first type, modeling barriers that increase fixed cost.

Market equilibrium requires that consumers be willing to purchase the output sold by firms. In addition, each country is governed by a balance-of-trade constraint. Each country raises foreign exchange by selling products, collecting earnings on exported capital, receiving remittances of operating surpluses from foreign subsidiaries, and receiving subsidies from foreign headquarters for local subsidiaries that run an operating loss. A country that exports physical capital is paid interest each year. In addition, each MNC subsidiary is required to remit any operating profits back to headquarters. However, subsidiaries that lose money receive a subsidy from headquarters to cover operating expenses. Foreign exchange is spent on goods imports, interest paid on physical capital imports, and remittances of operating profits to headquarters.

Data, parameters, and solution procedure

The model comprises eighteen countries/regions. The industrialized countries include Australia, Canada, the EU, Japan, New Zealand, and the US. The Asian developing countries include China, Hong Kong, Indonesia, Korea, Malaysia, the Philippines, Singapore, Taiwan, and Thailand. The group of

Asian countries does not coincide with the countries included in our Version I model, since the FDI data have come from a source other than GTAP. The remaining countries in the Version II model are Chile, Mexico, and a group of Other Developing Countries. All other countries of the world are aggregated into a single rest-of-world (ROW). In order to keep the dimensions of the model manageable and to avoid lengthy solution time and associated computer capacity constraints, each country/region is assumed to produce and trade only three aggregates of agricultural products, manufactures, and services. The basic data used are the same as the GTAP-4 data in the Version I model. But in the Version II model, as noted, we need data on FDI, which have been provided by the Productivity Commission of the Australian government.

The barriers to FDI were provided by Hoekman (1999), who has estimated the margins between price and marginal cost. Some of this gap is attributable to fixed cost. However, Hoekman's estimates vary across countries. Therefore, in most cases, some of the price–cost gap can also be attributed to barriers to FDI. The price–cost gap is smallest (in most sectors) for Hong Kong, a country considered to be freely open to foreign firms. Hence we assume that the entire price–cost gap in Hong Kong is attributable to fixed cost. The excess in any other country in the model above the Hong Kong figures is taken to be due to barriers to establishment by foreign firms. Thus the barrier is modeled as the cost increase attributable to an increase in fixed cost borne by MNCs attempting to establish an enterprise locally. In the simulations presented below, liberalization of these barriers is assumed to consist of reducing the average fixed cost by 40 percent of the margin estimated by Hoekman (1999).

Scenarios

We have run the following computational scenarios with Version II:

A   Forty percent reduction in barriers to trade and FDI in agricultural products, manufactures, and services
B   Forty percent reduction in barriers to trade and FDI in agricultural products
C   Forty percent reduction in barriers to trade and FDI in manufactures
D   Forty percent reduction in barriers to trade and FDI in services

To recapitulate, the assumptions made in running the scenarios are:

1   The risk-premium elasticity is set at 0.5.
2   The world interest rate is set at 10 percent.
3   Barriers to trade and FDI in services are modeled as an additional cost to fixed investment.
4   The demand structure follows Dee and Hanslow (2000). In the utility function, expenditure is first allocated to place of production and then allocated across multinationals.

5 The number of firms is varied to hold MNC profits at zero.
6 The markup of price over marginal cost is fixed.

Version II results

Aggregate results A summary of results is presented in Table 5.1 for each of the four scenarios. The results for individual sectors are included in Table 5.2. The countries/regions are listed in column (1), absolute changes in imports and exports in columns (2) and (3), the percentage change in the terms of trade in column (4), welfare effects, as measured by the equivalent variation, as a percent of GNP and in absolute terms in columns (5) and (6), and the percent change in the real wage in column (7). It is immediately apparent in columns (5) and (6) of Table 5.1(A), which refers to a 40 percent reduction in barriers to trade in agricultural products, manufactures, and services, that the welfare consequences are very large in both percentage and absolute terms and that they vary markedly across countries.

Total global welfare is shown to increase by US$454.0 billion. For the group of industrialized countries shown, Japan's welfare increase is

Table 5.1(A) The Michigan CGE model II, 40 percent reduction in barriers to trade and FDI: percentage change in imports, exports, the terms of trade, welfare, and wages. (a) Agriculture, manufacturing, and services

			Terms of trade	Equivalent variation		Wages
Country (1)	Imports (2)	Exports (3)	% change (4)	% (5)	US$ million (6)	% change (7)
Industrialized countries						
Australia	7,494.09	6,402.97	0.95	6.63	22,733.78	4.79
Canada	607.48	4,782.40	0.10	−0.95	−5,392.39	1.22
European Union	38,382.52	25,147.13	0.71	0.70	57,076.28	0.42
Japan	50,628.61	25,168.16	1.24	3.95	200,448.67	2.25
New Zealand	2,374.46	2,067.96	1.17	16.97	9,734.51	12.38
United States	26,331.44	34,979.92	0.44	−0.17	−11,743.04	0.31
Developing countries						
Asia						
China	27,829.56	47,310.83	−5.42	15.47	109,537.81	15.58
Hong Kong	9,038.20	6,769.45	0.77	9.95	10,012.26	10.78
Indonesia	1,082.57	4,132.10	−0.38	−2.46	−4,870.27	0.79
Korea	13,613.54	15,926.34	−1.41	7.88	35,028.17	7.02
Malaysia	8,110.13	10,376.67	−2.09	11.04	10,308.19	12.15
Philippines	3,192.60	4,138.77	−3.59	6.43	4,435.49	8.91
Singapore	9,284.22	10,588.19	−0.37	7.23	4,198.43	8.93
Taiwan	13,559.40	17,625.83	−0.79	10.13	27,750.09	8.57
Thailand	6,211.59	7,564.09	−1.73	5.34	8,588.71	5.96
Other						
Chile	1,199.81	1,029.79	−0.59	3.62	2,268.49	3.08
Mexico	−89.18	−477.36	0.12	−2.98	−8,206.86	−2.39
Rest of Cairns	6,463.22	4,717.70	−0.02	−1.69	−17,925.11	−1.83
Total	225,314.26	228,250.94			453,983.21	

Source: see note 3.

US$200.4 billion, which is equal to 3.95 percent of GNP. The welfare increase for the European Union (EU) is US$57.1 billion (0.70 percent of GNP) and for the United States, US$–11.7 billion (–0.17 percent of GNP). For the developing countries in Asia, the welfare increase for China is US$109.5 billion (15.47 percent of GNP); for Korea, US$35.0 billion (7.88 percent of GNP); for Taiwan, US$27.8 billion (10.13 percent of GNP); for Thailand, US$8.6 billion (5.34 percent of GNP); for Hong Kong, US$10.0 billion (9.95 percent of GNP); and for Malaysia, US$10.3 billion (11.04 percent of GNP). It is noteworthy that most of the countries/regions shown experience positive welfare gains from the assumed liberalization of the three main categories of trade being modeled.

It should be evident from these results that the welfare effects are an order of magnitude larger than we are accustomed to seeing from trade liberalization experiments in CGE models, such as our Version I and similar models. We know from earlier CGE analyses of trade liberalization that the largest welfare gains stem from the capital flows that are generated by changes in rates of return due to liberalization rather than from the removal of consumer distortions in trade. In particular, what our Version II model is capturing is the behavior of multinational firms in which the international allocation of physical capital plays a central role.

Turning now to scenario B, which refers to a 40 percent reduction in post-Uruguay Round trade barriers for agricultural products only, it can be seen in Table 5.1(B) that global welfare rises by US$58.3 billion. Among the industrialized countries, the largest gainers are the US, with a welfare increase of US$48.1 billion (0.68 percent of GNP), Australia, with a welfare increase of US$5.6 billion (1.62 percent of GNP), and Canada, with a welfare increase of US$4.2 billion (0.73 percent of GNP). Among the Asian developing countries, the largest gains from agricultural liberalization are for China, US$3.2 billion (0.45 percent of GNP), and Korea, US$2.5 billion (0.57 percent of GNP). These results reflect the effects of reducing the relatively high agricultural protection that exists in these countries and hence the importance for them of pursuing agricultural liberalization in the forthcoming WTO negotiating round.

It is evident in scenario C (Table 5.1C), which refers to a 40 percent reduction in post-Uruguay Round tariffs on manufactures, that the greatest source of welfare gain comes from the liberalization of manufactures. That is, global welfare is seen to increase by US$396.7 billion. Among the industrialized countries, the largest gains are recorded for: Japan, US$99.2 billion (1.95 percent of GNP); the EU, US$40.2 billion (0.49 percent of GNP); and the US, US$11.7 billion (0.16 percent of GNP). Among the Asian developing countries, the largest gains shown are for: China, US$148.7 billion (21.01 percent of GNP); Taiwan, US$34.0 billion (12.42 percent of GNP); and Korea, US$31.0 billion (6.98 percent of GNP). These results for the liberalization of trade in manufactures

Table 5.1(B) The Michigan CGE model II, 40 percent reduction in barriers to trade and FDI: percentage change in imports, exports, the terms of trade, welfare, and wages. (b) Agriculture

			Terms of trade	Equivalent variation		Wages
Country	Imports	Exports	% change	%	US$ million	% change
(1)	(2)	(3)	(4)	(5)	(6)	(7)
Industrialized countries						
Australia	1,426.70	1,468.04	0.50	1.62	5,560.59	0.98
Canada	1,186.37	1,066.93	0.12	0.73	4,173.93	0.42
European Union	4,463.15	2,282.20	0.13	0.00	384.05	0.02
Japan	5,988.48	6,063.29	−0.32	−0.32	−16,151.87	−0.07
New Zealand	91.86	93.85	0.10	0.43	247.88	0.34
United States	9,537.41	9,154.34	0.26	0.68	48,074.06	0.46
Developing countries						
Asia						
China	1,178.28	914.04	0.09	0.45	3,209.29	0.18
Hong Kong	409.83	398.18	0.07	0.25	252.33	0.44
Indonesia	150.42	160.42	0.07	0.04	81.43	−0.18
Korea	1,615.30	2,362.05	−0.48	0.57	2,523.90	0.73
Malaysia	948.75	1,172.90	−0.21	0.74	694.26	0.76
Philippines	330.01	406.63	−0.20	0.89	612.38	0.65
Singapore	821.57	1,003.89	−0.07	0.46	268.45	0.84
Taiwan	1,324.20	1,672.69	−0.25	0.46	1,265.55	0.63
Thailand	672.87	705.19	0.01	0.68	1,095.81	0.65
Other						
Chile	68.02	68.38	−0.05	0.10	63.60	0.11
Mexico	318.91	192.88	0.11	0.61	1,668.85	0.29
Rest of Cairns	770.38	757.90	0.17	0.41	4,300.93	0.25
Total	31,302.50	29,943.78			58,325.42	

Source: see note 3.

underscore the importance of including such liberalization as one of the highest priority items on the agenda of a new trade round.

In scenario D (Table 5.1D), which refers to the liberalization of services, global welfare is estimated to increase by US$10.1 billion. Among the industrialized countries, Japan has a welfare gain of US$115.7 billion (2.28 percent of GNP), and the EU, US$16.1 billion (0.20 percent of GNP). It is interesting to note that welfare declines for services liberalization are indicated for Canada, the US, China, Indonesia, Taiwan, and Mexico. The welfare effects in the Version II model are associated primarily with whether or not a country attracts or loses capital as a result of liberalization. Countries that experience an outflow of capital become "smaller" in the economic sense of the word. As the economy contracts, surviving firms produce less than before. The fall in firm output generally occurs in order to avoid a large loss of variety among domestically produced goods. The subsequent economy-wide reduction in realized scale economies is usually the source of the welfare loss.

Table 5.1(C) The Michigan CGE model II, 40 percent reduction in barriers to trade and FDI: percentage change in imports, exports, the terms of trade, welfare, and wages. (c) Manufacturing

Country	Imports	Exports	Terms of trade % change	Equivalent variation %	Equivalent variation US$ million	Wages % change
(1)	(2)	(3)	(4)	(5)	(6)	(7)
Industrialized countries						
Australia	5,138.46	5,127.91	0.08	3.38	11,590.17	2.83
Canada	2,030.49	1,767.18	0.06	0.19	1,080.24	0.13
European Union	31,489.48	24,941.38	0.45	0.49	40,194.96	0.16
Japan	31,580.77	27,932.71	1.06	1.95	99,158.09	1.17
New Zealand	1,745.86	1,889.97	0.86	10.56	6,057.12	7.93
United States	28,285.42	20,156.63	0.48	0.16	11,687.27	0.09
Developing countries						
Asia						
China	31,762.37	47,998.00	−5.69	21.01	148,706.32	19.91
Hong Kong	7,014.61	6,570.85	0.57	6.09	6,123.31	6.68
Indonesia	2,824.34	2,601.92	0.24	1.171	3,386.00	1.11
Korea	11,717.87	13,967.81	−0.98	6.98	31,021.63	6.21
Malaysia	7,136.00	9,373.07	−1.87	9.42	8,799.69	10.90
Philippines	2,857.55	3,701.40	−3.41	4.97	3,426.37	7.73
Singapore	8,275.20	9,315.16	−0.28	5.76	3,348.05	6.69
Taiwan	14,229.78	15,785.83	−0.26	12.42	34,035.28	8.97
Thailand	5,704.09	6,839.63	−1.74	4.57	7,351.05	5.27
Other						
Chile	897,29	993.78	−0.73	1.59	1,000.16	1.75
Mexico	411.73	61.91	0.03	−1.43	−3,943.13	−1.38
Rest of Cairns	5,677.10	4,356.44	−0.31	−1.54	−16,342.90	−1.61
Total	198,778.41	203,381.58			396,679.70	

Source: see note 3.

The percentage change in wages is shown in column (7) of the tables. Wage changes generally reflect the changes in economic welfare. For the liberalization of barriers to trade in agricultural products, manufactures, and services combined in scenario A, it can be seen that the increase in the real wage ranges from more than 0.3 percent to over 12 percent in the industrialized countries. The increases are somewhat greater for the Asian developing countries, ranging from 0.79 percent in Indonesia to 15.58 percent in China. The wage changes relating to agricultural liberalization by itself in scenario B are in the 1–2 percent range. For manufactures liberalization in scenario C, the wage changes range up to nearly 6 percent in the industrialized countries, and from 1 percent to 20 percent in the Asian developing countries. For services liberalization in scenario D, the wage changes are all less than 5 percent, and some are negative.

The wage changes noted mirror capital flows. That is, it is generally the case that countries that acquire capital will see an increase in capital per

Table 5.1(D) The Michigan CGE model II, 40 percent reduction in barriers to trade and FDI: percentage change in imports, exports, the terms of trade, welfare, and wages. (d) Services

Country	Imports	Exports	Terms of trade % change	Equivalent variation %	US$ million	Wages % change
(1)	(2)	(3)	(4)	(5)	(6)	(7)
Industrialized countries						
Australia	928.93	−192.98	0.37	1.48	5,092.12	0.98
Canada	−2,609.38	1,948.30	−0.09	−1.84	−10,477.17	0.66
European Union	2,429.88	−2,076.45	0.13	0.20	16,055.21	0.24
Japan	13,059.36	−8,827.84	0.49	2.28	115,713.57	1.15
New Zealand	536.74	84.15	0.21	5.34	3,063.27	4.12
United States	−11,491.39	5,668.94	−0.30	−1.00	−70,647.37	−0.24
Developing countries						
Asia						
China	−5,111.09	−1,601.20	0.17	−4.97	−35,191.28	−4.52
Hong Kong	1,613.76	−199.58	0.13	3.35	3,365.93	3.66
Indonesia	−1,892.20	1,369.76	−0.69	−4.15	−8,206.90	−0.14
Korea	280.38	−403.53	0.05	0.29	1,282.43	0.08
Malaysia	25.38	−169.29	−0.01	0.72	674.33	0.48
Philippines	5.05	30.74	0.01	0.52	360.32	0.53
Singapore	187.45	269.14	−0.02	0.91	527.84	1.39
Taiwan	−1,994.59	167.31	−0.29	−2.48	−6,798.53	−1.02
Thailand	−165.37	19.27	0.00	0.05	80.44	0.04
Other						
Chile	234.49	−32.37	0.19	1.88	1,179.06	1.22
Mexico	−819.81	−732.15	−0.02	−2.17	−5,992.84	−1.31
Rest of Cairns	5.14	8,271.56	0.12	−0.58	−6,095.72	−0.47
Total	−4,777.26	3,593.80			10,080.44	

Source: see note 3.

worker. The consequent rise in the marginal value product of workers will thus raise wages. By contrast, wages are lower in countries where an outflow of capital occurs.

Sectoral results   The results for the three aggregated sectors – agriculture, manufactures, and services – are shown for the scenario A liberalization in Table 5.2. For each of the three sectors, we report the percentage changes in exports and imports, sectoral output, the number of firms, and the output of foreign-owned affiliates. Output increases economy-wide in almost all sectors in many countries. For example, output rises in all three sectors in Australia, New Zealand, China, Hong Kong, Korea, Malaysia, the Philippines, Singapore, Taiwan, Thailand, and Chile. By contrast, output in the US declines in both manufacturing and services. Similarly, all three sectors contract in Indonesia, Mexico, and Rest of Cairns.[4]

The international movement of capital determines whether an economy will expand or contract. Those countries that attract capital may expand production in all sectors, whereas those that lose capital will contract in many, if not all, sectors. In addition, there are generally significant increases in activity by foreign-owned affiliates, especially in those countries that record large increases in output. There are significant lessons for the developing economies here.

5.6.3 Revelations from the Michigan model

The foregoing presentation of our Version II CGE model has focused on the behavior of MNCs in response to an assumed 40 percent reduction in post-Uruguay Round barriers to trade and FDI for agricultural products, manufactures, and services. The welfare effects in most cases were found to be large. The Version II model makes it clear that capital formation can play a far more important and substantive role than consumer distortions in determining the welfare effects of trade liberalization. Therefore, investment regulations and MNC investment should be paid adequate attention in the new round. Also, in analyzing the behavior of MNCs, the international allocation of physical capital should play a central role.

In Brown and Stern (1999), results are presented for a variety of other demand configurations and market structures as compared with what we have reported above. It is clear from the Brown and Stern analyses that the model results are extremely sensitive to the assumed demand structure, and also to whether or not entry can occur in the individual sectors. Much more research needs to be done therefore to understand fully the mechanics of the model, especially the characterization of the competing assumptions concerning consumer preferences.

We now summarize our main conclusions and the implications for the priorities and strategies that the developing countries should formulate in preparing for and participating in the forthcoming WTO negotiations.

5.7 Summing up

We have presented several simulation analyses of trade liberalization in the forthcoming WTO round to assess its potential economic effects. Both static and dynamic CGE models were used for these simulations. As the preceding sections are replete with quantitative details, our summing up must be qualitative. Although estimates vary, all the simulation results point in the same direction, that the forthcoming round and the liberalization of trade in goods and services will have large welfare effects on the global economy. In some cases the welfare gains are larger for the developing economies while in others they are larger for the industrial economies.

Notwithstanding the snags, the Uruguay Round accomplished a great deal for the developing economies, much of it to the benefit of the Asian developing economies. For some developing countries, including the Asian economies, these benefits arise to a considerable extent from the promised

Table 5.2 Sectoral change in exports, imports, output, number of firms, and output of foreign-owned firms due to 40 percent reduction in barriers to trade and FDI in agriculture, manufacturing, and services (%)

Country (1)	Sector (2)	Exports (3)	Imports (4)	Output (5)	No. of firms (6)	Output of foreign-owned firms (7)
Industrialized countries						
Australia	Agr.	11.84	4.76	6.22	7.06	1.86
	Mfr.	13.63	12.87	3.17	−1.00	3.61
	Ser.	2.30	6.02	3.13	0.64	−0.26
	Total	10.50	10.90	3.39	0.01	1.97
Canada	Agr.	3.90	1.6	1.40	0.74	3.06
	Mfr.	2.40	0.25	0.73	7.48	−1.34
	Ser.	0.41	0.42	−0.95	−1.73	−1.37
	Total	2.41	0.35	−0.16	2.65	−1.30
European Union	Agr.	3.74	1.12	−0.29	−1.3	2.60
	Mfr.	3.59	6.51	0.09	−0.32	0.28
	Ser.	0.26	1.61	0.02	−0.30	−0.38
	Total	2.81	4.52	0.03	−0.32	0.84
Japan	Agr.	2.49	15.92	−1.36	−2.22	1.61
	Mfr.	5.82	13.09	1.87	0.10	1.90
	Ser.	0.60	7.51	1.79	0.32	−0.05
	Total	5.20	12.14	1.71	0.19	1.30
New Zealand	Agr.	6.16	10.48	8.17	10.77	5.75
	Mfr.	18.42	15.20	12.08	4.50	10.76
	Ser.	−0.70	14.86	9.24	2.39	3.37
	Total	12.16	14.85	9.97	3.71	5.10
United States	Agr.	26.36	−0.17	2.71	2.4	3.55
	Mfr.	4.02	4.15	−0.17	−0.22	0.47
	Ser.	1.60	−0.16	−0.22	−0.56	−0.44
	Total	4.87	3.10	−0.09	−0.38	0.19
Developing countries						
Asia						
China	Agr.	16.64	5.27	13.14	1.72	13.51
	Mfr.	23.31	20.91	14.67	2.21	19.07
	Ser.	17.43	−1.25	13.46	1.85	10.09
	Total	22.50	17.35	14.01	2.08	14.73
Hong Kong	Agr.	8.79	7.07	9.76	48.87	9.16
	Mfr.	20.13	8.57	15.49	17.50	9.42
	Ser.	1.39	7.96	6.05	0.13	5.G6
	Total	9.09	8.37	8.07	6.58	8.06
Indonesia	Agr.	6.90	−1.78	−0.68	13.20	−2.40
	Mfr.	8.90	4.25	−0.23	−2.15	0.95
	Ser.	3.67	−4.16	−2.17	−3.45	−1.50
	Total	7.81	2.27	−1.20	−1.97	−1.57

Source: see note 3.

Country (1)	Sector (2)	Exports (3)	Imports (4)	Output (5)	No. of firms (6)	Output of foreign-owned firms (7)
Korea	Agr.	8.91	14.14	4.36	0.62	1.51
	Mfr.	12.33	9.88	7.49	1.35	6.98
	Ser.	6.85	2.49	6.02	0.95	1.95
	Total	11.42	9.32	6.61	1.23	5.64
Malaysia	Agr.	6.19	27.77	6.89	1.78	2.54
	Mfr.	13.31	11.03	11.97	3.63	11.25
	Ser.	9.25	2.86	9.80	2.33	5.89
	Total	12.30	10.71	10.49	2.91	8.55
Philippines	Agr.	17.26	6.17	6.40	1.27	2.04
	Mfr.	18.29	13.12	7.51	0.34	7.36
	Ser.	11.32	−5.00	6.35	0.05	0.97
	Total	16.03	9.02	6.79	0.21	5.66
Singapore	Agr.	20.66	6.75	14.40	25.09	5.49
	Mfr.	9.39	7.87	8.84	2.44	8.86
	Ser.	5.78	4.58	6.74	1.18	5.92
	Total	8.79	7.38	7.98	1.98	7.36
Taiwan	Agr.	8.30	24.42	4.57	−2.72	6.77
	Mfr.	14.55	12.90	10.20	2.35	10.53
	Ser.	1.24	8.69	6.39	0.90	−0.06
	Total	13.58	12.96	8.22	2.02	10.06
Thailand	Agr.	13.02	5.67	4.65	1.34	19.37
	Mfr.	12.06	10.56	4.34	−0.18	2.93
	Ser.	8.27	−2.55	4.05	0.06	0.28
	Total	11.43	7.76	4.25	−0.06	3.70
Developing countries Non-Asia						
Chile	Agr.	3.99	3.94	2.34	−0.10	1.95
	Mfr.	6.78	8.88	1.83	−0.81	2.26
	Ser.	4.82	−0.09	2.13	0.12	0.12
	Total	5.78	6.83	2.05	−0.33	1.46
Mexico	Agr.	0.66	−3.06	−2.04	−1.09	−0.08
	Mfr.	−0.99	0.47	−2.86	−2.40	−1.67
	Ser.	0.85	−3.12	−2.54	−1.89	−0.90
	Total	−0.57	−0.13	−2.62	−2.18	−0.90
Rest of Cairns	Agr.	4.85	0.10	−1.31	−1.05	2.56
	Mfr.	6.98	10.61	−2.23	−1.70	−0.40
	Ser.	2.52	−2.51	−1.90	−1.31	−0.56
	Total	5.88	7.04	−1.98	−1.57	−0.18

elimination of the MFA, backloading of which means that these gains remain to be realized. However, all developing economies have gained or stand to gain from the other liberalization measures that have been the more immediate consequences of the Uruguay Round.

As for the forthcoming WTO round, the entire global economy stands to benefit substantially from the lowering or elimination of trade barriers. Agricultural liberalization alone in the forthcoming round could yield substantial welfare gains for the global economy. The five crisis-affected Asian economies would have benefited from trade liberalization. It would also have raised the level of investment in the five crisis economies of Asia. Different simulation analyses present estimates of welfare gains globally, regionally as well as country-wise. Estimates of global welfare gains, albeit large, vary with the methodology followed. Different country groups benefit to different degrees as varying areas of global trade are liberalized. Trade liberalization generates significant exports above those that would otherwise have occurred.

Developing economies must proactively participate in the new round and strive for continued reductions of barriers to trade in traditional areas like manufactures (particularly textiles and apparel, and footwear) and in agriculture. They should also co-operate fully in the liberalization of trade in services by changing their regulations regarding trade in services. In this case, industrial economies are likely to benefit far more than the developing economies. However, the developing economies stand to gain as suppliers.

Notes

1 Global trading system: contemporary scenario

1 The WTO, like the United Nations and the World Bank, has become a key institution of global governance. The Final Act of the Uruguay Round established the WTO as a fully fledged international governing institution recognized in international law.
2 Its date of birth is 1 January 1995; its annual budget is less than US$90 million and its total personnel strength is 500.
3 The Uruguay Round of multilateral trade negotiations took place during 1986–94.
4 Croatia became the 140th WTO member on 30 November 2000, and agreed to assume its entire range of WTO obligations upon accession. At this point in time twenty-eight countries were negotiating to join the WTO, among them the largest trading developing economy, the People's Republic of China, which was responsible for 3.5 percent of world merchandise exports. On 8 December 2000, the WTO General Council approved the accession of Lithuania. It would be the 141st member of the WTO after the ratification of the terms of accession by its parliament.
5 According to the 2000 annual report of the WTO, merchandise exports in 1999 were US$5.46 trillion, while trade in commercial services was US$1.34 trillion.
6 For instance, during the 1960s the International Monetary Fund required member countries to peg their currencies either to gold or to the US dollar.
7 For greater details on these issues readers are referred to Schott, 1996 and Sampson, 2000. A great deal more information is available in these two scholarly writings than provided here.
8 For instance, see Goldin *et al.* (1993), Ng and Yeates (1996), and OECD (1998).
9 It is good to define the term "commercial services". In the fifth edition of the Balance of Payments Manual of the WTO the commercial services category is defined to include transport, travel, communications, construction, insurance, financial services, computer and information services, royalties and license fees, trade-related services, and personal, cultural, and recreational services.
10 An amber signal is essential here. Modeling results should be taken with a pinch of salt because different modeling exercises throw up different numbers. Such debates on models and their results tend to be interminable.
11 A caveat is necessary here. Income per person in a country is typically positively correlated with trade but this may simply reflect the fact that countries whose incomes are higher for reasons other than trade may trade more. Countries that adopt free-market trade policies may also adopt free-market domestic policies as well as stable monetary and fiscal policies, which are also likely to affect income. Thus the correlation between trade and income does not establish the direction of causation.
12 This assertion has been challenged by Krishna *et al.* (1998), who posit that if GDP growth in countries with high trade exposure is modeled by including an index of global business cycle conditions – in addition to the normal variables – 70 percent of the countries in the sample exhibited unidirectional causality between trade and growth, and in turn *per capita* income.

13 It is true as a generalization only because sometimes opening up an economy can increase risk either because official stabilization schemes are undermined or because residents switch completely from one activity to another that offers higher average rewards but greater variability.

14 This issue has been touched here in a cursory manner. For a detailed account, readers are referred to chapter 1 of the *World Development Report 1999/2000*, pp. 33–51.

15 See chapters 14 and 15 in particular. See also chapter 17, which describes "a seamless world" economy, although the real world is anything but seamless.

16 In the industrial economies tariffs and most non-tariff barriers have fallen. But anti-dumping measures have been used as a "safety valve", notably against specific sectors like steel and textiles.

17 Refer to WTO (1999e), companion volume on *International Trade Statistics*, table IV.28, p. 91.

18 Cited by Krugman (1997).

19 This economic logic requires markets to be working well. However, in many developing economies, underdevelopment is an inherent reflection of poorly functioning markets.

20 In 1994, when the famous World Economic Forum was organized in Davos, Switzerland, Klaus Schwab, president of the Forum, described the changing global economy by saying that it could no longer be divided into two comfortable groups, rich countries with high productivity and high wages and poor countries with low productivity and low wages. He noted that a group of countries had emerged which combined high productivity with low wages. Schwab opined that the growing presence of those countries in world markets is leading to a "massive redeployment of productive assets" which is making it impossible for advanced countries to maintain their standard of living.

21 Formerly President of the European Commission.

22 If a product is exported at a price less than either the price in its home country or the average cost of production, it is said to be dumped in the importing country.

23 The International Labor Organization (ILO) has formulated international labor standards. The body of international labor standards is the main and unique instrument of the ILO to promote social justice on a global scale. These standards are in the form of conventions and recommendations. Conventions are legally binding on countries which ratify them, while recommendations provide guidance to policy, legislation, and practice. Labor standards include freedom of association, the right to organize, collective bargaining, the abolition of forced labor, equality of opportunity and treatment, and standards regulating conditions across the entire spectrum of work-related issues. Minimum international labor standards also include technical assistance, primarily in the fields of vocational training and vocational rehabilitation, labor law and industrial relations, working conditions, management development, social security, occupational safety, and health. If the assets and facilities provided to workers are increased, and working conditions are improved, they are sure to work more productively, which in turn improves labor standards.

24 The agreements on information technology products, basic telecommunications services, and financial services were part of the "built-in" agenda of the Uruguay Round and have been concluded on schedule. The Agreement on Agriculture and the General Agreement on Trade in Services called for negotiations to carry forward the process of liberalization embarked upon during the Uruguay Round. These negotiations, by general consent, were seen as the core subjects for the next round.

2   Seattle and its aftermath

1 According to the statistics published by OECD (2000b), over the decade of the 1990s the rate of unemployment declined in Denmark, the Netherlands, and the UK, but has either stayed at a high level or increased in Austria, Belgium, France, Italy, Germany, Portugal, Spain, and Sweden.

2 The French saying is *Quand on s'arrête, on tombe*, literally "When one stops, one falls".

3 The European Union (of fifteen), the United States, and Japan are the largest exporting countries or country groups in the global economy. In 1999, their combined share of global merchandise trade was 45.2 percent. The EU (of fifteen) accounted for 18.9 percent of global exports in 1999, the US for 16.4 percent, and Japan for 9.9 percent.

4 As noted in Chapter 1, as of December 2000 the WTO had 140 members. On 8 December Croatia became the 140th member, while Azerbaijan, Belarus, Bhutan, Kazakstan, Lithuania, Moldova, Russia, Ukraine, and Uzbekistan were in the process of negotiating the terms of their entry. At this point in time, twenty-eight countries were negotiating to join, including the People's Republic of China.

5 Sir Leon Brittan, Vice-president of the European Commission, was the first to use this nomenclature. Since then it has caught on with academics and the economic and financial press.

6 Indonesia, Korea (Republic of), Malaysia, the Philippines, and Thailand.

7 The mystery regarding what and where the Green Room is should be unraveled at this stage. At the Centre William Rappard in Geneva, where the former GATT and present WTO headquarters are located, there is a room decorated in an unattractive parrot-green next to the room of the Director General. Whenever the Director General wanted to have a small meeting with some delegations, he traditionally invited them into the Green Room. It was a matter of convenience. In these meetings delegations of large trading countries agreed on important issues and the consultation process moved forward. These Green Room meetings were criticized by many developing country delegations for lack of transparency.

8 After the collapse in Seattle, Pascal Lamy, the EU Trade Commissioner, called the WTO's negotiation process "medieval", as reported by the *Financial Times*, 6 December 1999.

9 Also known as the Seven Wise Men report. Its formal title was *Trade Policies for a Better Future: Proposals for Action*, and it was published by the GATT secretariat in 1985.

10 Technically a vote could be taken and it was resorted to at the time of new accessions. Technically there could also be a vote for other purposes, but it was done rarely. The new WTO system operates expressly by consensus.

11 As Archbishop of Cracow in Poland, Pope John Paul II was a passionate supporter of globalization. But as the 1990s wore on, the Pope became increasingly uneasy about "unbridled capitalism". He expressed his disapproval in his Apostolic Exhortation to the Catholic Church in the Americas in January 1999 by enumerating the following ill effects of globalization: "the absolutizing of the economy, unemployment, the reduction and deterioration of public services, the destruction of the environment and natural resources, the growing distance between the rich and the poor, unfair competition which puts poor nations in a situation of ever increasing inferiority . . ."

12 The US accounted for 16.4 percent of total merchandise exports in 1999; only the share of the European Union (of fifteen) was higher.

13 More manifestations of the same backlash against globalization were seen soon after Seattle in Davos (against the World Economic Forum), Bangkok (against the UNCTAD X conference) and Washington DC (against the spring meetings of the International Monetary Fund and the World Bank).

14 Jonathan Fried, Assistant Deputy Minister, Trade and Economic Policy, Government of Canada (2000), questioned the suitability of Charlene Barshefsky to chair the Committee of the Whole at Seattle.

15 Refer to a speech given by Michael Meacher, Britain's Environment Minister, on 27 March 2000 at the Royal Institute of International Affairs, London, where he urged political leaders from the industrial economies to make earnest endeavors "to overcome barriers of misunderstanding and mistrust". *Financial Times*, 28 March 2000.

3 The Uruguay Round

1 The Multifiber Arrangement (MFA) was an anathema to the spirit of the GATT. It allowed industrial economies to negotiate "voluntary" export restraint agreements – sometimes very comprehensive in scope – with developing countries. They effectively circumvented Article XI of the GATT. The MFA provided for country-specific quotas, which introduced discrimination across trading partners, thus effectively violating Article I.

2 The Final Act is 550 pages long and contains legal texts of the negotiations. In addition to the texts of the agreements, the Final Act also contains texts of Ministerial Decisions and Declarations which further clarify the Final Act.

3 The term "binding" is important in trade economics. It is used in the context of tariffs. If a tariff lowered during the GATT or WTO round is unilaterally raised again a few months later, that tariff will have little value for foreign or domestic producers. An exporting firm will be reluctant to pursue new markets if the treatment afforded to products it intends to export is uncertain. This is true if taking advantage of the lower tariff requires investment in plant, equipment, and distribution networks. This investment will become unprofitable if the tariff is raised. When a country agrees to bind in GATT or WTO tariff on a product at a certain level, say 20 percent, it commits itself not to increase the tariff above that level except by negotiation and with compensation for trading partners affected. Binding is considered so important that countries which agree to bind previously unbound tariffs are given "negotiating credit" for the decision even if the tariff is bound at a level above the currently applied level. This is called "ceiling binding", used by many developing country participants during the Uruguay Round.

4 See speech by Peter Sutherland, Director General of the GATT, cited in the *Financial Times,* 3–4 September 1994.

5 Some called it "dirty" tariffication because in many cases non-tariff barriers were converted into overly high bound tariffs. In many cases NTBs were converted into tariff quotas, thereby limiting the gains possible.

6 The statistics used in this section came from various WTO sources, in particular WTO (1994).

7 There is a contrary view on this, that is, commitment to TRIPs may encourage firms in the industrial economies to supply technology to developing economies, giving a stimulus to growth.

8 They first developed this typology in 1985 and refined it in *Measures of Non-tariff Barriers* (1997).

9 Expressed as a fixed monetary amount per physical unit or per unit of weight of an imported product.

10 Mixed duty contains elements of both *ad valorem* and specific duties.

11 An *ad valorem* tariff is calculated as a percentage of the value of goods cleared through customs.

12 Switzerland, which has only specific tariffs, claims that they are easier to operate than *ad valorem* tariffs and that they do not show significant bias if set appropriately.

13 This is a tariff rate applicable to quota of imports, with a higher rate charged on imports in excess of the quota. The quota tariff may be defined in terms of quantity or value.

14 "Core" NTBs consist of two broad kinds of measure: quantitative restrictions (QRs) and price control measures (PCMs).

15 The twenty-nine members of the OECD are the US, Japan, Germany, France, Italy, the UK, Canada, Australia, Austria, Belgium, the Czech Republic, Denmark, Finland, Greece, Hungary, Iceland, Ireland, Korea, Luxembourg, Mexico, Netherlands, New Zealand, Norway, Poland, Portugal, Spain, Sweden, Switzerland, and Turkey.

16 The thirteen non-OECD-member economies are Argentina, Brazil, Colombia, India, Indonesia, Malaysia, Mexico, the Philippines, Romania, Sri Lanka, Thailand, Tunisia, and Venezuela.

17 Usually any tariff barrier higher than 15 percent is considered a tariff spike.

18 This refers to tariff quotas where the tariff rate is applicable to a quota of imports in such a manner that higher rate is charged on imports in excess of the quota. The quota and tariff may be defined in terms of quantity or value.

19 There was only one exception to this, Nigerian restrictions on grain imports, for which no elimination date was specified.

4 An action agenda

1 The European Union, Canada, Japan, and the United States are the four members of the Quad.

2 Cairns is the name of a city in eastern Australia. All the eighteen members of Cairns Group, which does not include the US, are substantial exporters of farm products. The eighteen members of the Group are: Argentina, Australia, Bolivia, Brazil, Canada, Chile, Colombia, Costa Rica, Fiji, Guatemala, Indonesia, Malaysia, New Zealand, Paraguay, the Philippines, South Africa, Thailand, and Uruguay.

3 The United Nations has put forty-eight countries in the category of the least developed economies of the world.

4 It implies that the results of the negotiations are adopted as a package and that they apply to all WTO members. Members could no longer take the *à la carte* approach. They are not given discretion to choose part or parts of the entire package. The Tokyo Round did have an *à la carte* approach. As opposed to that the Uruguay Round produced a fixed-price menu for all participants.

5 Using single undertaking strategy, the Uruguay Round featured grand bargains such as the simultaneous phase-out of the MFA and phase-in of intellectual property obligations.

6 In the past, the EU annually set indicative prices for individual farm products that were usually higher than the international prices. The rationale of fixing higher prices was the higher cost of production in the EU economies. When farm products were imported into the EU, the difference between the indicative price and the international price was levied like a tariff. Each agricultural product had a levy, depending upon the indicative price; it was called a "variable levy". Thus the EU markets were shielded from international competition. Such agricultural support measures worked as an incentive to higher production but led to overproduction. To export the overproduced agricultural items the CAP provided export subsidies. To undertake price support and subsidize exports the CAP had a large budget, two-thirds of total EU budget. The variable levies have now been eliminated.

7 See the communiqué of the Cairns Group Ministers, Sydney, 3 April 1998.

8 Under a tariff quota tariff rates are applicable to a quota of imports in such a manner that a higher rate is charged on imports in excess of the quota. The quota and tariff may be determined in terms of quantity or value.

9 The 5 percent consumption level was scheduled for 2000.

10 Refer to Part IV, Article XIX of the Articles of Agreement of the GATS.

11 The first Ministerial Conference was held in December 1996 in Singapore and the second in May 1998 in Geneva.

12 In reality, restrictions on textiles and apparel exports date back to the 1930s. Protectionist measures included high tariff protection and some voluntary restraints on exports, notably Japanese exports. A Short-term Arrangement (STA) in the cotton textile trade was reached in 1961 at the initiative of the US and under the auspices of the General Agreement on Tariffs and Trade. A Long-term Arrangement Regarding International Trade in Cotton and Textiles (LTA) was then concluded later in 1962 by imposing a 5 percent growth limit on imports of cotton products and placed a large share of developing country exports under the trade regime.

13 In March 1999.

14 The "green" subsidies or the "green" domestic policies are defined in the Uruguay Round agreement as those that have no or marginal trade distortion. They include, for example, services rendered by a government (research, inspection, stockpiling, domestic food aid). Direct payments to producers are allowed under the "green" subsidies, but they should be in the form of income support, with no link to production, or compensation for a substantial shortfall in income resulting from natural disasters. The "green" subsidies are granted as an exceptional measure.

15 See Article XXVI and Annex 2 of the WTO agreement.

16 Where a decision cannot be arrived at by consensus and a vote is unavoidable, Article IX of the Marrakesh Agreement provides that each member has one vote.

5   Implications of the forthcoming round

1 Indonesia, Korea (Republic of), Malaysia, the Philippines, Thailand.

2 Stoeckel's simulation included the US, Japan, Australia, Indonesia, Malaysia, the Philippines, Thailand, China, India, Taiwan, Korea, and all the remaining OECD economies.

3 This simulation analysis was a part of an Asian Development Bank project on the new round. This simulation was completed in March 2000 by Drusilla K. Brown of Tufts University, Dilip K. Das of the Asian Development Bank, Alan V. Deardorff of the University of Michigan, and Robert M. Stern of the University of Michigan. The author was project director. Permission of the co-authors was sought before citing.

4 See Chapter 4, note 2.

Bibliography

Abreu, M.D. 1996. "Trade in Manufactures: the Outcome of the Uruguay Round", in W. Martin and L.A. Winters (eds) *The Uruguay Round and the Developing Countries*, Cambridge: Cambridge University Press, pp. 59–88.

Adamantopoulos, K. 1997. *An Anatomy of the World Trade Organization*, London: Kluwer Law International.

Anderson, K. 1996. "The Intrusion of Environmental and Labour Standards into Trade Policy", in W. Martin and L.A. Winters (eds) *The Uruguay Round and the Developing Countries*, Cambridge: Cambridge University Press, pp. 435–62.

Anderson, K. 1998. "Domestic Agricultural Policy Objectives and Trade Liberalization: Synergies and Trade-offs", Paris: Organization for Economic Co-operation and Development. COM/AGR/CA/TD/WS(98)101.

Anderson, K. 1999. "The WTO Agenda for the New Millennium", *Economic Record*, 76(228), pp. 77–88. March.

Anderson, K., B. Hoekman and A. Strutt. 1999. "Agriculture and the WTO: Next Steps", Washington DC: World Bank. Mimeo. Available at http://www.worldbank.org/trade

Asian Development Bank (ADB). 2000. *Asian Development Outlook 2000*, New York: Oxford University Press.

Asia Pacific Economic Co-operation (APEC). 2000. *Twelfth APEC Meeting*, Brunei Darussalam, 12–13 November.

Australian Department of Foreign Affairs and Trade (ADFAT). 1999. *Global Trade Reform: Maintaining Momentum*, Canberra.

Australian Productivity Commission (APC). 2000. "Review of Australia's General Tariff Arrangements", Canberra and Melbourne, May.

Baldwin, R.E. 1970. *Non-tariff Distortions of International Trade*, Washington DC: Brookings Institution.

Baldwin, R.E. and A.J. Venables. 1995. "Regional Economic Integration", in G. Grossman and K. Rogoff (eds) *Handbook of International Economics*, Amsterdam: Elsevier Science, pp. 1597–643.

Barro, R. 1998. "Recent Developments in Growth Theory and Empirics", Cambridge MA: Harvard University. Mimeo.

Ben-David, D., H. Nordstrom and L.A. Winters. 1999. *Trade, Income Disparities and Poverty*, Geneva: World Trade Organization. Special Studies No. 5.

Ben-David, D. and M.B. Loewy. 2000. "Knowledge Dissemination, Capital Accumulation, Trade and Endogenous Growth", *Oxford Economic Papers*, 33(2), pp. 433–58.

Bergsten, C.F. 1996. "Competitive Liberalization and Global Trade", Washington DC: Institute for International Economics. APEC Working Paper No. 96-15. Available at http://www.iie.com/CATALOG/WP/1996/9615.htm

Bergsten, C.F. 2000. "The Backlash against Globalization". Testimony before the Trilateral Commission, Tokyo, 9 May.

Bhagwati, J.N. 1995. "US Trade Policy: the Infatuation with Free Trade Areas", in J.N. Bhagwati and A.O. Krueger (eds) *Dangerous Drift to Preferential Trade Agreements*, Washington DC: American Enterprise Institute, pp. 1–18.

Bhagwati, J.N., D. Greenaway and A. Panagariya. 1998. "Trading Preferentially: Theory and Policy", *Economic Journal*, 34(5), pp. 1128–48.

Binswanger, H. and E. Lutz. 2000. "Agricultural Trade Barriers, Trade Negotiations, and the Interests of Developing Countries", paper presented at UNCTAD X on 12 February at Bangkok.

Blackhurst, R. 1998. "The Capacity of the WTO to Fulfill its Mandate", in A.O. Krueger (ed.) *The WTO as an International Organization*, Chicago: University of Chicago Press, pp. 88–106.

Blackhurst, R., A. Enders and J.F. Francois. 1996. "The Uruguay Round and Market Access", in W. Martin and L.A. Winters (eds) *The Uruguay Round and the Developing Countries*, Cambridge: Cambridge University Press, pp. 125–55.

Bordo, M.D., B. Eichengreen and D.A. Irwin. 1999. "Is Globalization Today really Different than Globalization a Hundred Years Ago?", paper presented at Brookings Trade Policy Forum, Washington DC, 15–16 April.

Brown, D.K., A.V. Deardorff, A.K. Fox and R.M. Stern. 1996. "Computational Analysis of Goods and Services Liberalization in the Uruguay Round", in W. Martin and L.A. Winters (eds) *The Uruguay Round and the Developing Countries,* Cambridge: Cambridge University Press, pp. 240–72.

Brown, D.K. and R.M. Stern. 1999. "Measurement and Modeling of the Economic Effects of Trade and Investment Barriers in Services", paper presented at the World Services Congress, Atlanta, 1–3 November.

Brown, D.K., A.V. Deardorff and R.M. Stern. 2000. "Computational Analysis of the Accession of Chile to the NAFTA and Western Hemisphere Integration", *The World Economy*, 23(1), pp. 145–74.

Bryant, R., P. Hooper and C. Mann. 1993. *Evaluating Policy Regimes: New Research in Empirical Macroeconomics*, Washington DC: Brookings Institution.

Buehrer, T. and F. Di Mauro. 1994. *Computable General Equilibrium Models as Tools for Policy Analysis in Developing Countries*, Rome: Banca d'Italia.

Burtless, G., R. Lawrence, R.E. Litan and R.J. Shapiro. 1998. *Globophobia: Confronting Fears about Open Trade*, Washington DC: Brookings Institution.

Business Week (BW). 1999. "Trade: Global Growing Pains", 13 December, pp. 40–3.

Cameron, J. and K. Campbell. 1997. "Dispute Resolution in the World Trade Organization". Mimeo.

Clarida, R.H. 1996. "Dumping: In Theory, in Policy, and in Practice", in J. Bhagwati and R.E. Hudec (eds) *Fair Trade and Harmonization* I, Cambridge MA and London: MIT Press, pp. 120–44.

Cline, W.R. 1997. *Trade and Income Distribution*, Washington DC: Institute for International Economics.

Coe, D.T. and E. Helpman. 1995. "International R&D Spillovers", *European Economic Review*, 39(5), pp. 859–87.

Coppel, J. and M. Durand. 1999. "Trends in Market Openness", Paris: Organization for Economic Co-operation and Development. Economics Department Working Paper No. 221. August.

Croome, J. 1998. "The Present Outlook for Trade Negotiations in the World Trade Organization", Policy Research Working Paper No. 1932, Washington DC: World Bank.

Daly, M. and H. Kuwahara. 1998. "The Impact of the Uruguay Round on Tariff and Non-tariff Barriers to Trade in the 'Quad'", *The World Economy*, 21(2), pp. 207–34.

Das, Dilip K. 1990. *International Trade Policy*, London: Macmillan.

Das, Dilip K. 1991. *Import Canalization*, London: Sage Publications.

Das, Dilip K. 1998. "Trade in Financial Services and the Role of the GATS: Against the Backdrop of the Asian Crisis", *Journal of World Trade*, 32(6), pp. 79–114.

Das, Dilip K. 1999. "The Millennium Round and the Asian Economies: An Introduction", Manila: Asian Development Bank. Occasional Paper No. 20. November.

Das, Dilip K. 2000. "The Asian Financial Crisis: Distilling Critical Lessons", Manila: Asian Development Bank. Occasional Paper No. 22. May.

Deardorff, A.V. and R.M. Stern. 1990. *Computational Analysis of Global Trading Arrangements*, Ann Arbor MI: University of Michigan Press.

Deardorff, A.V. and R.M. Stern. 1997. *Measures of Non-tariff Barriers*, Paris: Organization for Economic Co-operation and Development.

Dee, P. 2000. "Modelling the Liberalization of Services", paper presented at the joint Australian National University and Productivity Commission conference "Achieving Better Regulation of Services", Canberra, 27–8 October.

Dee, P. and K. Hanslow. 2000. "Multilateral Liberalization of Services Trade", Melbourne: Australian Productivity Commission. Staff Research Paper. March.

Dollar, D. 1992. "Outward Oriented Economies Really do Grow More Rapidly: Evidence from 95 LDCs, 1976–85", *Economic Development and Cultural Change*, April, pp. 523–44.

Economist. 1999. "Trade in Parentheses", 13 November, p. 64.

Economist. 2000. "The Merit of Trading Quietly", 12 August, pp. 9–10.

Edwards, S. 1998. "Openness, Productivity, and Growth: What do we Really Know?", *Economic Journal*, 108(447), pp. 383–98.

Ethier, W.J. 1998. "The International Commercial System", Princeton NJ: International Finance Section, Princeton University. Essays in International Finance No. 210. September.

European Economic Commission (EEC). 1993. *Growth, Competitiveness and Employment*, Brussels.

Evenett, S.J. 1999. "The World Trading System: The Road Ahead", *Finance and Development*, 36(4), pp. 13–17.

Fallen, P. and Z. Tzannatos. 1998. "Child Labor: Issues and Directions for the World Bank", Washington DC: World Bank. Processed.

Feenstra, R.C. 1998. "Integration of Trade and Disintegration of Production in the Global Economy", *Journal of Economic Perspective*, 12(4), pp. 31–50.

Feketekuty, G. 1998. "Defining Subsidies in the Global System: Economic, Legal, and Political Criteria", in M.A. Swoolcock (ed.) *Subsidies in the Governance of the Global Economy*, New York: Oxford University Press, pp. 142–74.

Fernandez, R. and J. Ports. 1998. "Returns to Regionalism: An Analysis of Non-traditional Gains from Regional Trade Agreements", *World Bank Economic Review*, 12(2), pp. 197–220.

Finger, J.M. and A. Olechowski. 1987. *The Uruguay Round: a Handbook for the Multilateral Trade Negotiations*, Washington DC: World Bank.

Finger, J.M. and L. Schuknecht. 1999. "Market Access Advances and Retreats: the Uruguay Round and Beyond", Washington DC: World Bank. Policy Research Working Paper No. 2232. November.

Francois, J.F. and W. Martin. 1995. "Multilateral Trade Rules and the Expected Cost of Protection", London: Centre for Economic Policy Research. Discussion Paper No. 1214.

Francois, J.F., B. McDonald and H. Nordstrom. 1996. "The Uruguay Round: a Numerically Based Qualitative Assessment", in W. Martin and L.A. Winters (eds) *The Uruguay Round and the Developing Countries*, Cambridge: Cambridge University Press, pp. 224–46.

Frankel, J.A. 1997. *Regional Trading Blocs in the World Economic System*, Washington DC: Institute for International Economics.

Frankel, J.A. and D. Romer. 1999. "Does Trade Cause Growth?", *American Economic Review*, 89(3), pp. 379–99.

Fried, J. 2000. "The WTO after Seattle and the Role of Multilateral Financial Institutions", paper presented at the Asian Development Bank, Manila, 26 July.

Fujita, M., P.R. Krugman and A.J. Venables. 1999. *The Spatial Economy: Cities, Regions and International Trade*, Cambridge MA: MIT Press.

General Agreement on Tariffs and Trade (GATT). 1985. *Trade Policies for a Better Future: Proposals for Action*, Geneva.

General Agreement on Tariffs and Trade (GATT). 1994. *The Results of the Uruguay Round of Multilateral Trade Negotiations: The Legal Texts*, Geneva.

General Agreement on Trade in Services (GATS). 1994. *General Agreement on Trade in Services and Related Instruments*, Geneva.

Gilli, M. 1996. *Computational Economic Systems: Models, Methods and Econometrics*, Dordrecht: Kluwer Academic Publishers.

Goldin, I., O. Knudsen and D. van der Mensbrugghe. 1993. *Trade Liberalization: Global Economic Implications*, Paris: OECD and World Bank.

Greenaway, D., W. Morgan and P. Wright. 1998. "Trade Reform, Adjustment and Growth: What Does the Evidence Tell Us?", *Economic Journal*, 108(450), pp. 1547–61.

Griswold, D.T. 2000a. "WTO Report Card: America's Economic Stakes in Open Economy", Washington DC: Cato Institute. Trade Briefing Paper No. 8. April.

Griswold, D.T. 2000b. "Whatever Happened to the 'Giant Sucking Sound'?", Washington DC: Cato Institute. Available at http://www.freetrade.org/pubs/articles/dg-6-600.html (6 June).

Group of Eight (G-8). 2000. Communiqué. Kyushu–Okinawa. 23 July.

Harrison, G.W., T.F. Rutherford and D.G. Tarr. 1996. "Quantifying the Uruguay Round", in W. Martin and L.A. Winters (eds) *The Uruguay Round and the Developing Countries*, Cambridge: Cambridge University Press, pp. 215–84.

Harrison, W.J. and K. Pearson. 1996. "Computing Solutions for Large General Equilibrium Models using GEMPACK", *Computational Economics*, 9(2), pp. 83–127.

Hertel, T.W. 1997. *Global Trade Analysis: Modeling and Applications*, Cambridge and New York: Cambridge University Press.

Hertel, T.W. and W. Martin. 1999a. "Developing Countries' Interests in Liberalizing Manufactures Trade", paper presented at the CERP Workshop, London, 19–20 February.

Hertel, T.W. and W. Martin. 1999b. "Would Developing Countries Gain from Inclusion of Manufactures in the WTO Negotiations?", paper presented at the conference on the "WTO and the Millennium Round", Geneva, 20–1 September.

Hertel, T.W., K. Anderson, J.P. Francois and W. Martin. 2000. *Agriculture and Non-agricultural Liberalization in the Millennium Round*, Adelaide: Centre for International Studies, University of Adelaide. CIES Discussion Paper No. 00/16. March.

Hertel, T.W., W. Martin, K. Yanagishima and B. Dimaranan. 1996. "Liberalizing Manufactures Trade in a Changing World Economy", in W. Martin and L.A. Winters (eds) *The Uruguay Round and the Developing Countries*, Cambridge: Cambridge University Press, pp. 48–74.

Hill, R. 2000. "Cairns Group Statement on Multifunctionality", New York: Eighth Meeting of the Commission on Sustainable Development, 26 April.

Hoekman, B. 1996. "Assessing the General Agreement on Trade in Services", in W. Martin and L.A. Winters (eds) *The Uruguay Round and the Developing Countries*, Cambridge: Cambridge University Press, pp. 24–47.

Hoekman, B. 1999. "The Next Round of Services Negotiations: Identifying Priorities and Options", paper presented at the Federal Reserve Bank of St Louis conference "Multilateral Trade Negotiations: Issues for the Millennium Round", 21–2 October.

Hoekman, B. and K. Saggi. 1999. "Multilateral Disciplines for Investment-related Policies?", paper presented at the conference on "Global Regionalism", Istituto Affari Internazionali, Rome, 8–9 February.

Ingco, M. 1996. "Tariffication in the Uruguay Round: How Much Liberalization?", *The World Economy*, 19(4), pp. 425–46.

International Centre for Trade and Sustainable Development (ICTSD). 1999. *Bridges: Daily Update on the Third Ministerial Conference*, Geneva. Issue 1. 30 November.

International Monetary Fund (IMF). 1993. "Trade as an Engine of Growth", *World Economic Outlook 1993*, Washington DC: International Monetary Fund. May.

Irwin, D.A. 1999. "How Clinton Botched the Seattle Summit", *Asian Wall Street Journal*, 7 December.

Irwin, D.A. 2000. *Does Trade Raise Income?*, Cambridge MA: National Bureau of Economic Research.

Jackson, J.H. 1989. *The World Trading System*, Cambridge MA: MIT Press.

Jonquieres, G. and F. Williams. 1999. "A Goal beyond Reach", *Financial Times*, 6 December.

Josling, T. 1998. *Agricultural Trade Policy: Completing the Reforms*, Washington DC: Institute for International Economics.

Khan, S.A. 1998. *Policing the Global Economy: Why, How, and for Whom*, London: Cameron & May.

Koupparitsas, M. 1997. "A Dynamic Macroeconomic Analysis of NAFTA", *Economic Perspective*, Chicago: Federal Reserve Bank of Chicago, January–February, pp. 14–35.

Krishna, K., A. Ozyildirim and N.R. Swanson. 1998. "Trade, Investment, and Growth: Nexus, Analysis, and Prognosis", NBER Working Paper No. 6861. Cambridge MA: National Bureau of Economic Research.

Krueger, A.O. 1998. "Why Trade Liberalization is Good for Growth", *Economic Journal*, 108 (September), pp. 1513–22.

Krueger, A.O. 1999a. "The Developing Countries in the Next Round of Multilateral Trade Negotiations", Washington DC: World Bank. Policy Research Working Paper No. 2118.

Krueger, A.O. 1999b. "Are Preferential Trading Arrangements Trade-liberalizing or Protectionist?", *Journal of Economic Perspective*, 13(4), pp. 105–24.

Krueger, A.O. 2000. "Factors Affecting Export Growth and Performance and the Asian Case", in Dilip K. Das (ed.) *Asian Exports*, Oxford: Oxford University Press, pp. 25–74.

Krugman, P. 1996. "Does Third World Growth Hurt First World Prosperity?", *Harvard Business Review*, 72 (July–August), pp. 113–21.

Krugman, P. 1997. "What Should Trade Negotiations Negotiate About?", *Journal of Economic Literature*, 35 (March), pp. 113–20.

Krugman, P. 1999. *The Return of Depression Economics*, New York: Norton.

Krugman, P. 2000. "The Dismal Science: Enemies of the WTO". 23 November. Available at http://slate.msn.com/code/story/actions/print.asp?strURL=/XML/Dismal.xml&iMsg=

Laird, S. 1999. "Multinational Approaches to Market Access Negotiations", in M.R. Mendoza, P. Low and B. Kotschwar (eds) *Trade Rules in the Making*, Washington DC: Brookings Institution.

Leamer, E.E. 1996. "In Search of Solper–Samuelson Effects on US Wages", Cambridge MA: National Bureau of Economic Research. Working Paper No. 5427.

Lindsey, B. 1999. "The US Antidumping Law: Rhetoric versus Reality", Washington DC: Cato Institute. Center for Trade Policy Studies No. 7.

Lindsey, B. 2000. "Globalization in the Streets Again", Washington DC: Cato Institute. Center for Trade Policy Studies, 27 May. Available at http://www.freetrade.org/pubs/articles/bl-4–15–00.html

Lindsey, B., D.T. Griswold, M.A. Groombridge and A. Lukas. 1999. "Seattle and Beyond: A WTO Agenda for the New Millennium", Washington DC: Cato Institute. Center for Trade Policy Studies, Working Paper No. 8. 4 November.

Low, P. and A. Mattoo. 1999. "Is There a Better Way? Alternative Approaches to Liberalization under the GATS". Available at http://www.cid.harvard.edu/cidtrade/

Mandel, M.J. and P. Magnusson. 1999. "Global Growing Pains", *Business Week*, 13 December, pp. 40–5.

Mann, C.L. 2000. "Electronic Commerce in Developing Countries", Washington DC: Institute for International Economics. Working Paper No. 3. March.

Marceau, G. and P.N. Pedersen. 1999. "Is the WTO Open and Transparent? A Discussion of the Relationship of the WTO with Non-governmental Organizations and Civil Society's Claims for More Transparency and Public Participation", *Journal of World Trade*, 33(1), pp 33–60.

Markusen, J.R., T.F. Rutherford and D. Tarr. 1999. "Foreign Direct Investment in Services and the Domestic Market for Expertise", paper presented at the second annual conference on "Global Economic Analysis", Ebberuk, Denmark, 20–2 June.

Martin, W. and L.A. Winters. 1995a. "The Uruguay Round and the Developing Economies", Washington DC: World Bank. Discussion Paper No. 307.

Martin, W. and L.A. Winters (eds). 1995b. Executive Summary. "The Uruguay Round and the Developing Countries", Washington DC: World Bank. World Bank Discussion Paper No. 307.

Martin, W. and L.A. Winters. 1996. "The Uruguay Round: A Milestone for the Developing Countries", in W. Martin and L.A. Winters (eds) *The Uruguay Round and the Developing Countries*, Cambridge: Cambridge University Press, pp. 1–29.

Maskus, K.E. 1998. "The International Regulation of Intellectual Property", *Weltwirtschaftliches Archiv*, 134(2), pp. 205–29.

Matusz, S.J. 1997. *Adjusting to Trade Liberalization*, East Lansing MI: Michigan State University.

Matusz, S.J. and D. Tarr. 2000. "Adjusting to Trade Policy Reforms", in A.O. Krueger (ed.) *Economic Policy Reform: The Second Stage*, Chicago: University of Chicago Press.

McDougall, R. 1998. *Global Trade: Assistance and Protection: GTAP-4 Database*, West Lafayette IN: Purdue University.

McKibbin, W.J. 1997. "Global Consequences of Financial Market Liberalization", paper presented at the EMBA conference on Investment Liberalization and Financial Reform in the Asia–Pacific Region, Sydney, 29–31 August.

McKibbin, W.J. 1999. "Trade Liberalization in a Dynamic Setting: Implications of a New WTO Round", paper presented at the second annual conference on Global Economic Analysis held in Copenhagen, 19–21 September.

McKibbin, W.J. and P. Wilcoxen. 1998. "The Theoretical and Empirical Structure of the G-cubed Model", *Economic Modelling*, 16(1), pp. 123–48.

McKibbin, W.J. and P. Wilcoxen. 1999. "Macroeconomic Volatility in General Equilibrium", Washington DC: Brookings Institution. Discussion Paper in International Economics No. 140.

Michalopoulos, C. 1999a. "Developing Country Goals and Strategies for the Millennium Round", Washington DC: World Bank. Policy Research Working Paper No. 2147. July.

Michalopoulos, C. 1999b. "Trade and Market Access Issues for Developing Countries", Washington DC: World Bank. Policy Research Working Paper No. 2214. October.

Micklethwait, J. and A. Wooldridge. 2000. *A Future Perfect*, New York. Random House.

Moore, M. 1999. "Message from the Director General", *WTO Focus*, 43 (November), p. 1.

Moore, M. 2000. "Reflections on the Global Trading System", speech at Symposium on Global Economic Integration, Jackson Hole WY, 25 August.

Morgan, C. 1999. "Safeguard and Competition Policy", paper presented at the WTO–ADB seminar on "Trade Remedies and Competition Policy", Chiang Mai, Thailand, 11–13 May.

Mussa, M. 1998. "Trade Liberalization", in Z. Iqbal and M.S. Khan (eds) *Trade Reform and Regional Integration in Africa*, Washington DC: International Monetary Fund, pp. 19–65.

Ng, F. and A. Yeates. 1996. *Open Markets Work Better! Did Africa's Protectionist Policies cause its Marginalization in World Trade?*, Washington DC: World Bank. Policy Research Working Paper No. 1636.

Oman, C. 2000. *Policy Competition for Foreign Direct Investment*, Paris: Development Research Centre, Organization for Economic Co-operation and Development.

Organization for Economic Co-operation and Development (OECD). 1997. *Indicators of Tariff and Non-tariff Barriers*, Paris.

Organization for Economic Co-operation and Development (OECD). 1998. *Open Markets Matter: The Benefits of Trade and Investment Liberalization*, Paris.

Organization for Economic Co-operation and Development (OECD). 1999a. *Agricultural Trade Policies in OECD Countries: Monitoring and Evaluation*, Paris.

Organization for Economic Co-operation and Development (OECD). 1999b. *The Economic and Social Impact of Electronic Commerce*, Paris.

Organization for Economic Co-operation and Development (OECD). 1999c. *Post-Uruguay Round Tariff Regimes: Achievements and Outlook*, Paris.

Organization for Economic Co-operation and Development (OECD). 2000a. *Evaluation and Monitoring Report for 2000*, Paris.

Organization for Economic Co-operation and Development (OECD). 2000b. *OECD Economic Outlook*, June, Paris.

Organization for Economic Co-operation and Development (OECD). 2000c. Communiqué, Paris: OECD Council Meeting at Ministerial Level, 27 June.

Otten, A. and H. Wager. 1996. "Compliance with TRIPs: The Emerging World View", *Vanderbilt Journal of Transnational Law*, 29(3), pp. 391–413.

Overseas Development Institute (ODI). 1995. "Developing Countries in the WTO", London.

Oyejide, T.A. 2000. "Interests and Options of Developing and Least-developed Countries in a New Round of Multilateral Trade Negotiations", New York: United Nations.

Pacific Economic Co-operation Council (PECC). 2000. "Non-tariff Measures in Goods and Services Trade", Canberra. Available at http://www.pecc.net/

Page, S. 2000. *Regionalism among Developing Countries*, Basingstoke: Macmillan.

Page, S. and M. Davenport. 1994. *World Trade Reform*, London: Overseas Development Institute.

Panagariya, A. 1999. "TRIPs and the WTO: An Uneasy Marriage", paper presented at a seminar at the World Trade Organization, Geneva, 20 July.

Panagariya, A. 2000. "The Millennium Round and Developing Countries: Negotiating Strategies and Areas of Benefit", Cambridge MA: Center for International Development, Harvard University.

Petri, P.A. 1997. "Foreign Direct Investment in a Computable General Equilibrium Framework", paper presented at the conference "Making APEC Work: Economic Challenges and Policy Alternatives", 13–14 March.

Primo Braga, C.A., C. Fink and C.P. Sepulveda. 1999. "International Property Rights and Economic Development", TechNet Working Paper, Washington DC: World Bank.

Robinson, S. and K. Thierfelder. 1999. "Trade Liberalization and Regional Integration: the Search for Large Numbers", Washington DC: International Food Policy Research Institute.

Sachs, J.D. and A. Warner. 1997. "Fundamental Sources of Long-run Growth", *American Economic Review*, 87(2), pp. 184–8.

Sala-I-Martin, X. 1997. "I Just Ran Four Million Regressions", Cambridge, MA: National Bureau of Economic Research. NBER Working Paper Series 6252.

Sampson, G.P. 2000. *Trade, Environment, and the WTO: the post-Seattle Agenda*, Baltimore MD: Johns Hopkins University Press.

Sazanami, Y., S. Urata and H. Kawai. 1995. *Measuring the Cost of Protection in Japan*, Washington DC: Institute for International Economics.

Schott, J.J. 1996. "WTO 2000: Setting the Course for World Trade", Washington DC: Institute for International Economics.

Schott, J.J. and J. Watal. 2000. "Decision Making in the WTO", Washington DC: Institute for International Economics. Policy Brief No. 00–2. March.

Short, C. 1999. "Making the Next Trade Round Work for the World's Poor", London: Department for International Development.

Smith, M., M. Suzman and G. Jonquieres. 1999. "Anything but Agriculture", *Financial Times*, 19 November.

Snape, R.H. 1998. "Reaching Effective Agreements Covering Services", in A.O. Krueger (ed.) *The WTO as an International Organization*, Chicago: University of Chicago Press, pp. 279–96.

Soloaga, I. and L. Alan Winters. 1999. "Regionalism in the Nineties: What Effect on Trade?", World Bank. Washington DC: Mimeo.

Solow, R. 1956. "A Contribution to the Theory of Economic Growth", *Quarterly Journal of Economics*, 37(7), pp. 1501–25.

Spinanger, D. 1999. "Faking Liberalization and Finagling Protectionism: the ATC at its Best", Kiel: Kiel Institute of World Economics. 14 July.

Srinivasan, T.N. 1998. *Developing Countries and the Multilateral Trading System*, Boulder CO: Westview Press.

Stiglitz, J.E. 1999a. "Two Principles for the Next Round: or, How to Bring Developing Countries in from the Cold", Washington DC, 21 September. Mimeo.

Stiglitz, J.E. 1999b. "Addressing Developing Country Priorities and Needs in the Millennium Round", speech delivered at the Harvard University Center for Business and Government, Cambridge MA, 29 November.

Stoeckel, A. 2000. "Removing the Hidden Taxes on Exports", in *Reasons versus Emotions: Requirements for a Successful WTO Round*, Canberra: Centre for International Economics.

Stoeckel, A., K.K. Tang and W. McKibbin. 2000. "Productivity, Risk and the Gains from Trade Liberalization", Melbourne: Melbourne Business School. Pelham Paper No. 9. May.

Stolper, W. and P.A. Samuelson. 1941. "Protection and Real Wages", *Review of Economic Studies*, 9, 58–73.

Summers, L. 1999. "A Trade Round that Works for People", *Financial Times*, 29 November.

Taylor, C.O. 1997. "The Limits of Economic Power: Section 301 and the World Trade Organization Dispute Settlement System", *Vanderbilt Journal of Transnational Law*, 30(2), pp. 201–43.

United Nations (UN). 1993. *Liberalizing International Transactions in Services*, New York: UN Conference on Trade and Development and World Bank.

United Nations Conference on Trade and Development (UNCTAD). 2000a. Bangkok Declaration: "Global Dialogue and Dynamic Engagement", Bangkok, 12 February.

United Nations Conference on Trade and Development (UNCTAD). 2000b. *World Investment Report*. New York.

United Nations Conference on Trade and Development/World Trade Organization (UNCTAD/WTO). 1997. "Post-Uruguay Round Tariff Environment for Developing Country Exports", Geneva: UNCTAD/WTO joint study. TD/B/COM. 1/14.

United Nations Industrial Development Organization (UNIDO). 1995. *International Yearbook of Industrial Statistics*. Vienna.

United States Information Agency (USIA). 1998. "Intellectual Property in the TRIPs Era", *Economic Perspective*, 4(2), pp. 44–6. Available at http://usia.gov/journals/journals.htm

Vamvakidis, A. 1999. "Regional Trade Arrangements or Broad Liberalization: Which Path Leads to Faster Growth?", *IMF Staff Papers* 46 (March), pp. 42–68.

Warren, T. and C. Findlay. 1999. "Measuring Impediments to Trade in Services", Adelaide: Centre for International Economic Studies, University of Adelaide. Discussion Paper No. 99/19.

Whalley, J. 1996. "Developing Countries and System Strengthening in the Uruguay Round", in W. Martin and L.A. Winters (eds) *The Uruguay Round and the Developing Countries*, Cambridge: Cambridge University Press, pp. 409–35.

Whalley, J. 1999. "Notes on Textiles and Apparel in the Next Trade Round", paper presented at a conference on "Developing Countries in the Next WTO Trade Round", held at Harvard University, 5–6 November.

Whalley, J. and C. Hamilton. 1996. *The Trading System after the Uruguay Round*, Washington DC: Institute for International Economics.

World Bank (WB). 1987. *World Development Report 1987*, Washington DC.

World Bank (WB). 1997. *World Development Report 1997*, Washington DC.

World Bank (WB). 2000a. "Small States: Meeting Challenges in the Global Economy", Washington DC. March.

World Bank (WB). 2000b. *Global Economic Prospects and the Developing Countries*, Washington DC.

World Development Report 1999/2000 (WDR). 2000. New York: Oxford University Press for the World Bank.

World Economic Outlook 2000 (WEO). 2000, Washington DC: International Monetary Fund. May.

World Trade Organization (WTO). 1994. "Developing Countries and the Uruguay Round: an Overview", Geneva: Committee on Trade and Development, Seventy-seventh Session, 25 November.

World Trade Organization (WTO). 1998a. "Tariffs: More Bindings and Closer to Zero", 16 January. http://www.wto.org/about/agmnts2.htm

World Trade Organization (WTO). 1998b. *Electronic Commerce and the Role of the WTO*, Geneva.

World Trade Organization (WTO). 1998c. "Declaration on Global Electronic Commerce", WT/MIN/(98)/DEC/2, 26 May.

World Trade Organization (WTO). 1998d. *Annual Report 1998*, Geneva.

World Trade Organization (WTO). 1999a. "Preparation for the 1999 Ministerial Conference: Regional Trade Agreements", WT/GC/W/213, Geneva.

World Trade Organization (WTO). 1999b. "Work Programme on Electronic Commerce", Geneva. S/C/8. March.

World Trade Organization (WTO). 1999c. "Communication from the European Union and their Member States on the WTO Work Programme on Electronic Commerce", Geneva. 9 August.

World Trade Organization (WTO). 1999d. "Preparation for the 1999 Ministerial Conference", Geneva. JOB(99)/5868/Rev.1(6223). October.

World Trade Organization (WTO). 1999e. *Annual Report 1999*, Geneva.

World Trade Organization (WTO). 2000a. Press Release. Press/175. April, Geneva.

World Trade Organization (WTO). 2000b. Press Release. Press/185. July, Geneva.

World Trade Organization (WTO). 2000c. "DG Moore Welcomes G-8 Statement on Launch of New Trade Round", *WTO News*, 23 July. Available at http://www.wto.org/english/news_e/news00_e/g82000_e.htm

World Trade Organization (WTO). 2000d. *Overview of Developments in the International Trading Environment*, Geneva. WT/TPR/OV/6. 22 November.

World Trade Organization (WTO). 2000e. *Annual Report 2000*, Geneva.

Wyatt, S. 2000. "APEC agrees on Trade Talks but Not on Agenda", *Financial Times*, 8 June, p. 4.

Index